An Essay on the History of Civil Society

An Essay on the History of Civil Society

Adam Ferguson

With a New Introduction by
Louis Schneider

Transaction Books
New Brunswick (U.S.A.) and London (U.K.)

Library of Congress Catalog Number: 79-64856
ISBN: 0-87855-314-2 (cloth), 0-87855-696 (paper)
Printed in the United States of America

Library of Congress Cataloging in Publication Data
Ferguson, Adam, 1723-1816.
    An essay on the history of civil society, 1767.
    (Social science classics series)

    Includes bibliographical references and index.
    1. Civilization—History. I. Title. II. Series.
[CB25.F4 1979]   909   79-64856
ISBN 0-87855-696-6

Introduction to the Transaction Edition

Adam Ferguson is one of a number of men who won renown for eighteenth-century Scotland in philosophy and social science. Ferguson's name is easily associated with those of others of his time whose endeavors were related to his. The names of Adam Smith and David Hume are the most salient. Considerably less prominent, but certainly worthy of mention, is John Miller, holder of the chair of Civil Law at Glasgow from 1761. Another man of the law who is not intellectually far from Ferguson is the jurist Henry Home, Lord Kames. In the background is the figure of Francis Hutcheson, the philosopher and disciple of Shaftesbury, who (although himself of Irish birth) was an important early thinker among these Scots and also the teacher of Adam Smith. William Robertson, the historian, also has his plain affinities with these men. Somewhat aside from the social-science current is the philosopher Thomas Reid. And pursuing his own eccentric way is the anthropologist James Burnett, Lord Monboddo, who with all his bizarre notions about men with tails and "sea men" and mermaids, had something of an authentic sense for problems of human evolution. Late in the Scottish development comes Dugald Stewart, who, at considerable length and sometimes a bit dully, summarizes much that came before him.

The Scottish Enlightenment includes more than philosophy and social science. It is also marked by notable achievements in science, technology, and literature. But this local enlightenment as a whole runs its course within rather less than a century. A fairly good point at which to mark the termination of a remarkable Scottish development of ideas that began to gather real force around the middle of the eighteenth century is the death of Dugald Stewart in 1828. In round figures, it lasted from 1750 to 1830. David Hume's *Treatise of Human Nature* appeared as early as 1739, but Hume was then only twenty-eight and he lived to publish significant work well beyond 1750. Even the early Francis Hutcheson's *System of Moral Philosophy* was published (posthumously: Hutcheson died in 1746) in 1755. Adam Smith's *Theory of Moral Sentiments* appeared originally in 1759 and his *Wealth of Nations* in 1776. Ferguson's main books came out between 1767 and 1792. When Ferguson died in 1816 at the age of ninety-two, the stream in which he had been included was close to its end.

We have here, in the persons of the Scottish philosophers and scientists, one of those striking clusters of very able men working out the possibilities of philosophical scientific or artistic ideas that so intrigued the anthropologist Kroeber in his *Configurations of Culture Growth.* Kroeber notes how with the Union of Scotland and England in 1707, a change in the relative cultural contributions of the two countries occurs. Scotland becomes more productive, and, writes Kroeber, "Scotch births of genius show a definite constellation. There are Hume. . . Adam Smith."[1] When the Scottish achievements attain their peak, they are outstanding by any reasonable criterion. There were gifted economists before Adam Smith, but there are some good reasons to regard his *Wealth of Nations* as marking the foundation of economic science in its modern form. Not the least of the achievements is the making of an early sociology, not yet so named of course but still sufficiently close in its concerns to the modern subject to allow it the same label in retrospect; and here Adam Ferguson is one of the most significant figures. The economics and the sociology are not unconnected by any means. Adam Smith was unequivocally a sociologist as well as an economist, as much of the content of the *Wealth of Nations* indicates, and there was a broad Scottish persuasion of the crucial importance of economic factors in social life.

It is often asked what there was about Scotland in the eighteenth century that might have occasioned its striking production of leading social scientists. One answer was suggested by Meek some twenty years ago when he pointed to the possible stimulation to social thought coming from a combination of rapid economic development in some places in Scotland with retention of older economic patterns or forms of organization in the Scottish Highlands.[2] But much remains to be done in comparing great creative periods in different times and places, and it is perhaps easier to explain how the potential of important cultural patterns carried by human clusters is ultimately exhausted as the problem-possibilities of the patterns are worked out, than it is to explain the rise of the patterns themselves.

In any case, Adam Ferguson, with his participation in the eighteenth-century Scottish cluster with a special contribution to sociological thought, was born in 1723 (the same year as Adam Smith), in the manse of Logierait at Perthshire. He studied at the University of Saint Andrews and subsequently at Edinburgh. He saw service as an army chaplain, acquiring acquaintanceship with military matters that stood him in good stead when he came later to write his history of the Roman Republic, just as the historian Edward Gibbon's experience as a militiaman helped him in the composition of his own great history of the decline and fall of the Roman Empire. Although Ferguson had been educated for the ministry, his qualifications for being a Scottish clergyman were evidently rather less than ideal, for, as his biographer John Small tells us, "he was deficient in the gifts necessary for the popular preacher" and "his sermons were elaborate disquisitions showing more acquaintance with systems of philosophy than with the wants of common hearers."[3]

It was no doubt well for Ferguson and those who might have been his parishioners that he turned elsewhere for a life's vocation. He was appointed successor to David Hume as keeper of the Advocates Library at the beginning of 1757. But he quit this office abruptly and in 1759 succeeded John Stewart in the chair of natural philosophy at Edinburgh. It is a bit curious to think of Ferguson, preeminently the moral philosopher and historian, as a teacher of physical science subjects, but he continued in the natural philosophy post for some five years until in 1764 he was appointed to the chair at Edinburgh that enabled him to teach moral philosophy. He had found his métier and he had a distinguished career. If he has not the caliber of men like David Hume and Adam Smith, he is still a sturdy figure in his own right.

The scope of moral philosophy taught in Ferguson's day is worth recalling. Ferguson wrote, "for the use of students in the College of Edinburgh," a small volume entitled *Institutes of Moral Philosophy,* published in 1769, which gives a notion of the range of his teaching. But this little book was only the forerunner of a far more extensive, richer production published at Edinburgh in 1792, a two-volume affair entitled *Principles of Moral and Political Science.* Like the *Institutes,* this carried a subtitle indicating that it was designed for student use ("chiefly a retrospect of lectures delivered in the College of Edinburgh"). But it was not a "textbook," at least not in the often pejorative sense of that term. Rather, it was on the order of an authentic treatise. What does Ferguson take up in it? Simply a huge variety of subjects. Volume One of the *Principles* presents us with one chapter entitled "Of Man's Description and Place in the Scale of Being," with another entitled "Of Mind or the Characteristics of Intelligence," and with a third called "Of Man's Progressive Nature." The third chapter alone includes discussions of habit, ambition, the commercial and political arts, science and the fine arts, and "the progress of moral apprehension"; it concludes grandly, and most optimistically, with a disquisition on human immortality ("of a future state"). But we still face Volume Two (considerably longer than Volume One), which in its first chapter deals with pleasure and pain, beauty and deformity, prosperity and adversity, virtue and vice, and more. Later chapters take up morality and politics again and deal with jurisprudence and with the virtuous life.

Given this range, inevitably not everything could be covered in depth. But the reader alert to the outlines of Ferguson's incipient sociology will find much that is far from superficial. There are shrewd passages that stress unintended, or unanticipated (or unrecognized), consequences of social action, a well known and significant theme in many sociological works (although not occurring in sociological works alone in the social sciences), tracing back in its modern form for a number of centuries to some of the historical work of Niccolo Machiavelli. The theme of unintended, or unanticipated consequences, has been very much part of so-called functional analysis, it is well to observe that some of its most salient components antedate certain formulations in contemporary biology or the productions of sociology departments at Harvard or Columbia a generation or so ago. In the *Principles,* Ferguson will tell us that "the barons of England, in time of high feudal aristocracy, knew not that the charters which they extorted from their sovereign were to become foundations of freedom to the people over whom they themselves wished to tyrannize" (I, 314). The theme also figures eloquently in the *Essay* before us. "Nations," Ferguson tells us here, "stumble upon establishments which are indeed the result of human action but not the execution of any human design" (*Essay,* Part III, Section II). Friedrich Hayek, who has been profoundly influenced by the Scottish moral philosophers and by the theme often set out by them, follows deliberately in Ferguson's track, entitling one of his papers "The Results of Human Action but not of Human Design."[4]

Ferguson also exhibits in his *Principles* a powerful sense of what may be called the nonrational foundations of society. (Indeed, this ties in with the theme just mentioned.) Societies are not created wholecloth out of processes of reasoning. "Laws and institutions, in every community, contain articles of agreements entered into by the parties with whom they originated, and by their posterity who accede to them; but such agreements are all of them posterior to the existence of society, and not the foundations upon which society was erected" (*Principles* II, 220). The observation is a fundamental one for Ferguson. It, too, had been anticipated in the *Essay,* where he writes, "Like the winds that come we know not whence and blow whithersoever they list, the forces of society are derived from an obscure and distant origin. They arise long before the date of philosophy, from the instincts, not the speculations of men" (Part III, Section II). We may not now especially favor the term "instincts" in such a context, but Ferguson is broadly referring to impulse and emotion deeply grounded in and intertwined with custom and tradition. He urges us in the *Essay* to be cautious about stories of oldtime legislators and founders of states, for these often attribute large deliberate plans to such figures where there was probably little or no plan or "design."

Various other Scottish writers, like John Millar in his *Historical View of the English Government* or the less well known Gilbert Stewart, in his *View of Society in Europe,* also expressed strong skepticism of the supposed sagacity and all-foreseeing ability of ancient legislators. Lycurgus and Solon were often designated as men to whom far too much responsibility for the formation of society or constitutions, by philosophy and by speculation, had been imputed. Over-attribution of rational design ties in again with the sense of the Scots that much that occurs in human societies was never intended or deliberately wrought. Society, at any time of which we can imagine an account of it, is already "there," already present with its "establishments," with their grounding in custom, sentiments, values, interests, and conflicts. Reason may work upon these things, but then it works with given materials that are certainly not themselves outright products of "reason." Even where there are explicit contracts, there are, in Ferguson's view, precontractual realities that environ and influence contract itself. Human beings are in society together before they enter upon contracts. Contract rests on a base of a noncontractual character. It does not start from scratch. It is hedged and limited (although it may also be sustained) by noncontractual, nonrational elements. Ferguson conducts in his *Principles* a sharp polemic against Hobbes in the matter of a supposed original compact. He shadows forth ideas on contract set out by Durkheim in the *Division of Labor.*

Ferguson's theoretical views are not unconnected with his practical attitudes. Thus, the sense of substance of society existent prior to rational deliberations and plans for society as a whole could induce in him, and other Scottish thinkers of his time, a considerable reverence for the forms of the past. Near the end of his *Principles,* Ferguson commented that "it may be safely assumed as a maxim under every establishment whatever, that the present [political] order, if tolerable, is to be preferred to innovation, of which, even in very small matters, it may be difficult, and is often above the reach of human wisdom, to foresee all the consequences or effects" (II, p. 498). He adds at once that under the fairest government grievances may come up and "must be redressed." But he was not disposed to subvert the social order and shared with other Scottish students of society a suspicion of political "projectors," persons with ready schemes to change society and polity for the better, incognizant, in the view of men like Ferguson, of the value and viability of established forms and vain of their own hare-brained schemes. It is a question whether a realistic view of nonrational elements in society must induce a conservative position. John Millar's sociology was not very different from Ferguson's and he too was critical of "projectors," but he sustained a more unambiguously "liberal" position than Ferguson did. And Ferguson himself is by no means passively affirmative of all he sees in the way of major social arrangements. The skeptical stance toward wealth and competition that we shall comment on later, and that appears in the *Essay,* is also maintained in the *Principles.*

The persuasion that society is, and always has been, man's habitat is set out forcefully in Ferguson's early sociology. "The atmosphere of society. . . is the element in which the human mind must draw the first breath of intelligence itself," he tells us in the *Principles,* as at an earlier point he had assured us that "man is made for society" (I, 268, 199). And in the *Essay* the statements bearing on man's sociality present the same general message. With man, "society appears to be as old as the individual," and if there was a time when "he had his acquaintance with his own species to make," when he supposedly lived in a nonsocial state, then that is "a time of which we have no record" and about which Ferguson suggests it is useless to speculate (Part I, Section III). The further notion that theorists may project their image of human nature in the present into the past lurks just beneath the surface. Ferguson might well have agreed with Rousseau in his dissertation on the origin of inequality of mankind, when the latter argued that philosophers inquiring into the nature of society had transferred to the "savage" in the state of nature ideas that had taken form only after that state had ended.

These and numerous other notions of a sociological character occur in the midst of Ferguson's moral philosophy. Ferguson was not a sociologist in a strict modern sense if only because he conducted no sociological inquiry conceived as separate from moral philosophy. But this calls for additional comment. There is widespread appreciation today of the historical integrity of past writings. Ferguson had his purposes and his intellectual environment and we must not read him in terms that divest him of his historical place and significance if we wish to understand him. This is entirely just. But we must not carry it to the point where we fail to see that at times past writers are talking about precisely the things we are talking about, even if in somewhat different language, or allow it to induce us to find differences that do not exist.

In her fine book on Ferguson, Jogland has argued for a view of Scottish moral philosophy, including that of Ferguson, that would stimulate "a critical stance toward the present day state of sociological thought."[5] This would require that we consider that moral philosophy again in its historical integrity, allow it to speak for itself, with at least an initial reserve about invading it with present-day sociological notions. The past has to be permitted its proper confrontation with the present. This is granted. Yet must not the present also be permitted its confrontation with the past? We may well "listen" to Ferguson by letting him tell his own story, but we may hear just what he himself has to say more acutely and even understand some of his own gropings better than he did if we also "listen" with a set of ideas deriving from a time subsequent to his own.

At the same time, as we "listen" to the old moral philosophy it is decidedly worth noting that one of its looming components is an ethical concern. We can clearly see processes of differentiation at work as modern social-science subject matters emerge from the matrix of moral philosophy. The history of the social sciences is various and not everything in it is traceable to moral philosophy, but some differentiation of particular social-science subject matters did indeed take place as moral philosophy lost its original scope or fullness. In the differentiation a great deal of ethical concern was lost. Virtue and vice, justice and goodness, and benevolence are topics discussed in the works of men like Hume, Smith, and Ferguson. While the discussion is often of high analytical quality, it does not suggest anything like a refusal to make value-commitments.

This points to matters about which there is considerable argument in sociology, as well as other social-science areas, today. This is not the place to carry on the argument. But it may still be suggested that in this area of ethical concern and value commitment we deal with matters on which Jogland's view of relevant Scottish work in the eighteenth century as something that may induce "a critical stance toward the present day state of sociological thought" is particularly apt. Perhaps one may be indulged if he says flatly that we have seen enough of absurdities and vicious notions stemming from a brand of "cultural relativism" that would in the end, if consistently pursued, exhort us to embrace something on the order of, say, Nazism as a "way of life" equally valid with others, no matter how nauseating the exhortion. There has been too much squirming away by sociologists (and others) from forthright consideration of moral questions of justice, of right and wrong, with resultant "answers" (for answers of some sort are repeatedly unavoidable) that are not one whit better for being surreptitious or or self-concealing. Social science, sociology included, can still learn from the eighteenth-century Scots in these premises (although we may surely learn from other and later sources too). When the Scots wrote of justice, they really meant to refer to justice, not to some pleasant sounding but deceptive or meaningless noise produced by a glandular quirk, or an "interest" refusing to come into the open.

If the sheer range of moral philosophy is worth remarking upon, and the shrewd development of a number of significant sociological ideas within that range is notable, another significant feature of the endeavor of the Scottish moral philosophers is their large preoccupation with history. David Hume wrote a substantial, multivolume history of England. Adam Smith and Lord Kames (author of several volumes of *Sketches of the History of Man*) had unmistakable historical interests. William Robertson, so often associated with these men, was "purely" an historian, with histories of Scotland, the emperor Charles V, and America to his credit. Even that "minor" figure, Gilbert Stuart, was interested in European history and wrote extensively on the history of Scotland. Ferguson presents no exception to the broad Scottish interest in history. In 1783 he published his large *History of the Progress and Termination of the Roman Republic* which is not a work to be overlooked if we are interested in his achievement in social science.[6] While much of this work is straightforward history, it also has a general tone and various passages that establish its close connection with Ferguson's other work, especially the *Essay*.

The political moralist in Ferguson, evident in the *Essay*, also comes out very clearly in the work on Rome. In the first century B. C. in Rome, Ferguson proposes that men became "glutted with material prosperity; they thought that they were born to enjoy what their fathers had won, and saw not the use of those austere and arduous virtues by which the state had increased to its present greatness" (169-70). Ferguson writes of Lutatius Catulus, in Caesar's day, as one of "great integrity, moderation, fortitude, and ability; a model of what the Romans in this age should have been, in order to have preserved their own republic" (179). He writes also of the "paltry ambition" of Pompey and Caesar, an ambition which, "some ages before, might have been held in contempt by the meanest of the people, or must have shrunk before that noble elevation of mind by which the statesman conceived no eminence besides that of high personal qualities employed in public services, or before the austere virtue which confined the public esteem to acts of public utility, supported by unblemished reputation in private life" (207). In the *Essay*, there is repeated reference to "corruption" and in the Roman history Ferguson refers to "the worst and most corrupting part" of the republican privileges of the Roman people as "that of receiving gratuities in money and corn, as well as that of being frequently amused with expensive shows" (413). It is generally evident from the Roman history that the whole business of "bread and circuses" strikes Ferguson as a particularly unhappy species of corruption, wooing people away from their propensity to act as responsible members of a public.

There is in the Roman history also the suggestion of a kind of dialectical theme that had been intimated in the *Essay*. In the latter, Ferguson remarks, for example, "the virtues of men have shone most during their struggles, not after the attainment of their ends. Those ends themselves, though attained by virtue, are frequently the causes of corruption and vice" (Part V, Section I). Thus, wealth, once it has been amassed, may induce much greater "corruption and vice" than ever led to its acquisition. It may even have been acquired to begin with by "virtuous" enough impulses. Then a product of virtue tempts to, and induces, vices. This sort of dialectic of wealth has of course also been suggested in modern sociology, as in the view coming from Max Weber's work that "virtues" like industry, thrift, and frugality may help produce a wealth that acts in disintegrating fashion on the very virtues mentioned, to which it owes so much, presenting an irresistible temptation to idleness, waste, and lavishness. The triumph of wealth in this sense entails the defeat of what made wealth initially.

Again Ferguson proposes a dialectical theme in the *Essay* when he writes:

> The Romans only meant by their armies to incroach on the freedom of other nations, while they preserved their own. They forgot that, in assembling soldiers of fortune, and in suffering any leader to be master of a disciplined army, they actually resigned political rights, and suffered a master to arise for the state. This people, in short, whose ruling passion was depredation and conquest, perished by the recoil of an engine which they themselves had erected against mankind (Part V, Section IV).

The dialectic whereby the instrumentality of "success" turns on those who employ it and brings them "failure" is thus touched upon. (And this is not greatly remote from what we have just noted in the case of wealth.) The "victory" the Romans achieved by their peculiar military devices contained the seeds of defeat marked by the emergence of "a master for the state." In the Roman history, Ferguson tries to show how the enlargement of the territory of the Romans and the success of their arms abroad "become the sources of a ruinous corruption at home," as if again to emphasize the recoil of an engine (83). But the dialectical notion that success can bring failure in its turn, or carry the seed thereof, is yet more widely suggested. Thus, in a passage in the Roman history that might have been written only yesteryear, we find this:

> The Romans, by the continual labors of seven centuries, had made their way from the Tiber to the Rhine and the Danube, through the territory of warlike hordes who opposed them, and over forests and rugged ways that were everywhere to be cleared at the expense of their labour and their blood; but the ways they had made to reach their enemies were now open, in their turns, for enemies to reach them. The ample resources which they had formed by their cultivation increased the temptation to invade them, and facilitated all the means of making war upon their country. By reducing the inhabitants of their provinces, in every part, to pacific subjects, they brought the defense of the empire to depend on a few professional soldiers who composed the legions (432). [Ferguson writes this under date U. C. 760, that is, 760 years after the supposed founding of Rome in 753 B. C.]

It will be noted that this sort of description again intimates the operation of unintended, or unanticipated, effects of social action. The Romans presumably never intended to rear an engine against mankind by whose recoil they themselves would perish. They presumably never intended, or foresaw, that the very ways they had cleared to reach their enemies would later serve their enemies to reach them. But it was remarked above that the sentences just quoted might have been written only yesteryear. In the very recent one-volume edition of his *Study of History,* Arnold Toynbee writes of the imperial Roman roads quite as if he had taken his cue from Ferguson. The resemblance is indeed striking enough to demand quotation from Toynbee:

> If the makers and panegyrists of the Roman imperial system of communications could have foreseen the future they would have found it intolerable, no doubt, but not unintelligible in a

world in which "all roads" led "to Rome," that the thoroughfares which in their time were bringing prisoners, petitioners and sightseers to the imperial city should one day convey barbarian war-bands or the armies of rival empires. These imperial highways certainly enabled, and possible inspired, the barbarian invaders to make straight for the heart of the Hellenic world.[7]

Thus does Ferguson appear to be peculiarly up-to-date in a book whose "day" is long gone. And it is evident that his history enriches his sociology—or that his sociology enriches his history.

The Roman history, like the *Essay,* strikes some somber notes. The strong theological optimism evident in Ferguson's *Principles,* which could lead him to write that "to those who are qualified with intelligence and grateful mind, every circumstance in the order of nature may serve to manifest and extol the supreme wisdom and goodness of God" (I, 187), did not prevent him from noting the reality of decadence in the history of nations, which can become weak and obscure as "naturally" as they can rise to the very heights. Gibbon had presented in the third chapter of his *Decline and Fall* the famous view that if one were asked to indicate the period of the happiest and most prosperous condition of humanity, he would unhesitatingly name the period between the death of Domitian and the accession of Commodus (98–180 A.D.). On just about the same period, Ferguson's bias is that "if a people could be happy by any other virtue than their own," this was indeed a time in which human happiness might be supposed "complete." But a people cannot really be happy "by any other virtue than their own." They may receive protection from the justice and humanity of single men; but can receive "independence, vigour, and peace of mind only from their own" (468). The opinion is clearly more "pessimistic" than Gibbon's, and the tone of the political moralist is again like that of the *Essay.*

One gets the powerful impression from the Roman history as a whole that Ferguson feels himself to be chronicling a great decline in political morality (as well as portraying a situation in which the Romans are defeated by their very successes). The decline is not entirely uniform or constant. Thus, Tiberius, Caligula, Claudius and Nero do go, and are in time succeeded by rulers like the Antonines. (Ferguson does touch somewhat on the Empire too.) But the general picture of decline remains. (The germ of recovery may be in decline, as the *Essay* suggests, but that is something else.) Perhaps above all one gets the impression that the political moralist Ferguson is revolted by what he sees as the sheer decline in Roman virtue. The continuities with the *Essay* are marked indeed.

It is certainly fair to call Ferguson a "historical sociologist." His historical and comparative interests are evident from the *Essay*, even if one puts the Roman history aside. For Ferguson and his contemporaries the classical world was still a great subject for study and a great source of instruction.

For us, a last bit of instruction may now be drawn from the Roman history. Ferguson writes with Olympian calm: "The distinctions of poor and rich are as necessary in states of considerable extent as labour and good government. The poor are destined to labour, and the rich, by the advantages of education, independence, and leisure, are qualified for superior stations" (85). It is once more quite clear that whatever else he may have been, Adam Ferguson was no revolutionary, no anarchist, no intransigent opponent of the status quo.

There are two other features, aside from the great range of moral philosophy (an important component of which is a sociology in process of formation) and keen interest in history, of the work of Ferguson and a number of his contemporaries that may be noted much more briefly. One is an interest in human nature that the Scots so strongly manifest. Human nature constitutes a preoccupation for Ferguson in both the *Essay* and the *Principles.* Adam Smith's *Theory of Moral Sentiments* deals extensively with human nature. Hume's great early *Treatise of Human Nature* has a title that speaks for itself. The Scots were indeed "psychologists," being especially concerned with psychology as it bore on moral issues. One of the outstanding contributions of Scottish social psychology was Adam Smith's treatment of the impartial spectator in the *Moral Sentiments.*

Ferguson has nothing comparable to show, but he made adroit use of stoic ideas to lay the foundations of a theory of human nature; and he constantly relates human nature to the circumstances of society.

The remaining feature to be noted is the empirical bias of Ferguson and others. The Scottish philosophers certainly had abstract interests, but in the midst of these they had a powerful tendency to rely on experience and observation. Their interest in human nature led them to, and was guided by, the view that human nature was rather universally the same, and their empirical-observational bias inclined them to take into account such information as was available from early anthropological reports and comparative materials. The combination of the interest in, and universalistic bias about, human nature with the empirical-observational bent often induced a sagacity of comment that anthropologists may still admire. Ferguson was not easily fooled by divergences in social or cultural forms that in the end amounted to little. He saw a constancy of motive and an incidental difference in form in phenomena which might have induced less sagacious observers to spin out dubious theories on a ground of questionable presumptions of basic divergence. Thus, he writes in his *Principles,* "it is the form of respect in Europe to uncover the head. In Japan, we are told, the corresponding form is to drop the slipper, or to uncover the foot. The physical action in these instances is different, but the moral action is the same" (II, 142). No distraction is allowed to be created here by a "physical difference" that in relation to the "moral" meaning is quite insignificant. Possibly, Ferguson was inspired to make this comment by Bernard Mandeville, whose spokesman in the second volume of the *Fable of the Bees* observes that "to show respect, a man as well might have pulled off one of his shoes as his hat."[8] It is noteworthy that Mandeville (whom Ferguson refers to more than once in his works) insisted again and again that human nature is universally the same.

The concern with human nature (together with the emphasis on its constancy) and the empirical bias lend eighteenth-century Scottish social science a certain realistic, almost earthy quality.

Social science does allow for "evolutionary" differences. Ferguson thus writes of "savages" and "barbarians," as Adam Smith writes of "the lowest and rudest state of society" or "a more advanced state of society." While such phrases inevitably imply some human differences, the general anthropological thrust is not toward vivid representation of, and great stress on differences but rather toward noting common features beneath variations. Ferguson and other like Smith provide an approach to human behavior and human societies that, one might argue even today, makes a strategic beginning with all-important commonalities. (Even the important evolutionary differences do not destroy the commonalities.)

Let us turn now more particularly to the *Essay*. The book's reputation has not been an altogether consistent one. Its value has been questioned by some eminent men. David Hume did not care for it, although we do not know why.[9] Leslie Stephen, a century after Hume, found it superficial, also remarking, however, that "here and there we come across an argument or an illustration which seems to indicate greater acuteness."[10] The economist Schumpeter commented something over two decades ago that the considerable reputation the *Essay* enjoyed in Germany (partly through the influence of Marx) appeared to him to be "unmerited."[11] These are considerable critics and something must be granted to them. The drift of a certain amount of the adverse criticism (for instance as coming from Leslie Stephen) suggests that one clear shortcoming of the *Essay* is a declamatory tendency: declamatory rather than explanatory, oratorical rather than analytical. But this does not always hold and there are passages that exhibit depth (as indeed Stephen himself half acknowledged). Also, it is again merely accurate to note that the book has received decidedly favorable notice from other thinkers of stature. Karl Marx quoted (approvingly) from it at some length in his *The Poverty of Philosophy*.[11] The able Austrian sociologist Ludwig Gumplowicz regarded it as "the first natural history of society" and the man who composed it as "the first sociologist."[13]

The *Essay* has shown considerable stamina and has again come into some prominence in the world of recent scholarship.

It presents a number of themes, or emphases, that various present day scholars evidently find compelling. One of these is already referred to as the evolution of society, and Part II of the *Essay*, on this theme, is one of the better realized portions of the book.

When Ferguson suggests that Thucydides understood that he would find in the ways of barbarous nations in his own day indications of what the ancient manners of the Greeks themselves had been, and affirms, more generally, that if "in advanced years" we would know about the earlier social conditions from which we came, we must look to "the example of those who are still in the period of life we mean to describe" (Part II, Section I), he is now less likely to meet with the unfriendly criticism he once might have met. He is not saying that all particular societies must necessarily go through the same stages precisely and down to the least detail. Ferguson's contemporary, John Millar, did write that "the similarity of his [*vis.* man's] wants, as well as of the faculties by which those wants are supplied, has everywhere produced a remarkable uniformity in the several stages of his progression."[14] But just what does "uniformity" mean? Millar was too knowledgeable historically to allow himself belief in an inflexible evolutionary scheme. An "original similarity in all the governments of modern Europe" did not prevent him from seeing certain divergences in the development of the European states.[15] There is no reason to think that Ferguson was more naive, or ignorant, in such matters generally than Millar. It seems quite plausible to suggest that Ferguson is telling us that there is likely to be some sort of pattern, or order, in major social sequences, at least when there are no potent special influences from "outside." (Given the actual chances of "outside" influence, we must say today, "laws" of evolutionary stages, or sequences, are to be regarded with utmost caution.)

There are scholars who continue to be interested in social evolution in terms of a broad view of societal "steps," or "stages," as Ferguson was, and there is some looking back with interest to what Ferguson, or his contemporaries, did in this regard.[16] But the more general idea of evolution has also been evoking a measure of interest and Ferguson's pages that are explicitly on evolution in the *Essay* might elicit intellectual sympathy even from scholars whose particular orientation in respect to evolution is not very much like that set out in the *Essay*. It must also be remarked, however, that the *Essay* is suggestive of an "evolutionary" sense in more than one way. Through long development and "successive improvement," human institutions may develop to a point of usefulness for meeting a variety of social necessities that could never have been provided for by a deliberate, conscious facing up to these necessities. Social establishments thereby carry a notable freight of gradually evolved "wisdom." This is Ferguson's bias, as when he writes "those [human] establishments arose from successive improvements that were made, without any sense of their general effect; and they bring human affairs to a state of complication, which the greatest reach of capacity with which human nature was ever adorned, could not have projected." (Part IV, Section I). This is an aspect of Ferguson's evolutionary outlook that ties him to the earlier theories of Bernard Mandeville and the much later ones of Friedrich Hayek rather than to "step" or "stage" theorists.

Another feature of the *Essay* that attracts attention today is the place it makes for conflict in human social life. One contemporary commentator observes, "Ferguson's analysis of the nature and function of conflict is well known; it deserves to be, for its cool detachment is as impressive as it is chilling."[17] Ferguson himself writes at the end of Section IV of Part I that "it is vain to expect that we can give to the multitude of a people a sense of union among themselves without admitting hostility to those who oppose them." Or he will tell us that "the frequent practice of war tends to strengthen the bands of society, and the practice of depredation itself engages men in trials of mutual attachment and courage" (Part I, Section IX). Or again he will say that "Athens was necessary to Sparta, in the exercise of her virtue, as steel is to flint in the production of fire" (adding that "if the cities of Greece had been united under one head, we should never have heard of Epaminondas or Thrasybulus, of Lycurgus or Solon"—Part I, Section IX). Conflict, for Ferguson, clearly has its social uses and civic value. We may not share his tendency toward enthusiasm for conflict, but we must discern here something of the effect of that empirical-observational bias we have noted—a bias that would in any case make him stress the sheer reality of conflict whether one happens to like that reality or not.

The treatment of conflict in the *Essay* intersects with its treatment of the division of labor. Ferguson has misgivings, in respect to the latter, as did Adam Smith and John Millar. One of the significant statements in the *Essay* presents, with reference to the division of labor, a situation in which "society is made to consist of parts, of which none is animated with the spirit of society itself" (Part V, Section III). Adam Smith thought that as the division of labor advanced, the great body of laborers, coming to work as they did on a few simple operations, suffered in their understanding and experienced "torpor" of mind, while the strictly confined skills they acquired were accompanied not only by loss of intellectual but also of social and martial virtue's.[18] Millar sees the common workman of England as nearly "stripped of his mental powers" and "converted into the mere intrument of labor"[19] much more than the Scottish workman who was less subjected to the division of labor. Ferguson is no more blind to the advantageous side of the division of labor than Smith or Millar. He is well aware of the enhancement of productivity emergent with division of tasks. "By having separated the arts of the clothier and the tanner, we are the better supplied with shoes and with cloth." But then we are told that "to separate the arts which form the citizen and the statesman, the arts of policy and war, is an attempt to dismember the human character, and to destroy those very arts we mean to improve." This separation deprives a free people of "what is necessary to their safety," prepares "a [purchased] defence against invasions from abroad which gives a prospect of usurpation, and threatens the establishment of military government at home" (Part V, Section IV).

It is here that we see the intersection of the conflict and division of labor themes. Ferguson's concern over the removal from the citizen of all features of the soldier is expressed as a revulsion from what he evidently regarded as a diminution of full civic humanity, or full civic participation. He plainly indicates the fear of an inability of a people without soldierly experience to resist an enemy and an apprehension lest a citizenry deprived of all military engagement be subordinated by the agents it may procure to do its military work. (We have already noted similar intimations in the Roman history.) Adam Smith, for his part, favored the notion that "the security of every society must always depend, more or less, upon the martial spirit of the great body of the people."[20] This might be construed as a statement whose intent is purely empirical. But whether pertinent statements about the citizen's participation in military conflict are in the realm of political sociology, or of political ethics or morality, Ferguson, and Smith, are saying some things to us that are still important to consider.

Aside from its reflection on evolution, conflict, and the division of labor, perhaps the aspect of the *Essay* that accounts more for present day attention to it than any other, is its particular focus on wealth, or commerce, and civic life. We recall Ferguson's previously recorded sharp assertions that men's virtues have been most shining while they have struggled for their ends, not after they have attained them, and that "those ends themselves, though attained by virtue, are frequently the causes of corruption and vice." Ferguson very soon then refers suggestively to "neglects which prosperity itself had encouraged" (Part V, Section I). He is exercised above all over the pursuit of security, property, gain (and pleasure) while men lose their very political concerns and interests. To take advantage of the safety ostensibly rendered by certain political conditions merely in order to enjoy or advance fortune, is not to deserve the safety referred to, and is to decline into corruption. Wealth and commerce unreservedly pursued work insidiously to alienate humans from their own civic propensities.

Two recent commentators may be drawn upon to indicate something of the impression that these views of Ferguson's currently make upon scholars. The historian Pocock writes, precisely in context of discussion of Ferguson:

The paradigm of commerce presented the movement of history as being toward the indefinite multiplication of goods, and brought the whole progress of material, cultural, and moral civilization under this head. But so long as it did not contain any equivalent to the concept of the *zoon politikon,* of the individual as an autonomous, morally and politically choosing being, progress must appear to move away from something essential to human personality. And this corruption was self-generating; society as an engine for the production and multiplication of goods was inherently hostile to society as the moral foundation of personality. The history of commerce revealed once again that the republic had not solved the problem of existing as a universal value in particular and contingent time.[21]

The economist Hirschman also follows Ferguson on wealth, or commerce, and corruption. Ferguson, Hirschman notes, saw why preoccupation with individual wealth can lead to "despotical government," by way of corruption through luxury and prodigality. Hirschman observes that Ferguson added to that traditional argument and he alludes to Ferguson's touching upon fear of downward mobility, seen, in Hirschman's words, as "intimately bound up with the acquisitive society and its tumultuous ways" and as generating feelings of "relative deprivation and *ressentiment,*" which afford "a breeding ground for the ready acceptance of whatever 'strong' government promises to stave off such real or imagined dangers [of downward mobility]." Also, commerce, writes Hirschman, still expounding Ferguson, "creates a desire for tranquility and efficiency, and this may be another source of despotism."[22] Whatever the detailed mechanisms, the argument runs on the main line that wealth and commerce, once more, woo humans away from a civic disposition that would inhibit the inclination to despotism and constrain the people of possessions, the "beati possidentes," to put public concerns and involvement before those same possessions.

The loss of human political and civic essence thus stressed is spelled out by Ferguson in large generalizations that are less than ideally exemplified and systematically developed. The declamatory tendency in Ferguson unfortunately does not nourish his much more impressive empirical-observational bent. There are, moreover, tensions in his thought with regard to the "liberal" and toward the "conservative" side that he never resolves. But once more he has been provocative on some crucial matters in political sociology and political morality. His stature is a larger stature than the *Essay on the History of Civil Society* alone might indicate. No one interested in Ferguson and early modern social science can afford to neglect the *Essay.* Its considerable actual influence in social science would in itself demand attention to it. No work by a man who figures in the background of Hegel, Marx, Lessing, J.S. Mill, and Friedrich Schiller, among others, can possibly fail to appeal to us as culturally significant.

Bibiographical Note

Ferguson's main works are the *Essay on the History of Civil Society* (1767), the *Institutes of Moral Philosophy* (1769), the *History of the Progress and Terminationof the Roman Republic* (1783; subsequent editions), and the *Principles of Moral and Political Science* (1792; reprinted Hildesheim, New York: George Olms, 1975, with an Introduction by Jean Hecht).

Significant commentaries on Ferguson's work include William C. Lehmann, *Adam Ferguson and the Beginnings of Modern Sociology,* (New York: Columbia University Press, 1930); Herta H. Jogland, *Ursprünge und Grundlagen der Soziologie bei Adam Ferguson,* (Berlin: Duncker and Humblot, 1959); David Kettler, *The Social and Political Philosophy of Adam Ferguson,* (Ohio University Press, 1965). An older work, now in danger of being completely overlooked although it should not be, is Hermann Huth, *Soziale and Individualistische Auffassung, vornehmlich bei Adam Smith und Adam Ferguson,* (Leipzig: Duncker and Humblot, 1907). The most comprehensive book on Ferguson is Pasquale Salvucci, *Adam Ferguson: Sociologia e Philosophia Politica,* (Urbino: Argàlia, 1972).

A very brief but informative account of Ferguson is presented by William C. Lehmann in the *International Encyclopedia of the Social Sciences,* (New York: Macmillan and Free, 1968), vol. 5, pp. 369-71. Still important for Ferguson's life is the very readable but unfortunately not highly accessible account by John Small, *Biographical Sketch of Adam Ferguson,* (Edinburgh: Neill and Company, 1864).

Statements on eighteenth century Scottish thought, for those interested in social science in particular, may be found in Gladys Bryson, *Man and Society: The Scottish Inquiry of the Eighteenth Century,* (Princeton: Princeton University Press, 1945; reprinted New York: Augustus M. Kelley, 1968), and in William C. Lehmann, *John Millar of*

Glasgow, (Cambridge: The University Press, 1960). Both these books have things to say about Ferguson among others. Ferguson's writings may be seen in relation to the writings of fellow Scots preoccupied with like subjects in the selected readings in Louis Schneider, editor, *The Scottish Moralists on Human Nature and Society,* (Chicage: University of Chicago Press, 1967). There is an additional literature that continues to appear dealing with Scottish contemporaries other than Ferguson but containing references to him. Examples include Andrew S. Skinner and Thomas Wilson, editors, *Essays on Adam Smith,* (Oxford: Clarendon Press, 1975); David A Reisman, *Adam Smith's Sociological Economics,* (New York: Barnes and Noble, 1976); William C. Lehmann, *Henry Home, Lord Kames, and the Scottish Enlightenment,* (The Hague: Martinus Nijhoff, 1971); Ian S. Ross, *Lord Kames and the Scotland of his Day,* (Oxford: Clarendon Press, 1972).

A very detailed Ferguson bibliography appears in the Italian version of the *Essay,* the *Saggio sulla Storia della Società Civile,* (Florence: Vallecchi, 1973, under the editorship of Pasquale Salvucci), pp. 351-74.

NOTES

1. A. L. Kroeber, *Configurations of Culture Growth,* (Berkeley and Los Angeles: University of California Press, 1944), p. 713.
2. Ronald L. Meek, "The Scottish Contribution to Marxist Sociology," in John Saville, ed., *Democracy and the Labour Movement,* (London: Lawrence and Wishart, Ltd., 1954). pp. 84-102.
3. John Small, *Biographical Sketch of Adam Ferguson,* (Edinburgh: Neill and Company, 1964), pp. 4-5.
4. See F.A. Hayek, *Studies in Philosophy, Politics and Economies,* (Chicago: University of Chicago Press, 1967), ch. 6.
5. Herta H. Jogland, *Ursprünge und Grundlagen der Sociologie bei Adam Ferguson,* (Berlin: Duncker and Humblot, 1959). p. 164.
6. Of the numerous editions, we use here the one published at London by Jones and Co. in 1825. The book is very little read today but is described as that by which Ferguson was "best known in his own day," by James McGosh, *The Scottish Philosophy,* (New York: Robert Carter and Bros., 1874), p. 258.
7. Arnold Toynbee, *A Study of History,* new edition revised and abridged by the author and June Caplan, (New York: Weathervane Books, 1972), p. 292.
8. *The Fable of the Bees,* (Oxford: Clarendon Press, 1924), vol. II, p. 150.
9. For Hume's opinion, see Ernest C. Mossner, *The Life of David Hume,* (Austin: University of Texas Press, 1954), pp. 542-43. Mossner writes (p. 543), "Hume nowhere specifies his disap-

proval of Ferguson's reasonings, which were no little indebted to his own."

10. Leslie Stephen, *History of English Thought in the Eighteenth Century*, (New York: Harcourt, Brace and World, 1962), vol. II, p. 182.

11. Joseph A. Schumpeter, *History of Economic Analysis*, (New York: Oxford University Press, 1954), p. 184, footnote 16.

12. Karl Marx, *The Poverty of Philosophy*, (Moscow: Foreign Languages Publishing House, n.d.), p. 124. In both this work and in *Capital*, (New York: Random House (Modern Library), 1936), vol. I, p. 139, footnote Marx, curiously, harbors the notion that Ferguson was Adam Smith's teacher.

13. As quoted by William C. Lehmann, "Adam Ferguson," *International Encyclopedia of the Social Sciences*, (New York: Macmillan and Free Press, 1968), vol. 5, p. 369, from Gumplowicz, *Die Soziologische Staatsidee*, (Graz: Leuschner and Lubensky, 1892), p. 67.

14. John Millar, *The Origin of the Distinction of Ranks*, Part III in William C. Lehmann, *John Millar of Glasgow*, (Cambridge: The University Press, 1960), p. 176.

15. John Millar, *An Historical View of the English Government*, (London: J. Mawman, 1803), vol. III, pp. 10-11.

16. See Ronald L. Meek, *Social Science and the Ignoble Savage*, (London: Cambridge University Press, 1976).

17. Peter Gay, *The Enlightenment*, (New York: Knopf, 1969), vol. II, pp. 339-40.

18. Adam Smith, *The Wealth of Nations*, (Oxford: Clarendon Press, 1976), vol. 2, pp. 781-82.

19. *An Historical View of the English Government*, (London: J. Mawman, 1803), vol. IV, p. 152.

20. *The Wealth of Nations*, 1976, vol. 2, p. 787.

21. J.G.A. Pocock, *The Machiavellian Moment*, (Princeton: Princeton University Press, 1975), p. 501.

22. Albert O. Hirschman, *The Passions and the Interests*, (Princeton: Princeton University Press, 1977), p. 121.

Contents

PART III.
Of the History of Policy and Arts.

PART IV.
Of Consequences that result from the Advancement of Civil and Commercial Arts.

PART V.
Of the Decline of Nations.

PART VI.
Of Corruption and Political Slavery.

PART FIRST.

Of the General Characteristics of Human Nature.

SECTION I.

Of the question relating to the State of Nature.

Natural productions are generally formed by degrees. Vegetables grow from a tender shoot, and animals from an infant state. The latter being destined to act, extend their operations as their powers increase: they exhibit a progress, in what they perform, as well as in the faculties they acquire. This progress in the case of man is continued to a greater extent than in that of any other animal. Not only the individual advances from infancy to manhood, but the species itself from rudeness to civilization. Hence the supposed departure of mankind from the state of their nature; hence our conjectures and different opinions of what man must have been in the first age of his being. The poet, the historian, and the moralist, frequently allude to this ancient time; and under the emblems of gold, or of iron, represent a condition, and a manner of life, from which mankind have either degenerated, or on which they have greatly improved. On either supposition, the first state of our nature must have borne no resemblance to what men have exhibited in any subsequent period; historical monuments, even of the earliest date, are to be considered as novelties; and the most common establishments of human society are to be classed among the incroachments which fraud, oppression, or a busy invention, have made upon the reign of nature, by which the chief of our grievances or blessings were equally with-held.

Among the writers who have attempted to distinguish, in the human character, its original qualities, and to point out the limits between nature and art, some have represented mankind in their first condition, as possessed of mere animal sensibility, without any exercise of the faculties that render them superior to the brutes, without any political union, without any means of explaining their sentiments, and even without possessing any of the apprehensions and passions which the voice and the gesture are so well fitted to express. Others have made the state of nature to consist in perpetual wars, kindled by competition for dominion and interest, where every individual had a separate quarrel with his kind, and where the presence of a fellow-creature was the signal of battle.

The desire of laying the foundation of a favourite system, or a fond expectation, perhaps, that we may be able to penetrate the secrets of nature, to the very source of existence, have, on this subject, led to many fruitless inquiries, and given rise to many wild suppositions. Among the various qualities which mankind possess, we select one or a few particulars on which to establish a theory, and in framing our account of what man was in some imaginary state of nature, we overlook what he has always appeared within the reach of our own observation, and in the records of history.

In every other instance, however, the natural historian thinks himself obliged to collect facts, not to offer conjectures. When he treats of any particular species of animals, he supposes, that their present dispositions and instincts are the same they originally had, and that their present manner of life is a continuance of their first destination. He admits, that his knowledge of the material system of the world consists in a collection of facts, or at most, in general tenets derived from particular observations and experiments. It is only in what relates to himself, and in matters the most important, and the most easily known, that he substitutes hypothesis instead of reality, and confounds the provinces of imagination and reason, of poetry and science.

But without entering any farther on questions either in moral or physical subjects, relating to the manner or to the origin of our knowledge; without any disparagement to that subtilty which would analyze every sentiment, and trace every mode of being to its source; it may be safely affirmed, that the character of man, as he now exists, that the laws of this animal and intellectual system, on which his happiness now depends, deserve our principal study; and that general principles relating to this, or any other subject, are useful only so far as they are founded on just observation, and lead to the knowledge of important consequences, or so far as they enable us to act with success when we would apply either the intellectual or the physical powers of nature, to the great purposes of human life.

If both the earliest and the latest accounts collected from every quarter of the earth, represent mankind as assembled in troops and companies; and the individual always joined by affection to one party, while he is possibly opposed to another; employed in the exercise of recollection and foresight; inclined to communicate his own sentiments, and to be made acquainted with those of others; these facts must be admitted as the foundation of all our reasoning relative to man. His mixed disposition to friendship or enmity, his reason, his use of language and articulate sounds, like the shape and the erect position of his body, are to be considered as so many attributes of his nature: they are to be retained in his description, as the wing and the paw are in that of the eagle and the lion, and as different degrees of fierceness, vigilance, timidity, or speed, are made to occupy a place in the natural history of different animals.

If the question be put, What the mind of man could perform, when left to itself, and without the aid of any foreign direction? we are to look for our answer in the history of mankind. Particular experiments which have been found so useful in establishing the principles of other sciences, could probably, on this subject, teach us nothing important, or new: we are to take the history of every active being from his conduct in the situation to which he is formed, not from his appearance in any forced or uncommon condition; a wild man therefore, caught in the woods, where he had always lived apart from his species, is a singular instance, not a specimen of any general character. As the anatomy of an eye which had never received the impressions of light, or that of an ear which had never felt the impulse of sounds, would probably exhibit defects in the very structure of the organs themselves, arising from their not being applied to their proper functions; so any particular case of this sort would only shew in what degree the powers of apprehension and sentiment could exist where they had not been employed, and what would be the defects and imbecilities of a heart in which the emotions that pertain to society had never been felt.

Mankind are to be taken in groupes, as they have always subsisted. The history of the individual is but a detail of the sentiments and thoughts he has entertained in the view of his species: and every experiment relative to this subject should be made with entire societies, not with single men. We have every reason, however, to believe, that in the case of such an experiment made, we shall suppose, with a colony of children transplanted from the nursery, and left to form a society apart, untaught, and undisciplined, we should only have the same things repeated, which, in so many different parts of the earth, have been transacted already. The members of our little society would feed and sleep, would herd together and play, would have a language of their own, would quarrel and divide, would be to one another the most important objects of the scene, and, in the ardour of their friendships and competitions, would overlook their personal danger, and suspend the care of their self-preservation. Has not the human race been planted like the colony in question? Who has directed their course? whose instruction have they heard? or whose example have they followed?

Nature, therefore, we shall presume, having given to every animal its mode of existence, its dispositions and manner of life, has dealt equally with those of the human race; and the natural historian who would collect the properties of this species, may fill up every article now, as well as he could have done in any former age. Yet one property by which man is distinguished, has been sometimes overlooked in the account of his nature, or has only served to mislead our attention. In other classes of animals, the individual advances from infancy to age or maturity;

and he attains, in the compass of a single life, to all the perfection his nature can reach: but, in the human kind, the species has a progress as well as the individual; they build in every subsequent age on foundations formerly laid; and, in a succession of years, tend to a perfection in the application of their faculties, to which the aid of long experience is required, and to which many generations must have combined their endeavours. We observe the progress they have made; we distinctly enumerate many of its steps; we can trace them back to a distant antiquity; of which no record remains, nor any monument is preserved, to inform us what were the openings of this wonderful scene. The consequence is, that instead of attending to the character of our species, where the particulars are vouched by the surest authority, we endeavour to trace it through ages and scenes unknown; and, instead of supposing that the beginning of our story was nearly of a piece with the sequel, we think ourselves warranted to reject every circumstance of our present condition and frame, as adventitious, and foreign to our nature. The progress of mankind from a supposed state of animal sensibility, to the attainment of reason, to the use of language, and to the habit of society, has been accordingly painted with a force of imagination, and its steps have been marked with a boldness of invention, that would tempt us to admit, among the materials of history, the suggestions of fancy, and to receive, perhaps, as the model of our nature in its original state, some of the animals whose shape has the greatest resemblance to ours.*

It would be ridiculous to affirm, as a discovery, that the species of the horse was probably never the same with that of the lion; yet, in opposition to what has dropped from the pens of eminent writers, we are obliged to observe, that men have always appeared among animals a distinct and a superior race; that neither the possession of similar organs, nor the approximation of shape, nor the use of the hand†, nor the continued intercourse with this sovereign artist, has enabled any other species to blend their nature or their inventions with his; that in his rudest state, he is

* Rousseau, *sur l'origine de l'inégalité parmi les hommes.*
† *Traité de l'esprit.*

found to be above them; and in his greatest degeneracy, never descends to their level. He is, in short, a man in every condition; and we can learn nothing of his nature from the analogy of other animals. If we would know him, we must attend to himself, to the course of his life, and the tenor of his conduct. With him the society appears to be as old as the individual, and the use of the tongue as universal as that of the hand or the foot. If there was a time in which he had his acquaintance with his own species to make, and his faculties to acquire, it is a time of which we have no record, and in relation to which our opinions can serve no purpose, and are supported by no evidence.

We are often tempted into these boundless regions of ignorance or conjecture, by a fancy which delights in creating rather than in merely retaining the forms which are presented before it: we are the dupes of a subtilty, which promises to supply every defect of our knowledge, and, by filling up a few blanks in the story of nature, pretends to conduct our apprehension nearer to the source of existence. On the credit of a few observations, we are apt to presume, that the secret may soon be laid open, and that what is termed *wisdom* in nature, may be referred to the operation of physical powers. We forget that physical powers, employed in succession, and combined to a salutary purpose, constitute those very proofs of design from which we infer the existence of God; and that this truth being once admitted, we are no longer to search for the source of existence; we can only collect the laws which the author of nature has established; and in our latest as well as our earliest discoveries, only come to perceive a mode of creation or providence before unknown.

We speak of art as distinguished from nature; but art itself is natural to man. He is in some measure the artificer of his own frame, as well as his fortune, and is destined, from the first age of his being, to invent and contrive. He applies the same talents to a variety of purposes, and acts nearly the same part in very different scenes. He would be always improving on his subject, and he carries this intention where-ever he moves, through the streets of the populous city, or the wilds of the forest. While he appears equally fitted to every condition, he is upon this account unable to settle in any. At once obstinate and fickle, he complains of innovations, and is never sated with novelty. He is perpetually busied in reformations, and is continually wedded to his errors. If he dwell in a cave, he would improve it into a cottage; if he has already built, he would still build to a greater extent. But he does not propose to make rapid and hasty transitions; his steps are progressive and slow; and his force, like the power of a spring, silently presses on every resistance; an effect is sometimes produced before the cause is perceived; and with all his talent for projects, his work is often accomplished before the plan is devised. It appears, perhaps, equally difficult to retard or to quicken his pace; if the projector complain he is tardy, the moralist thinks him unstable; and whether his motions be rapid or slow, the scenes of human affairs perpetually change in his management: his emblem is a passing stream, not a stagnating pool. We may desire to direct his love of improvement to its proper object, we may wish for stability of conduct; but we mistake human nature, if we wish for a termination of labour, or a scene of repose.

The occupations of men, in every condition, bespeak their freedom of choice, their various opinions, and the multiplicity of wants by which they are urged: but they enjoy, or endure, with a sensibility, or a phlegm, which are nearly the same in every situation. They possess the shores of the Caspian, or the Atlantic, by a different tenure, but with equal ease. On the one they are fixed to the soil, and seem to be formed for settlement, and the accommodation of cities: The names they bestow on a nation, and on its territory, are the same. On the other they are mere animals of passage, prepared to roam on the face of the earth, and with their herds, in search of new pasture and favourable seasons, to follow the sun in his annual course.

Man finds his lodgment alike in the cave, the cottage, and the palace; and his subsistence equally in the woods, in the dairy, or the farm. He assumes the distinction of titles, equipage, and dress; he devises regular systems of government, and a complicated body of laws: or, naked in the woods, has no badge of superiority but the strength of his limbs and the sagacity of his mind; no rule of conduct but choice; no tie with his fellow-creatures but affection, the love of company, and the desire of safety. Capable of a great variety of arts, yet dependent on none in particular for the preservation of his being; to whatever length he has carried his artifice, there he seems to enjoy the conveniencies that suit his nature, and to have found the condition to which he is destined. The tree which an American, on the banks of the Oroonoko,* has chosen to climb for the retreat, and the lodgement of his family, is to him a convenient dwelling. The sopha, the vaulted dome, and the colonade, do not more effectually content their native inhabitant.

If we are asked therefore, Where the state of nature is to be found? we may answer, It is here; and it matters not whether we are understood to speak in the island of Great Britain, at the Cape of Good Hope, or the Straits of Magellan. While this active being is in the train of employing his talents, and of operating on the subjects around him, all situations are equally natural. If we are told, That vice, at least, is contrary to nature; we may answer, It is worse; it is folly and wretchedness. But if nature is only opposed to art, in what situation of the human race are the footsteps of art unknown? In the condition of the savage, as well as in that of the citizen, are many proofs of human invention; and in either is not any permanent station, but a mere stage through which this travelling being is destined to pass. If the palace be unnatural, the cottage is so no less; and the highest refinements of political and moral apprehension, are not more artificial in their kind, than the first operations of sentiment and reason.

If we admit that man is susceptible of improvement, and has in himself a principle of progression, and a desire of perfection, it appears improper to say, that he has quitted the state of his nature, when he has begun to proceed; or that he finds a station for which he was not intended, while, like other animals, he only follows the disposition, and employs the powers that nature has given.

The latest efforts of human invention are but a continuation of

* Lafitau, *Moeurs des sauvages.*

certain devices which were practised in the earliest ages of the world, and in the rudest state of mankind. What the savage projects, or observes, in the forest, are the steps which led nations, more advanced, from the architecture of the cottage to that of the palace, and conducted the human mind from the perceptions of sense, to the general conclusions of science.

Acknowledged defects are to man in every condition matter of dislike. Ignorance and imbecility are objects of contempt: penetration and conduct give eminence, and procure esteem. Whither should his feelings and apprehensions on these subjects lead him? To a progress, no doubt, in which the savage, as well as the philosopher, is engaged; in which they have made different advances, but in which their ends are the same. The admiration Cicero entertained for literature, eloquence, and civil accomplishments, was not more real than that of a Scythian for such a measure of similar endowments as his own apprehension could reach. 'Were I to boast,' says a Tartar prince,* 'it would be of that wisdom I have received from God. For as, on the one hand, I yield to none in the conduct of war, in the disposition of armies, whether of horse or of foot, and in directing the movements of great or small bodies; so, on the other, I have my talent in writing, inferior perhaps only to those who inhabit the great cities of Persia or India. Of other nations, unknown to me, I do not speak.'

Man may mistake the objects of his pursuit; he may misapply his industry, and misplace his improvements. If under a sense of such possible errors, he would find a standard by which to judge of his own proceedings, and arrive at the best state of his nature, he cannot find it perhaps in the practice of any individual, or of any nation whatever; not even in the sense of the majority, or the prevailing opinion of his kind. He must look for it in the best conceptions of his understanding, in the best movements of his heart; he must thence discover what is the perfection and the happiness of which he is capable. He will find, on the scrutiny, that the proper state of his nature, taken in this sense, is not a condition from which mankind are for ever removed, but one to

* Abulgaze Bahadur Chan, *History of the Tartars.*

which they may now attain; not prior to the exercise of their faculties, but procured by their just application.

Of all the terms that we employ in treating of human affairs, those of *natural* and *unnatural* are the least determinate in their meaning. Opposed to affectation, frowardness, or any other defect of the temper of character, the natural is an epithet of praise; but employed to specify a conduct which proceeds from the nature of man, can serve to distinguish nothing: for all the actions of men are equally the result of their nature. At most, this language can only refer to the general and prevailing sense or practice of mankind; and the purpose of every important inquiry on this subject may be served by the use of a language equally familiar and more precise. What is just, or unjust? What is happy, or wretched, in the manners of men? What, in their various situations, is favourable or adverse to their amiable qualities? are questions to which we may expect a satisfactory answer; and whatever may have been the original state of our species, it is of more importance to know the condition to which we ourselves should aspire, than that which our ancestors may be supposed to have left.

SECTION II.
Of the principles of Self-preservation.

If in human nature there are qualities by which it is distinguished from every other part of the animal creation, men are themselves in different climates and in different ages greatly diversified. So far as we are able to account for this diversity on principles either moral or physical, we perform a task of great curiosity or signal utility. It appears necessary, however, that we attend to the universal qualities of our nature, before we regard its varieties, or attempt to explain differences consisting in the unequal possession or application of dispositions and powers that are in some measure common to all mankind.

Man, like the other animals, has certain instinctive propensities, which, prior to the perception of pleasure or pain, and prior to the experience of what is pernicious or useful, lead him to perform mány functions of nature relative to himself and to his fellow-creatures. He has one set of dispositions which refer to his animal preservation, and to the continuance of his race; another which lead to society, and by inlisting him on the side of one tribe or community, frequently engage him in war and contention with the rest of mankind. His powers of discernment, or his intellectual faculties, which, under the appellatión of *reason*, are distinguished from the analogous endowments of other animals, refer to the objects around him, either as they are subjects of mere knowledge, or as they are subjects of approbation or censure. He is formed not only to know, but likewise to admire and to contemn; and these proceedings of his mind have a principal reference to his own character, and to that of his fellow-creatures, as being the subjects on which he is chiefly concerned to distinguish what is right from what is wrong. He enjoys his felicity likewise on certain fixed and determinate conditions; and either as an individual apart, or as a member of civil society, must take a particular course in order to reap the advantages of his nature. He is, withal, in a very high degree susceptible of habits; and can, by forbearance or exercise, so far weaken, confirm, or even diversify his talents, and his dispositions, as to appear, in a great measure, the arbiter of his own rank in nature, and the author of all the varieties which are exhibited in the actual history of his species. The universal characteristics, in the mean time, to which we have now referred, must, when we would treat of any part of this history, constitute the first subject of our attention; and they require not only to be enumerated, but to be distinctly considered.

The dispositions which refer to the preservation of the individual, while they continue to operate in the manner of instinctive desires, are nearly the same in man that they are in the other animals: but in him they are sooner or later combined with reflection and foresight; they give rise to his apprehensions on the subject of property, and make him acquainted with that object of care which he calls his interest. Without the instincts which teach the beaver and the squirrel, the ant and the bee, to make up their little hoards for winter, at first improvident, and, where no immediate object of passion is near, addicted to sloth, he becomes, in process of time, the great storemaster among animals. He finds in a provision of wealth, which he is probably never to employ, an object of his greatest solicitude, and the principal idol of his mind. He apprehends a relation between his person and his property, which renders what he calls his own in a manner a part of himself, a constituent of his rank, his condition, and his character, in which, independent of any real enjoyment, he may be fortunate or unhappy; and, independent of any personal merit, he may be an object of consideration or neglect; and in which he may be wounded and injured, while his person is safe, and every want of his nature completely supplied.

In these apprehensions, while other passions only operate occasionally, the interested find the object of their ordinary cares; their motive to the practice of mechanic and commercial arts; their temptation to trespass on the laws of justice; and, when extremely corrupted, the price of their prostitutions, and the standard of their opinions on the subject of good and of evil. Under this influence, they would enter, if not restrained by the laws of civil society, on a scene of violence or meanness, which would exhibit our species, by turns, under an aspect more terrible and odious, or more vile and contemptible, than that of any animal which inherits the earth.

Although the consideration of interest is founded on the experience of animal wants and desires, its object is not to gratify any particular appetite, but to secure the means of gratifying all; and it imposes frequently a restraint on the very desires from which it arose, more powerful and more severe than those of religion or duty. It arises from the principles of self-preservation in the human frame; but is a corruption, or at least a partial result, of those principles, and is upon many accounts very improperly termed *self-love*.

Love is an affection which carries the attention of the mind beyond itself, and has a quality, which we call *tenderness*, that never can accompany the considerations of interest. This affection being a complacency and a continued satisfaction in its object, independent of any external event, it has, in the midst of disappointment and sorrow, pleasures and triumphs unknown to those who act without any regard to their fellow-creatures; and in every change of condition, it continues entirely distinct from the sentiments which we feel on the subject of personal success or adversity. But as the care a man entertains for his own interest, and the attention his affection makes him pay to that of another, may have similar effects, the one on his own fortune, the other on that of his friend, we confound the principles from which he acts; we suppose that they are the same in kind, only referred to different objects; and we not only misapply the name of love, in conjunction with self, but, in a manner tending to degrade our nature, we limit the aim of this supposed selfish affection to the securing or accumulating the constituents of interest, or the means of mere animal life.

It is somewhat remarkable, that notwithstanding men value themselves so much on qualities of the mind, on parts, learning and wit, on courage, generosity, and honour, those men are still supposed to be in the highest degree selfish or attentive to themselves, who are most careful of animal life, and who are least mindful of rendering that life an object worthy of care. It will be difficult, however, to tell why a good understanding, a resolute and generous mind, should not, by every man in his senses, be reckoned as much parts of himself, as either his stomach or his palate, and much more than his estate or his dress. The epicure, who consults his physician, how he may restore his relish for food, and by creating an appetite, may increase the means of enjoyment, might at least with an equal regard to himself, consult how he might strengthen his affection to a parent or a child, to his country or to mankind; and it is probable that an appetite of this sort would prove a source of enjoyment not less than the former.

By our supposed selfish maxims, notwithstanding, we generally exclude from among the objects of our personal cares, many of the happier and more respectable qualities of human nature. We consider affection and courage as mere follies, that lead us to neglect or expose ourselves; we make wisdom consist in a regard to our interest; and without explaining what interest means, we would have it understood as the only reasonable motive of action with mankind. There is even a system of philosophy founded upon tenets of this sort, and such is our opinion of what men are likely to do upon selfish principles, that we think it must have a tendency very dangerous to virtue. But the errors of this system do not consist so much in general principles, as in their particular applications; not so much in teaching men to regard themselves, as in leading them to forget that their happiest affections, their candour, and their independence of mind, are in reality parts of themselves. And the adversaries of this supposed selfish philosophy, where it makes self-love the ruling passion with mankind, have had reason to find fault, not so much with its general representations of human nature, as with the obtrusion of a mere innovation in language for a discovery in science.

When the vulgar speak of their different motives, they are satisfied with ordinary names, which refer to known and obvious distinctions. Of this kind are the terms *benevolence* and *selfishness*, by which they express their desire of the welfare of others, or the care of their own. The speculative are not always satisfied with this proceeding; they would analyze, as well as enumerate the principles of nature; and the chance is, that, merely to gain the appearance of something new, without any prospect of real advantage, they will disturb the order of vulgar apprehension. In the case before us, they have actually found, that benevolence is no more than a species of self-love; and would oblige us, if possible, to look out for a new set of words, by which we may distinguish the selfishness of the parent when he takes care of his child, from his selfishness when he only takes care of himself. For according to this philosophy, as in both cases he only means to gratify a desire of his own, he is in both cases equally selfish. The term *benevolent*, in the mean time, is not employed to characterise persons who have no desires of their own, but persons whose own desires prompt them to procure the welfare of others. The fact is, that we should need only a fresh supply of language, instead of that which by this seeming discovery we should have lost, in order to make the reasonings of men proceed as they formerly did. But it is certainly impossible to live and to act with men, without employing different names to distinguish the humane from the cruel, and the benevolent from the selfish.

These terms have their equivalents in every tongue; they were invented by men of no refinement, who only meant to express what they distinctly perceived or strongly felt. And if a man of speculation should prove that we are selfish in a sense of his own, it does not follow that we are so in the sense of the vulgar; or, as ordinary men would understand his conclusion, that we are condemned in every instance to act on motives of interest, covetousness, pusillanimity, and cowardice; for such is conceived to be the ordinary import of selfishness in the character of man.

An affection or passion of any kind is sometimes said to give us an interest in its object; and humanity itself gives an interest in the welfare of mankind. This term *interest*, which commonly implies little more than our regard to property, is sometimes put for utility in general, and this for happiness; insomuch that, under these ambiguities, it is not surprising we are still unable to determine, whether interest is the only motive of human action, and the standard by which to distinguish our good from our ill.

So much is said in this place, not from any desire to have a share in any controversy of this sort, but merely to confine the meaning of the term *interest* to its most common acceptation, and to intimate our intention of employing it in expressing those objects of care which refer to our external condition, and the preservation of our animal nature. When taken in this sense, it will not surely be thought to comprehend at once all the motives of human conduct. If men be not allowed to have disinterested benevolence, they will not be denied to have disinterested passions of another kind. Hatred, indignation, and rage, frequently urge them to act in opposition to their known interest, and even to hazard their lives, without any hopes of compensation in any future returns of preferment or profit.

SECTION III.

Of the principles of Union among Mankind.

Mankind have always wandered or settled, agreed or quarrelled, in troops and companies. The cause of their assembling, whatever it be, is the principle of their alliance or union.

In collecting the materials of history, we are seldom willing to put up with our subject merely as we find it. We are loth to be embarrassed with a multiplicity of particulars, and apparent inconsistencies. In theory we profess the investigation of general principles; and in order to bring the matter of our inquiries within the reach of our comprehension, are disposed to adopt any system. Thus, in treating of human affairs, we would draw every consequence from a principle of union, or a principle of dissension. The state of nature is a state of war or of amity, and men are made to unite from a principle of affection, or from a principle of fear, as is most suitable to the system of different writers. The history of our species indeed abundantly shews, that they are to one another mutual objects both of fear and of love; and they who prove them to have been originally either in a state of alliance, or of war, have arguments in store to maintain their assertions. Our attachment to one division, or to one sect, seems often to derive much of its force from an animosity conceived to an opposite one: and this animosity in its turn, as often arises from a zeal in behalf of the side we espouse, and from a desire to vindicate the rights of our party.

'Man is born in society,' says Montesquieu, 'and there he remains.' The charms that detain him are known to be manifold. We may reckon the parental affection, which, instead of deserting the adult, as among the brutes, embraces more close, as it becomes mixed with esteem, and the memory of its early effects; together with a propensity common to man and other animals, to mix with the herd, and, without reflection, to follow the croud of his species. What this propensity was in the first moment of its operation, we know not; but with men accustomed to company, its enjoyments and disappointments are reckoned among the principal pleasures or pains of human life. Sadness and melancholy are connected with solitude; gladness and pleasure with the concourse of men. The track of a Laplander on the snowy shore, gives joy to the lonely mariner; and the mute signs of cordiality and kindness which are made to him, awaken the memory of pleasures which he felt in society. In fine, says the writer of a voyage to the north, after describing a mute scene of this sort, 'We were extremely pleased to converse with men, since in thirteen months we had seen no human creature.'* But we need no remote observation to confirm this position: The wailings of the infant, and the languors of the adult, when alone; the lively joys of the one, and the chearfulness of the other, upon the return of company, are a sufficient proof of its solid foundations in the frame of our nature.

In accounting for actions we often forget that we ourselves have acted; and instead of the sentiments which stimulate the mind in the presence of its object, we assign as the motives of conduct with men, those considerations which occur in the hours of retirement and cold reflection. In this mood frequently we can find nothing important, besides the deliberate prospects of interest; and a great work, like that of forming society, must in our apprehension arise from deep reflections, and be carried on with a view to the advantages which mankind derive from commerce and mutual support. But neither a propensity to mix with the herd, nor the sense of advantages enjoyed in that condition, comprehend all the principles by which men are united together. Those bands are even of a feeble texture, when compared to the resolute ardour with which a man adheres to his friend, or to his tribe, after they have for some time run the career of fortune together. Mutual discoveries of generosity, joint trials of fortitude, redouble the ardours of friendship, and kindle a flame in the human breast, which the considerations of personal interest or safety cannot suppress. The most lively

* *Collection of Dutch Voyages.*

transports of joy are seen, and the loudest shrieks of despair are heard, when the objects of a tender affection are beheld in a state of triumph or of suffering. An Indian recovered his friend unexpectedly on the island of Juan Fernandes: He prostrated himself on the ground, at his feet: 'We stood gazing in silence,' says Dampier, 'at this tender scene.' If we would know what is the religion of a wild American, what it is in his heart that most resembles devotion: it is not his fear of the sorcerer, nor his hope of protection from the spirits of the air or the wood; it is the ardent affection with which he selects and embraces his friend; with which he clings to his side in every season of peril; and with which he invokes his spirit from a distance, when dangers surprise him alone.* Whatever proofs we may have of the social disposition of man in familiar and contiguous scenes, it is possibly of importance, to draw our observations from the examples of men who live in the simplest condition, and who have not learned to affect what they do not actually feel.

Mere acquaintance and habitude nourish affection, and the experience of society brings every passion of the human mind upon its side. Its triumphs and prosperities, its calamities and distresses, bring a variety and a force of emotion, which can only have place in the company of our fellow-creatures. It is here that a man is made to forget his weakness, his cares of safety, and his subsistence; and to act from those passions which make him discover his force. It is here he finds that his arrows fly swifter than the eagle, and his weapons wound deeper than the paw of the lion, or the tooth of the boar. It is not alone his sense of a support which is near, nor the love of distinction in the opinion of his tribe, that inspire his courage, or swell his heart with a confidence that exceeds what his natural force should bestow. Vehement passions of animosity or attachment are the first exertions of vigour in his breast; under their influence, every consideration, but that of his object, is forgotten; dangers and difficulties only excite him the more.

That condition is surely favourable to the nature of any being, in which his force is increased; and if courage be the gift of

* Charlevoix, *History of Canada*.

society to man, we have reason to consider his union with his species as the noblest part of his fortune. From this source are derived, not only the force, but the very existence of his happiest emotions; not only the better part, but almost the whole of his rational character. Send him to the desert alone, he is a plant torn from its roots: the form indeed may remain, but every faculty droops and withers; the human personage and the human character cease to exist.

Men are so far from valuing society on account of its mere external conveniencies, that they are commonly most attached where those conveniencies are least frequent; and are there most faithful, where the tribute of their allegiance is paid in blood. Affection operates with the greatest force, where it meets with the greatest difficulties: In the breast of the parent, it is most solicitous amidst the dangers and distresses of the child: In the breast of a man, its flame redoubles where the wrongs or sufferings of his friend, or his country, require his aid. It is, in short, from this principle alone that we can account for the obstinate attachment of a savage to his unsettled and defenceless tribe, when temptations on the side of ease and of safety might induce him to fly from famine and danger, to a station more affluent, and more secure. Hence the sanguine affection which every Greek bore to his country, and hence the devoted patriotism of an early Roman. Let those examples be compared with the spirit which reigns in a commercial state, where men may be supposed to have experienced, in its full extent, the interest which individuals have in the preservation of their country. It is here indeed, if ever, that man is sometimes found a detached and a solitary being: he has found an object which sets him in competition with his fellow-creatures, and he deals with them as he does with his cattle and his soil, for the sake of the profits they bring. The mighty engine which we suppose to have formed society, only tends to set its members at variance, or to continue their intercourse after the bands of affection are broken.

SECTION IV.

Of the principles of War and Dissension.

'There are some circumstances in the lot of mankind,' says Socrates, 'that shew them to be destined to friendship and amity: Those are, their mutual need of one another; their mutual compassion; their sense of mutual benefits; and the pleasures arising in company. There are other circumstances which prompt them to war and dissension; the admiration and the desire which they entertain for the same subjects; their opposite pretensions; and the provocations which they mutually offer in the course of their competitions.'

When we endeavour to apply the maxims of natural justice to the solution of difficult questions, we find that some cases may be supposed, and actually happen, where oppositions take place, and are lawful, prior to any provocation, or act of injustice; that where the safety and preservation of numbers are mutually inconsistent, one party may employ his right of defence, before the other has begun an attack. And when we join with such examples, the instances of mistake, and misunderstanding, to which mankind are exposed, we may be satisfied that war does not always proceed from an intention to injure; and that even the best qualities of men, their candour, as well as their resolution, may operate in the midst of their quarrels.

There is still more to be observed on this subject. Mankind not only find in their condition the sources of variance and dissension; they appear to have in their minds the seeds of animosity, and to embrace the occasions of mutual opposition, with alacrity and pleasure. In the most pacific situation there are few who have not their enemies, as well as their friends; and who are not pleased with opposing the proceedings of one, as much as with favouring the designs of another. Small and simple tribes, who in their domestic society have the firmest union, are in their state of opposition as separate nations, frequently animated with the most implacable hatred. Among the citizens of Rome, in the early ages of that republic, the name of a foreigner, and that of an enemy, were the same. Among the Greeks, the name of Barbarian, under which that people comprehended every nation that was of a race, and spoke a language, different from their own, became a term of indiscriminate contempt and aversion. Even where no particular claim to superiority is formed, the repugnance to union, the frequent wars, or rather the perpetual hostilities, which take place among rude nations and separate clans, discover how much our species is disposed to opposition, as well as to concert.

Late discoveries have brought us to the knowledge of almost every situation in which mankind are placed. We have found them spread over large and extensive continents, where communications are open, and where national confederacy might be easily formed. We have found them in narrower districts, circumscribed by mountains, great rivers, and arms of the sea. They have been found in small and remote islands, where the inhabitants might be easily assembled, and derive an advantage from their union. But in all those situations, alike, they were broke into cantons, and affected a distinction of name and community. The titles of *fellow-citizen* and *countryman*, unopposed to those of *alien* and *foreigner*, to which they refer, would fall into disuse, and lose their meaning. We love individuals on account of personal qualities; but we love our country, as it is a party in the divisions of mankind; and our zeal for its interest, is a predilection in behalf of the side we maintain.

In the promiscuous concourse of men, it is sufficient that we have an opportunity of selecting our company. We turn away from those who do not engage us, and we fix our resort where the society is more to our mind. We are fond of distinctions; we place ourselves in opposition, and quarrel under the denominations of faction and party, without any material subject of controversy. Aversion, like affection, is fostered by a continued direction to its particular object. Separation and estrangement, as well as opposition, widen a breach which did not owe its beginnings to any offence. And it would seem, that till we have reduced mankind to the state of a family, or found some external consideration to maintain their connection in greater numbers, they will be for ever separated into bands, and form a plurality of nations.

The sense of a common danger, and the assaults of an enemy, have been frequently useful to nations, by uniting their members more firmly together, and by preventing the secessions and actual separations in which their civil discord might otherwise terminate. And this motive to union which is offered from abroad, may be necessary, not only in the case of large and extensive nations, where coalitions are weakened by distance, and the distinction of provincial names; but even in the narrow society of the smallest states. Rome itself was founded by a small party, which took its flight from Alba; her citizens were often in danger of separating; and if the villages and cantons of the Volsci had been further removed from the scene of their dissensions, the Mons Sacer might have received a new colony before the mother-country was ripe for such a discharge. She continued long to feel the quarrels of her nobles and her people; and the gates of Janus were frequently opened, to remind her inhabitants of the duties they owed to their country.

If societies, as well as individuals, be charged with the care of their own preservation, and if in both we apprehend a separation of interest, which may give rise to jealousies and competitions, we cannot be surprised to find hostilities arise from this source. But were there no angry passions of a different sort, the animosities which attend an opposition of interest, should bear a proportion to the supposed value of the subject. 'The Hottentot nations,' says Kolben, 'trespass on one another by thefts of cattle and of women; but such injuries are seldom committed, except with a view to exasperate their neighbours, and bring them to a war.' Such depredations then are not the foundation of a war, but the effects of a hostile intention already conceived. The nations of North America, who have no herds to preserve, nor settlements to defend, are yet engaged in almost perpetual wars, for which they can assign no reason, but the point of honour, and a desire to continue the struggle their fathers maintained. They do not regard the spoils of an enemy; and the warrior who has seized any booty, easily parts with it to the first person who comes in his way.*

But we need not cross the Atlantic to find proofs of animosity, and to observe, in the collision of separate societies, the influence of angry passions, that do not arise from an opposition of interest. Human nature has no part of its character, of which more flagrant examples are given on this side of the globe. What is it that stirs in the breasts of ordinary men when the enemies of their country are named? Whence are the prejudices that subsist between different provinces, cantons, and villages, of the same empire and territory? What is it that excites one half of the nations of Europe against the other? The statesman may explain his conduct on motives of national jealousy and caution, but the people have dislikes and antipathies, for which they cannot account. Their mutual reproaches of perfidy and injustice, like the Hottentot depredations, are but symptoms of an animosity, and the language of a hostile disposition, already conceived. The charge of cowardice and pusillanimity, qualities which the interested and cautious enemy should, of all others, like best to find in his rival, is urged with aversion, and made the ground of dislike. Hear the peasants on different sides of the Alps, and the Pyrenees, the Rhine, or the British channel, give vent to their prejudices and national passions; it is among them that we find the materials of war and dissension laid without the direction of government, and sparks ready to kindle into a flame, which the statesman is frequently disposed to extinguish. The fire will not always catch where his reasons of state would direct, nor stop where the concurrence of interest has produced an alliance. 'My Father,' said a Spanish peasant, 'would rise from his grave, if he could foresee a war with France.' What interest had he, or the bones of his father, in the quarrels of princes?

These observations seem to arraign our species, and to give an unfavourable picture of mankind; and yet the particulars we have mentioned are consistent with the most amiable qualities of our nature, and often furnish a scene for the exercise of our

* See Charlevoix's *History of Canada.*

greatest abilities. They are sentiments of generosity and self-denial that animate the warrior in defence of his country; and they are dispositions most favourable to mankind, that become the principles of apparent hostility to men. Every animal is made to delight in the exercise of his natural talents and forces: The lion and the tyger sport with the paw; the horse delights to commit his mane to the wind, and forgets his pasture to try his speed in the field; the bull even before his brow is armed, and the lamb while yet an emblem of innocence, have a disposition to strike with the forehead, and anticipate, in play, the conflicts they are doomed to sustain. Man too is disposed to opposition, and to employ the forces of his nature against an equal antagonist; he loves to bring his reason, his eloquence, his courage, even his bodily strength, to the proof. His sports are frequently an image of war; sweat and blood are freely expended in play; and fractures or death are often made to terminate the pastimes of idleness and festivity. He was not made to live for ever, and even his love of amusement has opened a path that leads to the grave.

Without the rivalship of nations, and the practice of war, civil society itself could scarcely have found an object, or a form. Mankind might have traded without any formal convention, but they cannot be safe without a national concert. The necessity of a public defence, has given rise to many departments of state, and the intellectual talents of men have found their busiest scene in wielding their national forces. To overawe, or intimidate, or, when we cannot persuade with reason, to resist with fortitude, are the occupations which give its most animating exercise, and its greatest triumphs, to a vigorous mind; and he who has never struggled with his fellow-creatures, is a stranger to half the sentiments of mankind.

The quarrels of individuals, indeed, are frequently the operations of unhappy and detestable passions; malice, hatred, and rage. If such passions alone possess the breast, the scene of dissension becomes an object of horror; but a common opposition maintained by numbers, is always allayed by passions of another sort. Sentiments of affection and friendship mix with animosity; the active and strenuous become the guardians of their society; and violence itself is, in their case, an exertion of generosity as well as of courage. We applaud, as proceeding from a national or party spirit, what we could not endure as the effect of a private dislike; and amidst the competitions of rival states, think we have found, for the patriot and the warrior, in the practice of violence and stratagem, the most illustrious career of human virtue. Even personal opposition here does not divide our judgement on the merits of men. The rival names of Agesilaus and Epaminondas, of Scipio and Hannibal, are repeated with equal praise; and war itself, which in one view appears so fatal, in another is the exercise of a liberal spirit; and in the very effects which we regret, is but one distemper more by which the author of nature has appointed our exit from human life.

These reflections may open our view into the state of mankind; but they tend to reconcile us to the conduct of Providence, rather than to make us change our own: where, from a regard to the welfare of our fellow-creatures, we endeavour to pacify their animosities, and unite them by the ties of affection. In the pursuit of this amiable intention, we may hope, in some instances, to disarm the angry passions of jealousy and envy; we may hope to instil into the breasts of private men sentiments of candour toward their fellow-creatures, and a disposition to humanity and justice. But it is vain to expect that we can give to the multitude of a people a sense of union among themselves, without admitting hostility to those who oppose them. Could we at once, in the case of any nation, extinguish the emulation which is excited from abroad, we should probably break or weaken the bands of society at home, and close the busiest scenes of national occupations and virtues.

SECTION V.

Of Intellectual Powers.

Many attempts have been made to analyze the dispositions which we have now enumerated; but one purpose of science, perhaps the most important, is served, when the existence of a disposition is established. We are more concerned in its reality, and in its consequences, than we are in its origin, or manner of formation.

The same observation may be applied to the other powers and faculties of our nature. Their existence and use are the principal objects of our study. Thinking and reasoning, we say, are the operations of some faculty; but in what manner the faculties of thought or reason remain, when they are not exerted, or by what difference in the frame they are unequal in different persons, are questions which we cannot resolve. Their operations alone discover them: when unapplied, they lie hid even from the person to whom they pertain; and their action is so much a part of their nature, that the faculty itself, in many cases, is scarcely to be distinguished from a habit acquired in its frequent exertion.

Persons who are occupied with different subjects, who act in different scenes, generally appear to have different talents, or at least to have the same faculties variously formed, and suited to different purposes. The peculiar genius of nations, as well as of individuals, may in this manner arise from the state of their fortunes. And it is proper that we endeavour to find some rule, by which to judge of what is admirable in the capacities of men, or fortunate in the application of their faculties, before we venture to pass a judgment on this branch of their merits, or pretend to measure the degree of respect they may claim by their different attainments.

To receive the informations of sense, is perhaps the earliest function of an animal combined with an intellectual nature; and one great accomplishment of the living agent consists in the force and sensibility of his animal organs. The pleasures or pains to which he is exposed from this quarter, constitute to him an important difference between the objects which are thus brought to his knowledge; and it concerns him to distinguish well, before he commits himself to the direction of appetite. He must scrutinize the objects of one sense by the perceptions of another; examine with the eye, before he ventures to touch; and employ every means of observation, before he gratifies the appetites of thirst and of hunger. A discernment acquired by experience, becomes a faculty of his mind; and the inferences of thought are sometimes not to be distinguished from the perceptions of sense.

The objects around us, beside their separate appearances, have their relations to one another. They suggest, when compared, what would not occur when they are considered apart; they have their effects, and mutual influences; they exhibit, in like circumstances, similar operations, and uniform consequences. When we have found and expressed the points in which the uniformity of their operations consists, we have ascertained a physical law. Many such laws, and even the most important, are known to the vulgar, and occur upon the smallest degrees of reflection: but others are hid under a seeming confusion, which ordinary talents cannot remove; and are therefore the objects of study, long observation, and superior capacity. The faculties of penetration and judgement, are, by men of business, as well as of science, employed to unravel intricacies of this sort; and the degree of sagacity with which either is endowed, is to be measured by the success with which they are able to find general rules, applicable to a variety of cases that seemed to have nothing in common, and to discover important distinctions between subjects which the vulgar are apt to confound.

To collect a multiplicity of particulars under general heads, and to refer a variety of operations to their common principle, is the object of science. To do the same thing, at least within the range of his active engagements, pertains to the man of pleasure, or business: and it would seem, that the studious and the active are so far employed in the same task, from observation and experience, to find the general views under which their objects may be considered, and the rules which may be usefully applied in the detail of their conduct. They do not always apply their talents to different subjects; and they seem to be distinguished chiefly by the unequal reach and variety of their remarks, or by the intentions which they severally have in collecting them.

Whilst men continue to act from appetites and passions, leading to the attainment of external ends, they seldom quit the view of their objects in detail, to go far in the road of general inquiries.

They measure the extent of their own abilities, by the promptitude with which they apprehend what is important in every subject, and the facility with which they extricate themselves on every trying occasion. And these, it must be confessed, to a being who is destined to act in the midst of difficulties, are the proper test of capacity and force. The parade of words, and general reasonings, which sometimes carry an appearance of so much learning and knowledge, are of little avail in the conduct of life. The talents from which they proceed, terminate in mere ostentation, and are seldom connected with that superior discernment which the active apply in times of perplexity; much less with that intrepidity and force of mind which are required in passing through difficult scenes.

The abilities of active men, however, have a variety corresponding to that of the subjects on which they are occupied. A sagacity applied to external and inanimate nature, forms one species of capacity; that which is turned to society and human affairs, another. Reputation for parts in any scene is equivocal, till we know by what kind of exertion that reputation is gained. That they understand well the subjects to which they apply, is all that can be said, in commending men of the greatest abilities: and every department, every profession, would have its great men, if there were not a choice of objects for the understanding, and of talents for the mind, as well as of sentiments for the heart, and of habits for the active character.

The meanest professions, indeed, so far sometimes forget themselves, or the rest of mankind, as to arrogate, in commending what is distinguished in their own way, every epithet the most respectable claim as the right of superior abilities. Every mechanic is a great man with the learner, and the humble admirer, in his particular calling; and we can, perhaps, with more assurance pronounce what it is that should make a man happy and amiable, than what should make his abilities respected, and his genius admired. This, upon a view of the talents themselves, may perhaps be impossible. The effect, however, will point out the rule and the standard of our judgement. To be admired and respected, is to have an ascendant among men. The talents which most directly procure that ascendant, are those which operate on mankind, penetrate their views, prevent their wishes, or frustrate their designs. The superior capacity leads with a superior energy, where every individual would go, and shews the hesitating and the irresolute a clear passage to the attainment of their ends.

This description does not pertain to any particular craft or profession; or perhaps it implies a kind of ability, which the separate application of men to particular callings, only tends to suppress or to weaken. Where shall we find the talents which are fit to act with men in a collective body, if we break that body into parts, and confine the observation of each to a separate track?

To act in the view of his fellow-creatures, to produce his mind in public, to give it all the exercise of sentiment and thought, which pertain to man as a member of society, as a friend, or an enemy, seems to be the principal calling and occupation of his nature. If he must labour, that he may subsist, he can subsist for no better purpose than the good of mankind; nor can he have better talents than those which qualify him to act with men. Here, indeed, the understanding appears to borrow very much from the passions; and there is a felicity of conduct in human affairs, in which it is difficult to distinguish the promptitude of the head from the ardour and sensibility of the heart. Where both are united, they constitute that superiority of mind, the frequency of which among men, in particular ages and nations, much more than the progress they have made in speculation, or in the practice of mechanic and liberal arts, should determine the rate of their genius, and assign the palm of distinction and honour.

When nations succeed one another in the career of discoveries and inquiries, the last is always the most knowing. Systems of science are gradually formed. The globe itself is traversed by degrees, and the history of every age, when past, is an accession of knowledge to those who succeed. The Romans were more knowing than the Greeks; and every scholar of modern Europe is, in this sense, more learned than the most accomplished person that ever bore either of those celebrated names. But is he on that account their superior?

Men are to be estimated, not from what they know, but from

what they are able to perform; from their skill in adapting materials to the several purposes of life; from their vigour and conduct in pursuing the objects of policy, and in finding the expedients of war and national defence. Even in literature, they are to be estimated from the works of their genius, not from the extent of their knowledge. The scene of mere observation was extremely limited in a Grecian republic; and the bustle of an active life appeared inconsistent with study: but there the human mind, notwithstanding, collected its greatest abilities, and received its best informations, in the midst of sweat and of dust.

It is peculiar to modern Europe, to rest so much of the human character on what may be learned in retirement, and from the information of books. A just admiration of ancient literature, an opinion that human sentiment, and human reason, without this aid, were to have vanished from the societies of men, have led us into the shade, where we endeavour to derive from imagination and thought, what is in reality matter of experience and sentiment: and we endeavour, through the grammar of dead languages, and the channel of commentators, to arrive at the beauties of thought and elocution, which sprang from the animated spirit of society, and were taken from the living impressions of an active life. Our attainments are frequently limited to the elements of every science, and seldom reach to that enlargement of ability and power which useful knowledge should give. Like mathematicians, who study the Elements of Euclid, but never think of mensuration, we read of societies, but do not propose to act with men: we repeat the language of politics, but feel not the spirit of nations: we attend to the formalities of a military discipline, but know not how to employ numbers of men to obtain any purpose by stratagem or force.

But for what end, it may said, point out a misfortune that cannot be remedied? If national affairs called for exertion, the genius of men would awake; but in the recess of better employment, the time which is bestowed on study, if even attended with no other advantage, serves to occupy with innocence the hours of leisure, and set bounds to the pursuit of ruinous and frivolous amusements. From no better reason than this, we employ so many of our early years, under the rod, to acquire what it is not expected we should retain beyond the threshold of the school; and whilst we carry the same frivolous character in our studies that we do in our amusements, the human mind could not suffer more from a contempt of letters, than it does from the false importance which is given to literature, as a business for life, not as a help to our conduct, and the means of forming a character that may be happy in itself, and useful to mankind.

If that time which is passed in relaxing the powers of the mind, and in with-holding every object but what tends to weaken and to corrupt, were employed in fortifying those powers, and in teaching the mind to recognise its objects, and its strength, we should not, at the years of maturity, be so much at a loss for occupation; nor, in attending the chances of a gaming-table, misemploy our talents, or waste the fire which remains in the breast. They, at least, who by their stations have a share in the government of their country, might believe themselves capable of business; and while the state had its armies and councils, might find objects enough to amuse, without throwing a personal fortune into hazard, merely to cure the yawnings of a listless and insignificant life. It is impossible for ever to maintain the tone of speculation; it is impossible not sometimes to feel that we live among men.

SECTION VI.

Of Moral Sentiment.

Upon a slight observation of what passes in human life, we should be apt to conclude, that the care of subsistence is the principal spring of human actions. This consideration leads to the invention and practice of mechanical arts; it serves to distinguish amusement from business; and, with many, scarcely admits into competition any other subject of pursuit or attention. The mighty advantages of property and fortune, when stript of the recommendations they derive from vanity, or the more serious regards to independence and power, only mean a provision that is made for animal enjoyment; and if our solicitude on this subject were removed, not only the toils of the mechanic, but the studies of the learned, would cease; every department of public business would become unnecessary; every senate-house would be shut up, and every palace deserted.

Is man therefore, in respect to his object, to be classed with the mere brutes, and only to be distinguished by faculties that qualify him to multiply contrivances for the support and convenience of animal life, and by the extent of a fancy that renders the care of animal preservation to him more burdensome than it is to the herd with which he shares in the bounty of nature? If this were his case, the joy which attends on success, or the griefs which arise from disappointment, would make the sum of his passions. The torrent that wasted, or the inundation that enriched his possessions, would give him all the emotion with which he is seized, on the occasion of a wrong by which his fortunes are impaired, or of a benefit by which they are preserved and enlarged. His fellow-creatures would be considered merely as they affected his interest. Profit or loss would serve to mark the event of every transaction; and the epithets *useful* or *detrimental* would serve to distinguish his mates in society, as they do the tree which bears plenty of fruit, from that which serves only to cumber the ground, or intercept his view.

This, however, is not the history of our species. What comes from a fellow-creature is received with peculiar attention; and every language abounds with terms that express somewhat in the transactions of men, different from success and disappointment. The bosom kindles in company, while the point of interest in view has nothing to inflame; and a matter frivolous in itself, becomes important, when it serves to bring to light the intentions and characters of men. The foreigner, who believed that Othello, on the stage, was enraged for the loss of his handkerchief, was not more mistaken, than the reasoner who imputes any of the more vehement passions of men to the impressions of mere profit or loss.

Men assemble to deliberate on business; they separate from

jealousies of interest; but in their several collisions, whether as friends or as enemies, a fire is struck out which the regards to interest or safety cannot confine. The value of a favour is not measured when sentiments of kindness are perceived; and the term *misfortune* has but a feeble meaning, when compared to that of *insult* and *wrong*.

As actors or spectators, we are perpetually made to feel the difference of human conduct, and from a bare recital of transactions which have passed in ages and countries remote from our own, are moved with admiration and pity, or transported with indignation and rage. Our sensibility on this subject gives their charm, in retirement, to the relations of history, and to the fictions of poetry; sends forth the tear of compassion, gives to the blood its briskest movement, and to the eye its liveliest glances of displeasure or joy. It turns human life into an interesting spectacle, and perpetually solicits even the indolent to mix, as opponents or friends, in the scenes which are acted before them. Joined to the powers of deliberation and reason, it constitutes the basis of a moral nature; and whilst it dictates the terms of praise and of blame, serves to class our fellow-creatures by the most admirable and engaging, or the most odious and contemptible, denominations.

It is pleasant to find men, who, in their speculations, deny the reality of moral distinctions, forget in detail the general positions they maintain, and give loose to ridicule, indignation, and scorn, as if any of these sentiments could have place, were the actions of men indifferent; and with acrimony pretend to detect the fraud by which moral restraints have been imposed, as if to censure a fraud were not already to take a part on the side of morality.*

Can we explain the principles upon which mankind adjudge the preference of characters, and upon which they indulge such vehement emotions of admiration or contempt? If it be admitted that we cannot, are the facts less true? or must we suspend the movements of the heart until they who are employed in framing systems of science have discovered the principle from which

* Mandeville.

those movements proceed? If a finger burn, we care not for information on the properties of fire: if the heart be torn, or the mind overjoyed, we have not leisure for speculations on the subject of moral sensibility.

It is fortunate in this, as in other articles to which speculation and theory are applied, that nature proceeds in her course, whilst the curious are busied in the search of her principles. The peasant, or the child, can reason, and judge, and speak his language, with a discernment, a consistency, and a regard to analogy, which perplex the logician, the moralist, and the grammarian, when they would find the principle upon which the proceeding is founded, or when they would bring to general rules, what is so familiar, and so well sustained in particular cases. The felicity of our conduct is more owing to the talent we possess for detail, and to the suggestion of particular occasions, than it is to any direction we can find in theory and general speculations.

We must, in the result of every inquiry, encounter with facts which we cannot explain; and to bear with this mortification would save us frequently a great deal of fruitless trouble. Together with the sense of our existence, we must admit many circumstances which come to our knowledge at the same time, and in the same manner; and which do, in reality, constitute the mode of our being. Every peasant will tell us, that a man hath his rights; and that to trespass on those rights is injustice. If we ask him farther, what he means by the term *right?* we probably force him to substitute a less significant, or less proper term, in the place of this; or require him to account for what is an original mode of his mind, and a sentiment to which he ultimately refers, when he would explain himself upon any particular application of his language.

The rights of individuals may relate to a variety of subjects, and be comprehended under different heads. Prior to the establishment of property, and the distinction of ranks, men have a right to defend their persons, and to act with freedom; they have a right to maintain the apprehensions of reason, and the feelings of the heart; and they cannot for a moment converse with one another, without feeling that the part they maintain may be just or unjust. It is not, however, our business here to carry the notion of a right into its several applications, but to reason on the sentiment of favour with which that notion is entertained in the mind.

If it be true, that men are united by instinct, that they act in society from affections of kindness and friendship; if it be true, that even prior to acquaintance and habitude, men, as such, are commonly to one another objects of attention, and some degree of regard; that while their prosperity is beheld with indifference, their afflictions are considered with commiseration; if calamities be measured by the numbers and the qualities of men they involve; and if every suffering of a fellow-creature draws a croud of attentive spectators; if even in the case of those to whom we do not habitually wish any positive good, we are still averse to be the instruments of harm; it should seem, that in these various appearances of an amicable disposition, the foundations of a moral apprehension are sufficiently laid, and the sense of a right which we maintain for ourselves, is by a movement of humanity and candour extended to our fellow creatures.

What is it that prompts the tongue when we censure an act of cruelty or oppression? What is it that constitutes our restraint from offences that tend to distress our fellow-creatures? It is probably, in both cases, a particular application of that principle, which, in presence of the sorrowful, sends forth the tear of compassion; and a combination of all those sentiments, which constitute a benovolent disposition; and if not a resolution to do good, at least an aversion to be the instrument of harm.*

* Mankind, we are told, are devoted to interest; and this, in all commercial nations, is undoubtedly true: but it does not follow, that they are, by their natural dispositions, averse to society and mutual affection: proofs of the contrary remain, even where interest triumphs most. What must we think of the force of that disposition to compassion, to candour, and goodwill, which, notwithstanding the prevailing opinion that the happiness of a man consists in possessing the greatest possible share of riches, preferments, and honours, still keeps the parties who are in competition for those objects, on a tolerable footing of amity, and leads them to abstain even from their own supposed good, when their seizing it appears in the light of a detriment to others? What might we not expect from the human heart in circumstances which prevented this apprehension on the subject of fortune, or under the influence of an opinion as steady and general as the former, that human felicity does

It may be difficult, however, to enumerate the motives of all the censures and commendations which are applied to the actions of men. Even while we moralize, every disposition of the human mind may have its share in forming the judgement, and in prompting the tongue. As jealousy is often the most watchful guardian of chastity, so malice is often the quickest to spy the failings of our neighbour. Envy, affectation, and vanity, may dictate the verdicts we give, and the worst principles of our nature may be at the bottom of our pretended zeal for morality; but if we only mean to inquire, why they who are well disposed to mankind, apprehend, in every instance, certain rights pertaining to their fellow-creatures, and why they applaud the consideration that is paid to those rights, we cannot perhaps assign a better reason, than that the person who applauds, is well disposed to the welfare of the parties to whom his applauses refer.

When we consider, that the reality of any amicable propensity in the human mind has been frequently contested; when we recollect the prevalence of interested competitions, with their attendant passions of jealousy, envy, and malice; it may seem strange to alledge, that love and compassion are the most powerful principles in the human breast: but they are destined, on many occasions, to urge with the most irresistible vehemence; and if the desire of self-preservation be more constant, and more uniform, these are a more plentiful source of enthusiasm, satisfaction, and joy. With a power, not inferior to that of resentment and rage, they hurry the mind into every sacrifice of interest, and bear it undismayed through every hardship and danger.

The disposition on which friendship is grafted, glows with satisfaction in the hours of tranquillity, and is pleasant, not only in its triumphs, but even in its sorrows. It throws a grace on the external air, and, by its expression on the countenance, compensates for the want of beauty, or gives a charm which no complex-

---

not consist in the indulgences of animal appetite, but in those of a benevolent heart; not in fortune or interest, but in the contempt of this very object, in the courage and freedom which arise from this contempt, joined to a resolute choice of conduct, directed to the good of mankind, or to the good of that particular society to which the party belongs?

ion or features can equal. From this source the scenes of human life derive their principal felicity; and their imitations in poetry, their principal ornament. Descriptions of nature, even representations of a vigorous conduct, and a manly courage, do not engage the heart, if they be not mixed with the exhibition of generous sentiments, and the pathetic, which is found to arise in the struggles, the triumphs, or the misfortunes of a tender affection. The death of Polites, in the Aeneid, is not more affecting than that of many others who perished in the ruins of Troy; but the aged Priam was present when this last of his sons was slain; and the agonies of grief and sorrow force the parent from his retreat, to fall by the hand that shed the blood of his child. The pathetic of Homer consists in exhibiting the force of affections, not in exciting mere terror and pity; passions he has never perhaps, in any instance, attempted to raise.

With this tendency to kindle into enthusiasm, with this command over the heart, with the pleasure that attends its emotions, and with all its effects in meriting confidence, and procuring esteem, it is not surprising, that a principle of humanity should give the tone to our commendations and our censures, and even where it is hindered from directing our conduct, should still give to the mind, on reflection, its knowledge of what is desirable in the human character. *What hast thou done with thy brother Abel?* was the first expostulation in behalf of morality; and if the first answer has been often repeated, mankind have notwithstandstanding, in one sense, sufficiently acknowledged the charge of their nature. They have felt, they have talked, and even acted, as the keepers of their fellow-creatures: They have made the indications of candour and mutual affection the test of what is meritorious and amiable in the- characters of men: They have made cruelty and oppression the principal objects of their indignation and rage: Even while the head is occupied with projects of interest, the heart is often seduced into friendship; and while business proceeds on the maxims of self-preservation, the careless hour is employed in generosity and kindness.

Hence the rule by which men commonly judge of external actions, is taken from the supposed influence of such actions on the general good. To abstain from harm, is the great law of natural justice; to diffuse happiness is the law of morality; and when we censure the conferring a favour on one or a few at the expence of many, we refer to public utility, as the great object at which the actions of men should be aimed.

After all, it must be confessed, that if a principle of affection to mankind, be the basis of our moral approbation and dislike, we sometimes proceed in distributing applause or censure, without precisely attending to the degree in which our fellow-creatures are hurt or obliged; and that, besides the virtues of candour, friendship, generosity, and public spirit, which bear an immediate reference to this principle, there are others which may seem to derive their commendation from a different source. Temperance, prudence, fortitude, are those qualities likewise admired from a principle of regard to our fellow-creatures? Why not, since they render men happy in themselves, and useful to others? He who is qualified to promote the welfare of mankind, is neither a sot, a fool, nor a coward. Can it be more clearly expressed, that temperance, prudence, and fortitude, are necessary to the character we love and admire? I know well why I should wish for them in myself; and why likewise I should wish for them in my friend, and in every person who is an object of my affection. But to what purpose seek for reasons of approbation, where qualities are so necessary to our happiness, and so great a part in the perfection of our nature? We must cease to esteem ourselves, and to distinguish what is excellent, when such qualifications incur our neglect.

A person of an affectionate mind, possessed of a maxim, That he himself, as an individual, is no more than a part of the whole that demands his regard, has found, in that principle, a sufficient foundation for all the virtues; for a contempt of animal pleasures, that would supplant his principal enjoyment; for an equal contempt of danger or pain, that come to stop his pursuits of public good. 'A vehement and steady affection magnifies its object, and lessens every difficulty or danger that stands in the way.' 'Ask those who have been in love,' says Epictetus, 'they will know that I speak truth.'

'I have before me,' says another eminent moralist,* 'an idea of justice, which, if I could follow in every instance, I should think myself the most happy of men'. And it is, perhaps, of consequence to their happiness, as well as to their conduct, if those can be disjoined, that men should have this idea properly formed: It is perhaps but another name for that good of mankind, which the virtuous are engaged to promote. If virtue be the supreme good, its best and most signal effect is, to communicate and diffuse itself.

To love, and even to hate, on the apprehension of moral qualities, to espouse one party from a sense of justice, to oppose another with indignation excited by iniquity, are the common indications of probity, and the operations of an animated, upright, and generous spirit. To guard against unjust partialities, and ill-grounded antipathies; to maintain that composure of mind, which, without impairing its sensibility or ardour, proceeds in every instance with discernment and penetration, are the marks of a vigorous and cultivated spirit. To be able to follow the dictates of such a spirit through all the varieties of human life, and with a mind always master of itself, in prosperity or adversity, and possessed of all its abilities, when the subjects in hazard are life, or freedom, as much as in treating simple questions of interest, are the triumphs of magnanimity, and true elevation of mind. 'The event of the day is decided. Draw this javelin from my body now,' said Epaminondas, 'and let me bleed.'

In what situation, or by what instruction, is this wonderful character to be formed? Is it found in the nurseries of affectation, pertness, and vanity, from which fashion is propagated, and the genteel is announced? in great and opulent cities, where men vie with one another in equipage, dress, and the reputation of fortune? Is it within the admired precincts of a court, where we may learn to smile without being pleased, to caress without affection, to wound with the secret weapons of envy and jealousy, and to rest our personal importance on circumstances which we cannot always with honour command? No: but in a situation where the great sentiments of the heart are awakened; where the

* *Persian Letters.*

characters of men, not their situations and fortunes, are the principal distinction; where the anxieties of interest, or vanity, perish in the blaze of more vigorous emotions; and where the human soul, having felt and recognised its objects, like an animal who has tasted the blood of his prey, cannot descend to pursuits that leave its talents and its force unemployed.

Proper occasions alone operating on a raised and a happy disposition, may produce this admirable effect, whilst mere instruction may always find mankind at a loss to comprehend its meaning, or insensible to its dictates. The case, however, is not desperate, till we have formed our system of politics, as well as manners; till we have sold our freedom for titles, equipage, and distinctions; till we see no merit but prosperity and power, no disgrace but poverty and neglect. What charm of instruction can cure the mind that is tainted with this disorder? What syren voice can awaken a desire of freedom, that is held to be meanness, and a want of ambition? or what persuasion can turn the grimace of politeness into real sentiments of humanity and candour?

SECTION VII.
Of Happiness.

Having had under our consideration the active powers and the moral qualities which distinguish the nature of man, is it still necessary that we should treat of his happiness apart? This significant term, the most frequent, and the most familiar, in our conversation, is, perhaps, on reflection, the least understood. It serves to express our satisfaction, when any desire is gratified: It is pronounced with a sigh, when our object is distant: It means what we wish to obtain, and what we seldom stay to examine. We estimate the value of every subject by its utility, and its influence on happiness; but we think that utility itself, and happiness, require no explanation.

Those men are commonly esteemed the happiest, whose desires are most frequently gratified. But if, in reality, the possession of what we desire, and a continued fruition, were requisite to happiness, mankind for the most part would have reason to complain of their lot. What they call their enjoyments, are generally momentary; and the object of sanguine expectation, when obtained, no longer continues to occupy the mind: A new passion succeeds, and the imagination, as before, is intent on a distant felicity.

How many reflections of this sort are suggested by melancholy, or by the effects of that very languor and inoccupation into which we would willingly sink, under the notion of freedom from care and trouble?

When we enter on a formal computation of the enjoyments or sufferings which are prepared for mankind, it is a chance but we find that pain, by its intenseness, its duration, or frequency, is greatly predominant. The activity and eagerness with which we press from one stage of life to another, our unwillingness to return on the paths we have trod, our aversion in age to renew the frolics of youth, or to repeat in manhood the amusements of children, have been accordingly stated as proofs, that our memory of the past, and our feeling of the present, are equal subjects of dislike and displeasure.*

This conclusion, however, like many others, drawn from our supposed knowledge of causes, does not correspond with experience. In every street, in every village, in every field, the greater number of persons we meet, carry an aspect that is chearful or thoughtless, indifferent, composed, busy, or animated. The labourer whistles to his team, and the mechanic is at ease in his calling; the frolicsome and the gay feel a series of pleasures, of which we know not the source; even they who demonstrate the miseries of human life, when intent on their argument, escape from their sorrows, and find a tolerable pastime in proving that men are unhappy.

The very terms *pleasure* and *pain*, perhaps, are equivocal; but if they are confined, as they appear to be in many of our reasonings, to the mere sensations which have a reference to external objects, either in the memory of the past, the feeling of the present, or the apprehension of the future, it is a great error

* Maupertuis, *Essai de Morale.*

to suppose, that they comprehend all the constituents of happiness or misery; or that the good humour of an ordinary life is maintained by the prevalence of those pleasures which have their separate names, and are, on reflection, distinctly remembered.

The mind, during the greater part of its existence, is employed in active exertions, not in merely attending to its own feelings of pleasure or pain; and the list of its faculties, understanding, memory, foresight, sentiment, will, and intention, only contains the names of its different operations.

In the absence of every sensation to which we commonly give the names either of *enjoyment* or *suffering*, our very existence may have its opposite qualities of *happiness* or *misery*; and if what we call *pleasure* or *pain*, occupies but a small part of human life, compared to what passes in contrivance and execution, in pursuits and expectations, in conduct, reflection, and social engagements; it must appear, that our active pursuits, at least on account of their duration, deserve the greater part of our attention. When their occasions have failed, the demand is not for pleasure, but for something to do; and the very complaints of a sufferer are not so sure a mark of distress, as the stare of the languid.

We seldom, however, reckon any task which we are bound to perform, among the blessings of life. We always aim at a period of pure enjoyment, or a termination of trouble; and overlook the source from which most of our present satisfactions are really drawn. Ask the busy, Where is the happiness to which they aspire? they will answer, perhaps, That it is to be found in the object of some present pursuit. If we ask, Why they are not miserable in the absence of that happiness? they will say, That they hope to attain it. But is it hope alone that supports the mind in the midst of precarious and uncertain prospects? and would assurance of success fill the intervals of expectation with more pleasing emotions? Give the huntsman his prey, give the gamester the gold which is staked on the game, that the one may not need to fatigue his person, nor the other to perplex his mind, and both will probably laugh at our folly: the one will stake his money anew, that he may be perplexed; the other will turn his stag to the field, that he may hear the cry of the dogs, and follow through danger and hardship. Withdraw the occupations of men, terminate their desires, existence is a burden, and the iteration of memory is a torment.

The men of this country, says one lady, should learn to sow and to knit; it would hinder their time from being a burden to themselves, and to other people. That is true, says another; for my part, though I never look abroad, I tremble at the prospect of bad weather; for then the gentlemen come mopping to us for entertainment; and the sight of a husband in distress, is but a melancholy spectacle.

In devising, or in executing a plan, in being carried on the tide of emotion and sentiment, the mind seems to unfold its being, and to enjoy itself. Even where the end and the object are known to be of little avail, the talents and the fancy are often intensely applied, and business or play may amuse them alike. We only desire repose to recruit our limited and our wasting force: when business fatigues, amusement is often but a change of occupation. We are not always unhappy, even when we complain. There is a kind of affliction which makes an agreeable state of the mind; and lamentation itself is sometimes an expression of pleasure. The painter and the poet have laid hold of this handle, and find, among the means of entertainment, a favourable reception for works that are composed to awaken our sorrows.

To a being of this description, therefore, it is a blessing to meet with incentives to action, whether in the desire of pleasure, or the aversion to pain. His activity is of more importance than the very pleasure he seeks, and langour a greater evil than the suffering he shuns.

The gratifications of animal appetite are of short duration; and sensuality is but a distemper of the mind, which ought to be cured by remembrance, if it were not perpetually inflamed by hope. The chace is not more surely terminated by the death of the game, than the joys of the voluptuary by the means of completing his debauch. As a bond of society, as a matter of distant pursuit, the objects of sense make an important part in the system of human life. They lead us to fulfil the purpose of nature, in preserving the individual, and in perpetuating the species: but to rely on their use as a principal constituent of human felicity, were an error in speculation, and would be still more an error in practice. Even the master of the seraglio, for whom all the treasures of empire are extorted from the hoards of its frighted inhabitants, for whom alone the choicest emerald and the diamond are drawn from the mine, for whom every breeze is enriched with perfumes, for whom beauty is assembled from every quarter, and, animated by passions that ripen under the vertical sun, is confined to the grate for his use, is still, perhaps, more wretched than the very herd of the people, whose labours and properties are devoted to relieve him of trouble, and to procure him enjoyment.

Sensuality is easily overcome by any of the habits of pursuit which usually engage an active mind. When curiosity is awake, or when passion is excited, even in the midst of the feast when conversation grows warm, grows jovial, or serious, the pleasures of the table we know are forgotten. The boy contemns them for play, and the man of age declines them for business.

When we reckon the circumstances that correspond to the nature of any animal, or to that of man in particular, such as safety, shelter, food, and the other means of enjoyment or preservation, we sometimes think that we have found a sensible and a solid foundation on which to rest his felicity. But those who are least disposed to moralize, observe, that happiness is not connected with fortune, although fortune includes at once all the means of subsistence, and the means of sensual indulgence. The circumstances that require abstinence, courage, and conduct, expose us to hazard, and are in description of the painful kind; yet the able, the brave, and the ardent, seem most to enjoy themselves when placed in the midst of difficulties, and obliged to employ the powers they possess.

Spinola being told, that Sir Francis Vere died of having nothing to do, said, 'That was enough to kill a general.'* How many are there to whom war itself is a pastime, who chuse the life of a soldier, exposed to dangers and continued fatigues; of a mariner, in conflict with every hardship, and bereft of every conveniency;

* *Life of Lord Herbert.*

of a politician, whose sport is the conduct of parties and factions; and who, rather than be idle, will do the business of men and of nations for whom he has not the smallest regard. Such men do not chuse pain as preferable to pleasure, but they are incited by a restless disposition to make continued exertions of capacity and resolution; they triumph in the midst of their struggles; they droop, and they languish, when the occasion of their labour has ceased.

What was enjoyment, in the sense of that youth, who, according to Tacitus, loved danger itself, not the rewards of courage? What is the prospect of pleasure, when the sound of the horn or the trumpet, the cry of the dogs, or the shout of war, awaken the ardour of the sportsman and the soldier? The most animating occasions of human life, are calls to danger and hardship, not invitations to safety and ease: and man himself, in his excellence, is not an animal of pleasure, nor destined merely to enjoy what the elements bring to his use; but, like his associates, the dog and the horse, to follow the exercises of his nature, in preference to what are called its enjoyments; to pine in the lap of ease and of affluence, and to exult in the midst of alarms that seem to threaten his being. In all which, his disposition to action only keeps pace with the variety of powers with which he is furnished; and the most respectable attributes of his nature, magnanimity, fortitude, and wisdom, carry a manifest reference to the difficulties with which he is destined to struggle.

If animal pleasure becomes insipid when the spirit is roused by a different object, it is well known likewise, that the sense of pain is prevented by any vehement affection of the soul. Wounds received in a heat of passion, in the hurry, the ardour, or consternation of battle, are never felt till the ferment of the mind subsides. Even torments, deliberately applied, and industriously prolonged, are borne with firmness, and with an appearance of ease, when the mind is possessed with some vigorous sentiment, whether of religion, enthusiasm, or love to mankind. The continued mortifications of superstitious devotees in several ages of the Christian church; the wild penances, still voluntarily borne, during many years, by the religionists of the east; the contempt in which famine and torture are held by most savage nations; the chearful or obstinate patience of the soldier in the field; the hardships endured by the sportsman in his pastime, show how much we may err in computing the miseries of men, from the measures of trouble and of suffering they seem to incur. And if there be a refinement in affirming, that their happiness is not to be measured by the contrary enjoyments, it is a refinement which was made by Regulus and Cincinnatus before the date of philosophy; it is a refinement, which every boy knows at his play, and every savage confirms, when he looks from his forest on the pacific city, and scorns the plantation, whose master he cares not to imitate.

Man, it must be confessed, notwithstanding all this activity of his mind, is an animal in the full extent of that designation. When the body sickens, the mind droops; and when the blood ceases to flow, the soul takes its departure. Charged with the care of his preservation, admonished by a sense of pleasure or pain, and guarded by an instinctive fear of death, nature has not intrusted his safety to the mere vigilance of his understanding, nor to the government of his uncertain reflections.

The distinction betwixt mind and body is followed by consequences of the greatest importance; but the facts to which we now refer, are not founded on any tenets whatever. They are equally true, whether we admit or reject the distinction in question, or whether we suppose, that this living agent is formed of one, or is an assemblage of separate natures. And the materialist, by treating of man as of an engine, cannot make any change in the state of his history. He is a being, who, by a multiplicity of visible organs, performs a variety of functions. His joints are bent, and his muscles relax and contract in our sight; the heart beats in his breast, and the blood flows to every part of his frame. He performs other operations which we cannot refer to any corporeal organ. He perceives, he recollects, and forecasts; he desires, and he shuns; he admires, and he contemns. He enjoys his pleasures, or he endures his pain. All these different functions, in some measure, go well or ill together. When the motion of the blood is languid, the muscles relax, the understanding is tardy, and the fancy is dull: when distemper assails him, the physician must attend no less to what he thinks, than to what he eats, and examine the returns of his passion, together with the strokes of his pulse.

With all his sagacity, his precautions, and his instincts, which are given to preserve his being, he partakes in the fate of other animals, and seems to be formed only that he may die. Myriads perish before they reach the perfection of their kind; and the individual, with an option to owe the prolongation of his temporary course to resolution and conduct, or to abject fear, frequently chuses the latter, and by a habit of timidity, imbitters the life he is so intent to preserve.

Man, however, at times, exempted from this mortifying lot, seems to act without any regard to the length of his period. When he thinks intensely, or desires with ardour, pleasures and pains from any other quarter assail him in vain. Even in his dying hour, the muscles acquire a tone from his spirit, and the mind seems to depart in its vigour, and in the midst of a struggle to obtain the recent aim of its toils. Muley Moluck, borne on his litter, and spent with disease, still fought the battle, in the midst of which he expired; and the last effort he made, with a finger on his lips, was a signal to conceal his death: the precaution, perhaps, of all which he had hitherto taken, the most necessary to prevent a defeat.

Can no reflections aid us in acquiring this habit of the soul, so useful in carrying us through many of the ordinary scenes of life? If we say, that they cannot, the reality of its happiness is not the less evident. The Greeks and the Romans considered contempt of pleasure, endurance of pain, and neglect of life, as eminent qualities of a man, and a principal subject of discipline. They trusted, that the vigorous spirit would find worthy objects on which to employ its force; and that the first step towards a resolute choice of such objects was to shake off the meanness of a solicitous and timorous mind.

Mankind, in general, have courted occasions to display their courage, and frequently, in search of admiration, have presented a spectacle, which to those who have ceased to regard fortitude on its own account, becomes a subject of horror. Scevola held his arm in the fire, to shake the soul of Porsenna. The savage inures his body to the torture, that in the hour of trial he may exult over his enemy. Even the Mussulman tears his flesh to win the heart of his mistress, and comes in gaiety, streaming with blood, to shew that he deserves her esteem.*

Some nations carry the practice of inflicting, or of sporting with pain, to a degree that is either cruel or absurd; others regard every prospect of bodily suffering as the greatest of evils; and in the midst of their troubles, imbitter every real affliction, with the terrors of a feeble and dejected imagination. We are not bound to answer for the follies of either, nor, in treating a question which relates to the nature of man, make an estimate of its strength, or its weakness, from the habits or apprehensions peculiar to any nation or age.

SECTION VIII.

The same subject continued.

Whoever has compared together the different conditions and manners of men, under varieties of education or fortune, will be satisfied, that mere situation does not constitute their happiness or misery; nor a diversity of external observances imply any opposition of sentiments on the subject of morality. They express their kindness and their enmity in different actions; but kindness or enmity is still the principal article of consideration. in human life. They engage in different pursuits, or acquiesce in different conditions; but act from passions nearly the same. There is no precise measure of accommodation required to suit their conveniency, nor any degree of danger or safety under which they are peculiarly fitted to act. Courage and generosity, fear and envy, are not peculiar to any station or order of men; nor is there any condition in which some of the human race have not shewn, that it is possible to employ, with propriety, the talents and virtues of their species.

* Letters of the Right Honourable Lady M—y W——y M———e.

What, then, is that mysterious thing called *Happiness*, which may have place in such a variety of stations, and to which circumstances in one age or nation thought necessary, are in another held to be destructive, or of no effect? It is not the succession of mere animal pleasures, which, apart from the occupation or the company in which they serve to engage the mind, can fill up but a few moments in the duration of life. On too frequent a repetition, those pleasures turn to satiety and disgust; they tear the constitution to which they are applied in excess, and, like the lightning of night, only serve to darken the gloom through which they occasionally break. Happiness is not that state of repose, or that imaginary freedom from care, which at a distance is so frequent an object of desire, but with its approach brings a tedium, or a languor, more unsupportable than pain itself. If the preceding observations on this subject be just, it arises more from the pursuit, than from the attainment of any end whatever; and in every new situation to which we arrive, even in the course of a prosperous life, it depends more on the degree in which our minds are properly employed, than it does on the circumstances in which we are destined to act, on the materials which are placed in our hands, or the tools with which we are furnished.

If this be confessed in respect to that class of pursuits which are distinguished by the name of *amusement*, and which, in the case of men who are commonly deemed the most happy, occupy the greater part of human life, we may apprehend, that it holds, much more than is commonly suspected, in many cases of business, where the end to be gained, and not the occupation, is supposed to have the principal value.

The miser himself, we are told, can sometimes consider the care of his wealth as a pastime, and has challenged his heir, to have more pleasure in spending, than he in amassing his fortune. With this degree of indifference to what may be the conduct of others; with this confinement of his care to what he has chosen as his own province, more especially if he has conquered in himself the passions of jealousy and envy, which tear the covetous mind; why may not the man whose object is money, be understood to lead a life of amusement and pleasure, not only more entire than that of the spendthrift, but even as much as the virtuoso, the scholar, the man of taste, or any of that class of persons who have found out a method of passing their leisure without offence, and to whom the acquisitions made, or the works produced, in their several ways, perhaps, are as useless as the bag to the miser, or the counter to those who play from mere dissipation at any game of skill or of chance?

We are soon tired of diversions that do not approach to the nature of business, that is, that do not engage some passion, or give an exercise proportioned to our talents, and our faculties. The chace and the gaming-table have each their dangers and difficulties, to excite and employ the mind. All games of contention animate our emulation, and give a species of party-zeal. The mathematician is only to be amused with intricate problems, the lawyer and the casuist with cases that try their subtilty, and occupy their judgement.

The desire of active engagements, like every other natural appetite, may be carried to excess; and men may debauch in amusements, as well as in the use of wine, or other intoxicating liquors. At first, a trifling stake, and the occupation of a moderate passion, may have served to amuse the gamester; but when the drug becomes familiar, it fails to produce its effect: The play is made deep, and the interest increased, to awaken his attention; he is carried on by degrees, and in the end comes to seek for amusement, and to find it only in those passions of anxiety, hope, and despair, which are roused by the hazard into which he has thrown the whole of his fortunes.

If men can thus turn their amusements into a scene more serious and interesting than that of business itself, it will be difficult to assign a reason, why business, and many of the occupations of human life, independent of any distant consequences, or future events, may not be chosen as an amusement, and adopted on account of the pastime they bring. This is, perhaps, the foundation on which, without the aid of reflection, the contented and the chearful have rested the gaiety of their tempers. It is perhaps the most solid basis of fortitude which any reflection can lay; and happiness itself is secured, by making a certain species of conduct our amusement; and, by considering life, in the general estimate of its value, as well as on every particular occasion, as a mere scene for the exercise of the mind, and the engagements of the heart. 'I will try and attempt every thing,' says Brutus, 'I will never cease to recal my country from this state of servility. If the event be favourable, it will prove matter of joy to us all; if not, yet I, notwithstanding, shall rejoice.' Why rejoice in a disappointment? Why not be dejected, when his country was overwhelmed? Because sorrow, perhaps, and dejection, can do no good. Nay, but they must be endured when they come. And whence should they come to me? might the Roman say; I have followed my mind, and can follow it still. Events may have changed the situation in which I am destined to act; but can they hinder my acting the part of a man? Shew me a situation in which a man can neither act nor die, and I will own he is wretched.

Whoever has the force of mind steadily to view human life under this aspect, has only to chuse well his occupations, in order to command that state of enjoyment, and freedom of soul, which probably constitute the peculiar felicity to which his active nature is destined.

The dispositions of men, and consequently their occupations, are commonly divided into two principal classes; the selfish, and the social. The first are indulged in solitude; and if they carry a reference to mankind, it is that of emulation, competition, and enmity. The second incline us to live with our fellow-creatures, and to do them good; they tend to unite the members of society together; they terminate in a mutual participation of their cares and enjoyments, and render the presence of men an occasion of joy. Under this class may be enumerated the passions of the sexes, the affections of parents and children, general humanity, or singular attachments; above all, that habit of the soul by which we consider ourselves as but a part of some beloved community, and as but individual members of some society, whose general welfare is to us the supreme object of zeal, and the great rule of our conduct. This affection is a principle of candour, which knows no partial distinctions, and is confined to no bounds:

it may extend its effects beyond our personal acquaintance; it may, in the mind, and in thought, at least, make us feel a relation to the universe, and to the whole creation of God. 'Shall any one,' says Antoninus, 'love the city of Cecrops, and you not love the city of God?'

No emotion of the heart is indifferent. It is either an act of vivacity and joy, or a feeling of sadness; a transport of pleasure, or a convulsion of anguish: and the exercises of our different dispositions, as well as their gratifications, are likely to prove matter of the greatest importance to our happiness or misery.

The individual is charged with the care of his animal preservation. He may exist in solitude, and, far removed from society, perform many functions of sense, imagination, and reason. He is even rewarded for the proper discharge of those functions; and all the natural exercises which relate to himself, as well as to his fellow-creatures, not only occupy without distressing him, but in many instances are attended with positive pleasures, and fill up the hours of life with agreeable occupation.

There is a degree, however, in which we suppose that the care of ourselves becomes a source of painful anxiety and cruel passions; in which it degenerates into avarice, vanity, or pride; and in which, by fostering habits of jealousy and envy, of fear and malice, it becomes as destructive of our own enjoyments, as it is hostile to the welfare of mankind. This evil, however, is not to be charged upon any excess in the care of ourselves, but upon a mere mistake in the choice of our objects. We look abroad for a happiness which is to be found only in the qualities of the heart: we think ourselves dependent on accidents; and are therefore kept in suspense and solicitude: we think ourselves dependent on the will of other men; and are therefore servile and timid: we think our felicity is placed in subjects for which our fellow-creatures are rivals and competitors; and in pursuit of happiness, we engage in those scenes of emulation, envy, hatred, animosity, and revenge, that lead to the highest pitch of distress. We act, in short, as if to preserve ourselves were to retain our weakness, and perpetuate our sufferings. We charge the ills of a distempered imagination, and a corrupt heart, to the account of our fellow-creatures, to whom we refer the pangs of our disappointment or malice; and while we foster our misery, are surprised that the care of ourselves is attended with no better effects. But he who remembers that he is by nature a rational being, and a member of society; that to preserve himself, is to preserve his reason, and to preserve the best feelings of his heart; will encounter with none of these inconveniencies; and in the care of himself, will find subjects only of satisfaction and triumph.

The division of our appetites into benevolent and selfish, has probably, in some degree, helped to mislead our apprehension on the subject of personal enjoyment and private good; and our zeal to prove that virtue is disinterested, has not greatly promoted its cause. The gratification of a selfish desire, it is thought, brings advantage or pleasure to ourselves; that of benevolence terminates in the pleasure or advantage of others: whereas, in reality, the gratification of every desire is a personal enjoyment, and its value being proportioned to the particular quality or force of the sentiment, it may happen that the same person may reap a greater advantage from the good fortune he has procured to another, than from that he has obtained for himself.

While the gratifications of benevolence, therefore, are as much our own as those of any other desire whatever, the mere exercises of this disposition are, on many accounts, to be considered as the first and the principal constituent of human happiness. Every act of kindness, or of care, in the parent to his child; every emotion of the heart. in friendship or in love, in public zeal, or general humanity, are so many acts of enjoyment and satisfaction. Pity itself, and compassion, even grief and melancholy, when grafted on some tender affection, partake of the nature of the stock; and if they are not positive pleasures, are at least pains of a peculiar nature, which we do not even wish to exchange but for a very real enjoyment, obtained in relieving our object. Even extremes, in this class of our dispositions, as they are the reverse of hatred, envy, and malice, so they are never attended with those excruciating anxieties, jealousies, and fears, which tear the interested mind; or if, in reality, any ill passion arise from a pretended attachment to our fellow-creatures, that attachment may be safely condemned, as not genuine. If we be distrustful or jealous, our pretended affection is probably no more than a desire of attention and personal consideration, a motive which frequently inclines us to be connected with our fellow-creatures; but to which we are as frequently willing to sacrifice their happiness. We consider them as the tools of our vanity, pleasure, or interest; not as the parties on whom we may bestow the effects of our good-will, and our love.

A mind devoted to this class of its affections, being occupied with an object that may engage it habitually, is not reduced to court the amusements or pleasures with which persons of an ill temper are obliged to repair their disgusts: and temperance becomes an easy task when gratifications of sense are supplanted by those of the heart. Courage too is most easily assumed, or is rather inseparable from that ardour of the mind, in society, friendship, or in public action, which makes us forget subjects of personal anxiety or fear, and attend chiefly to the object of our zeal or affection, not to the trifling inconveniencies, dangers, or hardships, which we ourselves may encounter in striving to maintain it.

It should seem, therefore, to be the happiness of man, to make his social dispositions the ruling spring of his occupations; to state himself as the member of a community, for whose general good his heart may glow with an ardent zeal, to the suppression of those personal cares which are the foundation of painful anxieties, fear, jealousy, and envy; or, as Mr Pope expresses the same sentiment,

> 'Man, like the generous vine, supported lives;
> The strength he gains, is from th'embrace he gives.'*

If this be the good of the individual, it is likewise that of mankind; and virtue no longer imposes a task by which we are obliged to bestow upon others that good from which we ourselves refrain; but supposes, in the highest degree, as possessed by ourselves, that state of felicity which we are required to promote in the world.

---

* The same maxim will apply throughout every part of nature. *To love, is to enjoy pleasure: To hate, is to be in pain.*

We commonly apprehend, that it is our duty to do kindnesses, and our happiness to receive them: but if, in reality, courage, and a heart devoted to the good of mankind, are the constituents of human felicity, the kindness which is done infers a happiness in the person from whom it proceeds, not in him on whom it is bestowed; and the greatest good which men possessed of fortitude and generosity can procure to their fellow-creatures, is a participation of this happy character. 'You will confer the greatest benefit on your city,' says Epictetus, 'not by raising the roofs, but by exalting the souls of your fellow-citizens; for it is better that great souls should live in small habitations, than that abject slaves should burrow in great houses.'*

To the benevolent, the satisfaction of others is a ground of enjoyment; and existence itself, in a world that is governed by the wisdom of God, is a blessing. The mind, freed from cares that lead to pusillanimity and meanness, becomes calm, active, fearless, and bold; capable of every enterprise, and vigorous in the exercise of every talent, by which the nature of man is adorned. On this foundation was raised the admirable character, which, during a certain period of their story, distinguished the celebrated nations of antiquity, and rendered familiar and ordinary in their manners, examples of magnanimity, which, under governments less favourable to the public affections, rarely occur; or which, without being much practised, or even understood, are made subjects of admiration and swelling panegyric. 'Thus,' says Xenophon, 'died Thrasybulus; who indeed appears to have been a good man.' What valuable praise, and how significant to those who know the story of this admirable person! The members of those illustrious states, from the habit of considering themselves as part of a community, or at least as deeply involved with some order of men in the state, were regardless of personal considerations: they had a perpetual view to objects which excite a great ardour in the soul; which led them to act perpetually in the view of their fellow-citizens, and to practise those arts of deliberation, elocution, policy, and war, on which the fortunes of nations, or of men, in their collective body, depend. To the

* Mrs Carter's translation of the works of Epictetus.

force of mind collected in this career, and to the improvements of wit which were made in pursuing it, these nations owed, not only their magnanimity, and the superiority of their political and military conduct, but even the arts of poetry and literature, which among them were only the inferior appendages of a genius otherwise excited, cultivated, and refined.

To the ancient Greek, or the Roman, the individual was nothing, and the public every thing. To the modern, in too many nations of Europe, the individual is every thing, and the public nothing. The state is merely a combination of departments, in which consideration, wealth, eminence, or power, are offered as the reward of service. It was the nature of modern government, even in its first institution, to bestow on every individual a fixed station and dignity, which he was to maintain for himself. Our ancestors, in rude ages, during the recess of wars from abroad, fought for their personal claims at home, and by their competitions, and the balance of their powers, maintained a kind of political freedom in the state, while private parties were subject to continual wrongs and oppressions. Their posterity, in times more polished, have repressed the civil disorders in which the activity of earlier ages chiefly consisted; but they employ the calm they have gained, not in fostering a zeal for those laws, and that constitution of government, to which they owe their protection, but in practising apart, and each for himself, the several arts of personal advancement, or profit, which their political establishments may enable them to pursue with success. Commerce, which may be supposed to comprehend every lucrative art, is accordingly considered as the great object of nations, and the principal study of mankind.

So much are we accustomed to consider personal fortune as the sole object of care, that even under popular establishments, and in states where different orders of men are summoned to partake in the government of their country, and where the liberties they enjoy cannot be long preserved, without vigilance and activity on the part of the subject; still they, who, in the vulgar phrase, have not their fortunes to make, are supposed to be at a loss for occupation, and betake themselves to solitary pastimes, or cultivate what they are pleased to call a taste for gardening, building, drawing, or music. With this aid, they endeavour to fill up the blanks of a listless life, and avoid the necessity of curing their languors by any positive service to their country, or to mankind.

The weak or the malicious are well employed in any thing that is innocent, and are fortunate in finding any occupation which prevents the effects of a temper that would prey upon themselves, or upon their fellow-creatures. But they who are blessed with a happy disposition, with capacity and vigour, incur a real debauchery, by having any amusement that occupies an improper share of their time; and are really cheated of their happiness, in being made to believe, that any occupation or pastime is better fitted to amuse themselves, than that which at the same time produces some real good to their fellow-creatures.

This sort of entertainment, indeed, cannot be the choice of the mercenary, the envious, or the malignant. Its value is known only to persons of an opposite temper; and to their experience alone we appeal. Guided by mere disposition, and without the aid of reflection, in business, in friendship, and in public life, they often acquit themselves well; and borne with satisfaction on the tide of their emotions and sentiments, enjoy the present hour, without recollection of the past, or hopes of the future. It is in speculation, not in practice, they are made to discover, that virtue is a task of severity and self-denial.

SECTION IX.

Of National Felicity.

Man is, by nature, the member of a community; and when considered in this capacity, the individual appears to be no longer made for himself. He must forego his happiness and his freedom, where these interfere with the good of society. He is only part of a whole; and the praise we think due to his virtue, is but a branch of that more general commendation we bestow on the member of a body, on the part of a fabric or engine, for being well fitted to occupy its place, and to produce its effect.

If this follow from the relation of a part to its whole, and if the public good be the principal object with individuals, it is likewise true, that the happiness of individuals is the great end of civil society: for in what sense can a public enjoy any good, if its members, considered apart, be unhappy?

The interests of society, however, and of its members, are easily reconciled. If the individual owe every degree of consideration to the public, he receives, in paying that very consideration, the greatest happiness of which his nature is capable; and the greatest blessing that the public can bestow on its members, is to keep them attached to itself. That is the most happy state, which is most beloved by its subjects; and they are the most happy men, whose hearts are engaged to a community, in which they find every object of generosity and zeal, and a scope to the exercise of every talent, and of every virtuous disposition.

After we have thus found general maxims, the greater part of our trouble remains, their just application to particular cases. Nations are different in respect to their extent, numbers of people, and wealth; in respect to the arts they practise, and the accommodations they have procured. These circumstances may not only affect the manners of men; they even, in our esteem, come into competition with the article of manners itself; are supposed to constitute a national felicity, independent of virtue; and give a title, upon which we indulge our own vanity, and that of other nations, as we do that of private men, on the score of their fortunes and honours.

But if this way of measuring happiness, when applied to private men, be ruinous and false, it is so no less when applied to nations. Wealth, commerce, extent of territory, and the knowledge of arts, are, when properly employed, the means of preservation, and the foundations of power. If they fail in part, the nation is weakened; if they were entirely with-held, the race would perish: their tendency is to maintain numbers of men, but not to constitute happiness. They will accordingly maintain the wretched, as well as the happy. They answer one purpose, but are not therefore sufficient for all; and are of little significance, when only employed to maintain a timid, dejected, and servile people.

Great and powerful states are able to overcome and subdue the weak; polished and commercial nations have more wealth, and practise a greater variety of arts, than the rude: but the happiness of men, in all cases alike, consists in the blessings of a candid, an active, and strenuous mind. And if we consider the state of society merely as that into which mankind are led by their propensities, as a state to be valued from its effect in preserving the species, in ripening their talents, and exciting their virtues, we need not enlarge our communities, in order to enjoy these advantages. We frequently obtain them in the most remarkable degree, where nations remain independent, and are of a small extent.

To increase the numbers of mankind, may be admitted as a great and important object: but to extend the limits of any particular state, is not, perhaps, the way to obtain it; while we desire that our fellow-creatures should multiply, it does not follow, that the whole should, if possible, be united under one head. We are apt to admire the empire of the Romans, as a model of national greatness and splendour: but the greatness we admire in this case, was ruinous to the virtue and the happiness of mankind; it was found to be inconsistent with all the advantages which that conquering people had formerly enjoyed in the articles of government and manners.

The emulation of nations proceeds from their division. A cluster of states, like a company of men, find the exercise of their reason, and the test of their virtues, in the affairs they transact, upon a foot of equality, and of separate interest. The measures taken for safety, including great part of the national policy, are relative in every state to what is apprehended from abroad. Athens was necessary to Sparta, in the exercise of her virtue, as steel is to flint in the production of fire; and if the cities of Greece had been united under one head, we should never have heard of Epaminondas or Thrasybulus, of Lycurgus or Solon.

When we reason in behalf of our species, therefore, although we may lament the abuses which sometimes arise from independence, and opposition of interest; yet, whilst any degrees of virtue remain with mankind, we cannot wish to croud, under one establishment, numbers of men who may serve to constitute several; or to commit affairs to the conduct of one senate, one legislative or executive power, which, upon a distinct and separate footing, might furnish an exercise of ability, and a theatre of glory, to many.

This may be a subject upon which no determinate rule can be given, but the admiration of boundless dominion is a ruinous error; and in no instance, perhaps, is the real interest of mankind more entirely mistaken.

The measure of enlargement to be wished for any particular state, is often to be taken from the condition of its neighbours. Where a number of states are contiguous, they should be near an equality, in order that they may be mutually objects of respect and consideration, and in order that they may possess that independence in which the political life of a nation consists.

When the kingdoms of Spain were united, when the great fiefs in France were annexed to the crown, it was no longer expedient for the nations of Great Britain to continue disjoined.

The small republics of Greece, indeed, by their subdivisions, and the balance of their power, found almost in every village the object of nations. Every little district was a nursery of excellent men, and what is now the wretched corner of a great empire, was the field on which mankind have reaped their principal honours. But in modern Europe, republics of a similar extent, are like shrubs, under the shade of a taller wood, choked by the neighbourhood of more powerful states. In their case, a certain disproportion of force frustrates, in a great measure, the advantage of separation. They are like the trader in Poland, who is the more despicable, and the less secure, that he is neither master nor slave.

Independent communities, in the mean time, however weak, are averse to a coalition, not only where it comes with an air of imposition, or unequal treaty, but even where it implies no more than the admission of new members to an equal share of consideration with the old. The citizen has no interest in the annexation of kingdoms; he must find his importance diminished, as the state is enlarged: but ambitious men, under the enlargement of territory, find a more plentiful harvest of power, and of wealth, while government itself is an easier task. Hence the ruinous progress of empire; and hence free nations, under the shew of acquiring dominion, suffer themselves, in the end, to be yoked with the slaves they had conquered.

Our desire to augment the force of a nation is the only pretext for enlarging its territory; but this measure, when pursued to extremes, seldom fails to frustrate itself.

Notwithstanding the advantage of numbers, and superior resources in war, the strength of a nation is derived from the character, not from the wealth, nor from the multitude of its people. If the treasure of a state can hire numbers of men, erect ramparts, and furnish the implements of war; the possessions of the fearful are easily seized; a timorous multitude falls into rout of itself; ramparts may be scaled where they are not defended by valour; and arms are of consequence only in the hands of the brave. The band to which Agesilaus pointed as the wall of his city, made a defence for their country more permanent, and more effectual, than the rock and the cement with which other cities were fortified.

We should owe little to that statesman who were to contrive a defence that might supersede the external uses of virtue. It is wisely ordered for man, as a rational being, that the employment of reason is necessary to his preservation: it is fortunate for him, in the pursuit of distinction, that his personal consideration depends on his character; and it is fortunate for nations, that, in order to be powerful and safe, they must strive to maintain the courage, and cultivate the virtues, of their people. By the use of such means, they at once gain their external ends, and are happy.

Peace and unanimity are commonly considered as the principal foundations of public felicity; yet the rivalship of separate communities, and the agitations of a free people, are the principles of political life, and the school of men. How shall we reconcile these jarring and opposite tenets? It is, perhaps, not necessary to reconcile them. The pacific may do what they can to allay the animosities, and to reconcile the opinions, of men; and it will be happy if they can succeed in repressing their crimes, and in calming the worst of their passions. Nothing, in the mean time, but corruption or slavery can suppress the debates that subsist among men of integrity, who bear an equal part in the administration of state.

A perfect agreement in matters of opinion is not to be obtained in the most select company; and if it were, what would become of society? 'The Spartan legislator,' says Plutarch, 'appears to have sown the seeds of variance and dissension among his countrymen: he meant that good citizens should be led to dispute; he considered emulation as the brand by which their virtues were kindled; and seemed to apprehend, that a complaisance, by which men submit their opinions without examination, is a principal source of corruption.'

Forms of government are supposed to decide of the happiness or misery of mankind. But forms of government must be varied, in order to suit the extent, the way of subsistence, the character, and the manners of different nations. In some cases, the multitude may be suffered to govern themselves; in others, they must be severely restrained. The inhabitants of a village in some primitive age, may have been safely intrusted to the conduct of reason, and to the suggestion of their innocent views; but the tenants of Newgate can scarcely be trusted, with chains locked to their bodies, and bars of iron fixed to their legs. How is it possible, therefore, to find any single form of government that would suit mankind in every condition?

We proceed, however, in the following section, to point out the distinctions, and to explain the language which occurs in this place, on the head of different models for subordination and government.

SECTION X.
The same subject continued.

It is a common observation, That mankind were originally equal. They have indeed by nature equal rights to their preservation, and to the use of their talents; but they are fitted for different stations; and when they are classed by a rule taken from this circumstance, they suffer no injustice on the side of their natural rights. It is obvious, that some mode of subordination is as necessary to men as society itself; and this, not only to attain the ends of government, but to comply with an order established by nature.

Prior to any political institution whatever, men are qualified by a great diversity of talents, by a different tone of the soul, and ardour of the passions, to act a variety of parts. Bring them together, each will find his place. They censure or applaud in a body; they consult and deliberate in more select parties; they take or give an ascendant as individuals; and numbers are by this means fitted to act in company, and to preserve their communities, before any formal distribution of office is made.

We are formed to act in this manner; and if we have any doubts with relation to the rights of government in general, we owe our perplexity more to the subtilties of the speculative, than to any uncertainty in the feelings of the heart. Involved in the resolutions of our company, we move with the croud before we have determined the rule by which its will is collected. We follow a leader, before we have settled the ground of his pretensions, or adjusted the form of his election: and it is not till after mankind have committed many errors in the capacities of magistrate and subject, that they think of making government itself a subject of rules.

If therefore, in considering the variety of forms under which societies subsist, the casuist is pleased to inquire, What title one man, or any number of men, have to controul his actions? he may be answered, None at all, provided that his actions have no effect to the prejudice of his fellow-creatures; but if they have, the rights of defence, and the obligation to repress the commission of wrongs, belong to collective bodies, as well as to individuals. Many rude nations, having no formal tribunals for the judgement of crimes, assemble, when alarmed by any flagrant offence, and take their measures with the criminal as they would with an enemy.

But will this consideration, which confirms the title to sovereignty, where it is exercised by the society in its collective capacity, or by those to whom the powers of the whole are committed, likewise support the claim to dominion, where-ever it is casually lodged, or even where it is only maintained by force?

This question may be sufficiently answered, by observing, that a right to do justice, and to do good, is competent to every individual, or order of men; and that the exercise of this right has no limits but in the defect of power. But a right to do wrong, and commit injustice, is an abuse of language, and a contradiction in terms. It is no more competent to the collective body of a people, than it is to any single usurper. When we admit such a prerogative in the case of any sovereign, we can only mean to express the extent of his power, and the force with which he is enabled to execute his pleasure. Such a prerogative is assumed by the leader of banditti at the head of his gang, or by a despotic prince at the head of his troops. When the sword is presented by either, the traveller or the inhabitant may submit from a sense of necessity or fear; but he lies under no obligation from a motive of duty or justice.

The multiplicity of forms, in the mean time, which different societies offer to our view, is almost infinite. The classes into which they distribute their members, the manner in which they establish the legislative and executive powers, the imperceptible circumstances by which they are led to have different customs, and to confer on their governors unequal measures of power and authority, give rise to perpetual distinctions between constitutions the most nearly resembling one another, and give to human affairs a variety in detail, which, in its full extent, no understanding can comprehend, and no memory retain.

In order to have a general and comprehensive knowledge of the whole, we must be determined on this, as on every other subject, to overlook many particulars and singularities, distinguishing different governments; to fix our attention on certain points, in which many agree; and thereby establish a few general heads, under which the subject may be distinctly considered. When we have marked the characteristics which form the general points of coincidence; when we have pursued them to their consequences in the several modes of legislation, execution, and judicature, in the establishments which relate to police, commerce, religion, or domestic life; we have made an acquisition of knowledge, which, though it does not supersede the necessity of experience, may serve to direct our inquiries, and, in the midst of affairs, to give an order and a method for the arrangement of particulars that occur to our observation.

When I recollect what the President Montesquieu has written, I am at a loss to tell, why I should treat of human affairs: but I too am instigated by my reflections, and my sentiments; and I may utter them more to the comprehension of ordinary capacities, because I am more on the level of ordinary men. If it be necessary to pave the way for what follows on the general history of nations, by giving some account of the heads under which various forms of government may be conveniently ranged, the reader should perhaps be referred to what has been already delivered on the subject by this profound politician and amiable moralist. In his writings will be found, not only the original of what I am now, for the sake of order, to copy from him, but likewise probably the source of many observations, which, in different places, I may, under the belief of invention, have repeated, without quoting their author.

The ancient philosophers treated of government commonly under three heads; the Democratic, the Aristocratic, and the Despotic. Their attention was chiefly occupied with the varieties o republican government; and they paid little regard to a very important distinction, which Mr Montesquieu has made, between despotism and monarchy. He too has considered government as reducible to three general forms; and, 'to understand the nature of each,' he observes, 'it is sufficient to recal ideas which are familiar with men of the least reflection, who admit three definitions, or rather three facts: That a republic is a state in which the people in a collective body, or a part of the people, possess the sovereign power: That monarchy is that in which one man governs, according to fixed and determinate laws: And a despotism is that in which one man, without law, or rule of administration, by the mere impulse of will or caprice, decides, and carries every thing before him.'

Republics admit of a very material distinction, which is pointed out in the general definition; that between democracy and aristocracy. In the first, supreme power remains in the hands of the collective body. Every office of magistracy, at the nomination of this sovereign, is open to every citizen; who, in the discharge of his duty, becomes the minister of the people, and accountable to them for every object of his trust.

In the second, the sovereignty is lodged in a particular class, or order of men; who, being once named, continue for life; or by the hereditary distinctions of birth and fortune, are advanced to a station of permanent superiority. From this order, and by their nomination, all the offices of magistracy are filled; and in the different assemblies which they constitute, whatever relates to the legislation, the execution, or jurisdiction, is finally determined.

Mr Montesquieu has pointed out the sentiments or maxims from which men must be supposed to act under these different governments.

In democracy, they must love equality; they must respect the rights of their fellow-citizens; they must unite by the common ties of affection to the state. In forming personal pretensions, they must be satisfied with that degree of consideration they can procure by their abilities fairly measured with those of an opponent; they must labour for the public without hope of profit; they must reject every attempt to create a personal dependence. Candour, force, and elevation of mind, in short, are the props of democracy; and virtue is the principle of conduct required to its preservation.

How beautiful a pre-eminence on the side of popular government! and how ardently should mankind wish for the form, if it tended to establish the principle, or were, in every instance, a sure indication of its presence!

But perhaps we must have possessed the principle, in order, with any hopes of advantage, to receive the form; and where the first is entirely extinguished, the other may be fraught with evil, if any additional evil deserves to be shunned where men are already unhappy.

At Constantinople or Algiers, it is a miserable spectacle when men pretend to act on a foot of equality: they only mean to shake off the restraints of government, and to seize as much as they can of that spoil, which, in ordinary times, is ingrossed by the master they serve.

It is one advantage of democracy, that the principal ground of distinction being personal qualities, men are classed according to their abilities, and to the merit of their actions. Though all have equal pretensions to power, yet the state is actually governed by a few. The majority of the people, even in their capacity of sovereign, only pretend to employ their senses; to feel, when pressed by national inconveniencies, or threatened by public dangers; and with the ardour which is apt to arise in crouded assemblies, to urge the pursuits in which they are engaged, or to repel the attacks with which they are menaced.

The most perfect equality of rights can never exclude the ascendant of superior minds, nor the assemblies of a collective body govern without the direction of select councils. On this account, popular government may be confounded with aristocracy. But this alone does not constitute the character of aristocratical government. Here the members of the state are divided, at least, into two classes; of which one is destined to command, the other to obey. No merits or defects can raise or sink a person from one class to the other. The only effect of personal character is, to procure the individual a suitable degree of consideration with his own order, not to vary his rank. In one situation he is taught to assume, in another to yield the pre-eminence. He occupies the station of patron or client, and is either the sovereign or the subject of his country. The whole citizens may unite in executing the plans of state, but never in deliberating on its measures, or enacting its laws. What belongs to the whole people under democracy, is here confined to a part. Members of the superior order, are among themselves, possibly, classed according to their abilities, but retain a perpetual ascendant over those of inferior station. They are at once the servants and the masters of the state, and pay with their personal attendance and their blood for the civil or military honours they enjoy.

To maintain for himself, and to admit in his fellow-citizen, a perfect equality of privilege and station, is no longer the leading maxim of the member of such a community. The rights of men are modified by their condition. One order claims more than it is willing to yield; the other must be ready to yield what it does not assume to itself: and it is with good reason that Mr Montesquieu gives to the principle of such governments the name of *moderation*, not of *virtue*.

The elevation of one class is a moderated arrogance; the submission of the other a limited deference. The first must be careful, by concealing the invidious part of their distinction, to palliate what is grievous in the public arrangement, and by their education, their cultivated manners, and improved talents, to appear qualified for the stations they occupy. The other must be taught to yield, from respect and personal attachment, what could not otherwise be extorted by force. When this moderation fails on either side, the constitution totters. A populace enraged to mutiny, may claim the right of equality to which they are admitted in democratical states; or a nobility bent on dominion, may chuse among themselves, or find already pointed out to them, a sovereign, who, by advantages of fortune, popularity, or abilities, is ready to seize for his own family, that envied power, which has already carried his order beyond the limits of moderation, and infected particular men with a boundless ambition.

Monarchies have accordingly been found with the recent marks of aristocracy. There, however, the monarch is only the first among the nobles; he must be satisfied with a limited power; his subjects are ranged into classes; he finds on every quarter a pretence to privilege, that circumscribes his authority; and he finds a force sufficient to confine his administration within certain bounds of equity, and determinate laws.

Under such governments, however, the love of equality is preposterous, and moderation itself is unnecessary. The object of every rank is precedency, and every order may display its advantages to their full extent. The sovereign himself owes great part of his authority to the sounding titles and the dazzling equipage which he exhibits in public. The subordinate ranks lay claim to importance by a like exhibition, and for that purpose carry in every instant the ensigns of their birth, or the ornaments of their fortune. What else could mark out to the individual the relation in which he stands to his fellow-subjects, or distinguish the numberless ranks that fill up the interval between the state of the sovereign and that of the peasant? Or what else could, in states of a great extent, preserve any appearance of order, among members disunited by ambition and interest, and destined to form a community, without the sense of any common concern?

Monarchies are generally found, where the state is enlarged in population and in territory, beyond the numbers and dimensions that are consistent with republican government. Together with these circumstances, great inequalities arise in the distribution of property; and the desire of pre-eminence becomes the predominant passion. Every rank would exercise its prerogative, and the sovereign is perpetually tempted to enlarge his own; if subjects, who despair of precedence, plead for equality, he is willing to favour their claims, and to aid them in procuring what must weaken a force, with which he himself is, on many occasions, obliged to contend. In the event of such a policy, many invidious distinctions and grievances peculiar to monarchical government, may, in appearance, be removed; but the state of equality to which the subjects approach, is that of slaves, equally dependent on the will of a master, not that of freemen in a condition to maintain their own.

The principle of monarchy, according to Montesquieu, is honour. Men may possess good qualities, elevation of mind, and

fortitude; but the sense of equality, that will bear no incroachment on the personal rights of the meanest citizen; the indignant
spirit, that will not court a protection, nor accept as a favour, what
is due as a right; the public affection, which is founded on the
neglect of personal considerations, are neither consistent with
the preservation of the constitution, nor agreeable to the habits
acquired in any station assigned to its members.

Every condition is possessed of peculiar dignity, and points out
a propriety of conduct, which men of station are obliged to
maintain. In the commerce of superiors and inferiors, it is the
object of ambition, and of vanity, to refine on the advantages
of rank; while, to facilitate the intercourse of polite society, it is
the aim of good breeding, to disguise or reject them.

Though the objects of consideration are rather the dignities
of station than personal qualities; though friendship cannot be
formed by mere inclination, nor alliances by the mere choice
of the heart; yet men so united, and even without changing their
order, are highly susceptible of moral excellence, or liable to
many different degrees of corruption. They may act a vigorous
part as members of the state, an amiable one in the commerce of
private society; or they may yield up their dignity as citizens,
even while they raise their arrogance and presumption as private
parties.

In monarchy, all orders of men derive their honours from the
crown; but they continue to hold them as a right, and they
exercise a subordinate power in the state, founded on the permanent rank they enjoy, and on the attachment of those whom
they are appointed to lead and protect. Though they do not force
themselves into national councils, and public assemblies, and
though the name of senate is unknown; yet the sentiments they
adopt must have weight with the sovereign; and every individual,
in his separate capacity, in some measure, deliberates for his
country. In whatever does not derogate from his rank, he has
an arm ready to serve the community; in whatever alarms his
sense of honour, he has aversions and dislikes, which amount to
a negative on the will of his prince.

Intangled together by the reciprocal ties of dependence and

protection, though not combined by the sense of a common interest, the subjects of monarchy, like those of republics, find themselves occupied as the members of an active society, and engaged to treat with their fellow-creatures on a liberal footing. If those principles of honour which save the individual from servility in his own person, or from becoming an engine of oppression in the hands of another, should fail; if they should give way to the maxims of commerce, to the refinements of a supposed philosophy, or to the misplaced ardours of a republican spirit; if they are betrayed by the cowardice of subjects, or subdued by the ambition of princes; what must become of the nations of Europe?

Despotism is monarchy corrupted, in which a court and a prince in appearance remain, but in which every subordinate rank is destroyed; in which the subject is told, that he has no rights; that he cannot possess any property, nor fill any station, independent of the momentary will of his prince. These doctrines are founded on the maxims of conquest; they must be inculcated with the whip and the sword; and are best received under the terror of chains and imprisonment. Fear, therefore, is the principle which qualifies the subject to occupy his station: and the sovereign, who holds out the ensigns of terror so freely to others, has abundant reason to give this passion a principal place with himself. That tenure which he has devised for the rights of others, is soon applied to his own; and from his eager desire to secure, or to extend, his power, he finds it become, like the fortunes of his people, a creature of mere imagination and unsettled caprice.

Whilst we thus, with so much accuracy, can assign the ideal limits that may distinguish constitutions of government, we find them, in reality, both in respect to the principle and the form, variously blended together. In what society are not men classed by external distinctions, as well as personal qualities? In what state are they not actuated by a variety of principles; justice, honour, moderation, and fear? It is the purpose of science, not to disguise this confusion in its object, but, in the multiplicity and combination of particulars, to find the principal points which deserve our attention, and which, being well understood, save us from the embarrassment which the varieties of singular cases might otherwise create. In the same degree in which governments require men to act from principles of virtue, of honour, or of fear, they are more or less fully comprised under the heads of republic, monarchy, or despotism, and the general theory is more or less applicable to their particular case.

Forms of government, in fact, mutually approach or recede by many, and often insensible gradations. Democracy, by admitting certain inequalities of rank, approaches to aristocracy. In popular, as well as aristocratical governments, particular men, by their personal authority, and sometimes by the credit of their family, have maintained a species of monarchical power. The monarch is limited in different degrees: even the despotic prince is only that monarch whose subjects claim the fewest privileges, or who is himself best prepared to subdue them by force. All these varieties are but steps in the history of mankind, and mark the fleeting and transient situations through which they have passed, while supported by virtue, or depressed by vice.

Perfect democracy and despotism appear to be the opposite extremes to which constitutions of government are sometimes carried. Under the first, a perfect virtue is required; under the second, a total corruption is supposed: yet in point of mere form, there being nothing fixed in the ranks and distinctions of men, beyond the casual and temporary possession of power, societies easily pass from a condition in which every individual has an equal title to reign, into one in which they are equally destined to serve. The same qualities in both, courage, popularity, address, and military conduct, raise the ambitious to eminence. With these qualities, the citizen or the slave easily passes from the ranks to the command of an army, from an obscure to an illustrious station. In either, a single person may rule with unlimited sway; and in both, the populace may break down every barrier of order, and restraint of law.

If we suppose that the equality established among the subjects of a despotic state, has inspired its members with confidence, intrepidity, and the love of justice; the despotic prince, having ceased to be an object of fear, must sink among the croud. If, on the contrary, the personal equality which is enjoyed by the members of a democratical state, should be valued merely as an equal pretension to the objects of avarice and ambition, the monarch may start up anew, and be supported by those who mean to share in his profits. When the covetous and mercenary assemble in parties, it is of no consequence under what leader they inlist, whether Caesar or Pompey; the hopes of rapine or power are the only motives from which they become attached to either.

In the disorder of corrupted societies, the scene has been frequently changed from democracy to despotism, and from the last too, in its turn, to the first. From amidst the democracy of corrupt men, and from a scene of lawless confusion, the tyrant ascends a throne with arms reeking in blood. But his abuses, or his weaknesses, in the station which he has gained, in their turn, awaken and give way to the spirit of mutiny and revenge. The cries of murder and desolation, which in the ordinary course of military government terrified the subject in his private retreat, are carried through the vaults, and made to pierce the grates and iron doors of the seraglio. Democracy seems to revive in a scene of wild disorder and tumult: but both the extremes are but the transient fits of paroxysm or languor in a distempered state.

If men be any where arrived at this measure of depravity, there appears no immediate hope of redress. Neither the ascendency of the multitude, nor that of the tyrant, will secure the administration of justice: neither the licence of mere tumult, nor the calm of dejection and servitude, will teach the citizen that he was born for candour and affection to his fellow-creatures. And if the speculative would find that habitual state of war which they are sometimes pleased to honour with the name of *the state of nature*, they will find it in the contest that subsists between the despotical prince and his subjects, not in the first approaches of a rude and simple tribe to the condition and the domestic arrangement of nations.

PART SECOND.
Of the History of Rude Nations.

SECTION I.
*Of the Informations on this subject which are
derived from Antiquity.*

The history of mankind is confined within a limited period, and from every quarter brings an intimation that human affairs have had a beginning. Nations, distinguished by the possession of arts, and the felicity of their political establishments, have been derived from a feeble original, and still preserve in their story the indications of a slow and gradual progress, by which this distinction was gained. The antiquities of every people, however diversified, and however disguised, contain the same information on this point.

In sacred history, we find the parents of the species, as yet a single pair, sent forth to inherit the earth, and to force a subsistence for themselves amidst the briers and thorns which were made to abound on its surface. Their race, which was again reduced to a few, had to struggle with the dangers that await a weak and infant species; and after many ages elapsed, the most respectable nations took their rise from one or a few families that had pastured their flocks in the desert.

The Grecians derive their own origin from unsettled tribes, whose frequent migrations are a proof of the rude and infant state of their communities; and whose warlike exploits, so much celebrated in story, only exhibit the struggles with which they disputed for the possession of a country they afterwards, by their talent for fable, by their arts, and their policy, rendered so famous in the history of mankind.

Italy must have been divided into many rude and feeble cantons, when a band of robbers, as we are taught to consider them, found a secure settlement on the banks of the Tiber, and when a people, yet composed only of one sex, sustained the character of a nation. Rome, for many ages, saw, from her walls, on every side, the territory of her enemies, and found as little to check or to stifle the weakness of her infant power, as she did afterwards to restrain the progress of her extended empire. Like a Tartar or a Scythian horde, which had pitched on a settlement, this nascent community was equal, if not superior, to every tribe in its neighbourhood; and the oak which has covered the field with its shade, was once a feeble plant in the nursery, and not to be distinguished from the weeds by which its early growth was restrained.

The Gauls and the Germans are come to our knowledge with the marks of a similar condition; and the inhabitants of Britain, at the time of the first Roman invasions, resembled, in many things, the present natives of North America: they were ignorant of agriculture; they painted their bodies; and used for cloathing, the skins of beasts.

Such therefore appears to have been the commencement of history with all nations, and in such circumstances are we to look for the original character of mankind. The inquiry refers to a distant period, and every conclusion should build on the facts which are preserved for our use. Our method, notwithstanding, too frequently, is to rest the whole on conjecture; to impute every advantage of our nature to those arts which we ourselves possess; and to imagine, that a mere negation of all our virtues is a sufficient description of man in his original state. We are ourselves the supposed standards of politeness and civilization; and where our own features do not appear, we apprehend, that there is nothing which deserves to be known. But it is probable that here, as in many other cases, we are ill qualified, from our supposed knowledge of causes, to prognosticate effects, or to determine what must have been the properties and operations, even of our own nature, in the absence of those circumstances in which we have seen it engaged. Who would, from mere conjecture, suppose, that the naked savage would be a coxcomb and a gamester? that he would be proud and vain, without the distinctions of title and fortune? and that his principal care would be to adorn his person, and to find an amusement? Even if it could be supposed that he would thus share in our vices, and, in the midst of his forest, vie with the follies which are practised in the town; yet no one would be so bold as to affirm, that he would likewise, in any instance, excel us in talents and virtues; that he would have a penetration, a force of imagination and elocution, an ardour of mind, an affection and courage, which the arts, the discipline, and the policy of few nations would be able to improve. Yet these particulars are a part in the description which is delivered by those who have had opportunities of seeing mankind in their rudest condition: and beyond the reach of such testimony, we can neither safely take, nor pretend to give, information on the subject.

If conjectures and opinions formed at a distance, have not sufficient authority in the history of mankind, the domestic antiquities of every nation must, for this very reason, be received with caution. They are, for most part, the mere conjectures or the fictions of subsequent ages; and even where at first they contained some resemblance of truth, they still vary with the imagination of those by whom they are transmitted, and in every generation receive a different form. They are made to bear the stamp of the times through which they have passed in the form of tradition, not of the ages to which their pretended descriptions relate. The information they bring, is not like the light reflected from a mirrour, which delineates the object from which it originally came; but, like rays that come broken and dispersed from an opaque or unpolished surface, only give the colours and features of the body from which they were last reflected.

When traditionary fables are rehearsed by the vulgar, they bear the marks of a national character; and though mixed with absurdities, often raise the imagination, and move the heart:

when made the materials of poetry, and adorned by the skill and the eloquence of an ardent and superior mind, they instruct the understanding, as well as engage the passions. It is only in the management of mere antiquaries, or stript of the ornaments which the laws of history forbid them to wear, that they become even unfit to amuse the fancy, or to serve any purpose whatever.

It were absurd to quote the fable of the Iliad or the Odyssey, the legends of Hercules, Theseus, or Oedipus, as authorities in matter of fact relating to the history of mankind; but they may, with great justice, be cited to ascertain what were the conceptions and sentiments of the age in which they were composed, or to characterise the genius of that people, with whose imaginations they were blended, and by whom they were fondly rehearsed and admired.

In this manner fiction may be admitted to vouch for the genius of nations, while history has nothing to offer that is intitled to credit. The Greek fable accordingly conveying a character of its authors, throws light on an age of which no other record remains. The superiority of this people is indeed in no circumstance more evident than in the strain of their fictions, and in the story of those fabulous heroes, poets, and sages, whose tales, being invented or embellished by an imagination already filled with the subject for which the hero was celebrated, served to inflame that ardent enthusiasm with which this people afterwards proceeded in the pursuit of every national object.

It was no doubt of great advantage to those nations, that their system of fable was original, and being already received in popular traditions, served to diffuse those improvements of reason, imagination, and sentiment, which were afterwards, by men of the finest talents, made on the fable itself, or conveyed in its moral. The passions of the poet pervaded the minds of the people, and the conceptions of men of genius being communicated to the vulgar, became the incentives of a national spirit.

A mythology borrowed from abroad, a literature founded on references to a strange country, and fraught with foreign allusions, are much more confined in their use: they speak to the learned alone; and though intended to inform the understanding, and to mend the heart, may, by being confined to a few, have an opposite effect: they may foster conceit on the ruins of common sense, and render what was, at least innocently, sung by the Athenian mariner at his oar, or rehearsed by the shepherd in attending his flock, an occasion of vice, and the foundation of pedantry and scholastic pride.

Our very learning, perhaps, where its influence extends, serves, in some measure, to depress our national spirit. Our literature being derived from nations of a different race, who flourished at a time when our ancestors were in a state of barbarity, and consequently when they were despised by those who had attained to the literary arts, has given rise to a humbling opinion, that we ourselves are the offspring of mean and contemptible nations, with whom the human imagination and sentiment had no effect, till the genius was in a manner inspired by examples, and directed by lessons that were brought from abroad. The Romans, from whom our accounts are chiefly derived, have admitted, in the rudeness of their own ancestors, a system of virtues, which all simple nations perhaps equally possess; a contempt of riches, love of their country, patience of hardship, danger, and fatigue. They have, notwithstanding, vilified our ancestors for having perhaps only resembled their own; at least, in the defect of their arts, and in the neglect of conveniencies which those arts are employed to procure.

It is from the Greek and the Roman historians, however, that we have not only the most authentic and instructive, but even the most engaging, representations of the tribes from whom we descend. Those sublime and intelligent writers understood human nature, and could collect its features, and exhibit its characters in every situation. They were ill succeeded in this task by the early historians of modern Europe; who, generally bred to the profession of monks, and confined to the monastic life, applied themselves to record what they were pleased to denominate facts, while they suffered the productions of genius to perish, and were unable, either by the matter they selected, or the style of their compositions, to give any representation of the active spirit of mankind in any condition. With them, a narration was supposed to constitute history, whilst it did not convey any knowledge of men; and history itself was allowed to be complete, while, amidst the events and the succession of princes that are recorded in the order of time, we are left to look in vain for those characteristics of the understanding and the heart, which alone, in every human transaction, render the story either engaging or useful.

We therefore willingly quit the history of our early ancestors, where Caesar and Tacitus have dropped them; and perhaps, till we come within the reach of what is connected with present affairs, and makes a part in the system on which we now proceed, have little reason to expect any subject to interest or inform the mind. We have no reason, however, from hence to conclude, that the matter itself was more barren, or the scene of human affairs less interesting, in modern Europe, than it has been on every stage where mankind were engaged to exhibit the movements of the heart, the efforts of generosity, magnanimity, and courage.

The trial of what those ages contained, is not even fairly made, when men of genius and distinguished abilities, with the accomplishments of a learned and a polished age, collect the materials they have found, and, with the greatest success, connect the story of illiterate ages with transactions of a later date: it is difficult even for them, under the names which are applied in a new state of society, to convey a just apprehension of what mankind were in situations so different, and in times so remote from their own.

In deriving from historians of this character the instruction which their writings are fit to bestow, we are frequently to forget the general terms that are employed, in order to collect the real manners of an age, from the minute circumstances that are occasionally presented. The titles of *Royal* and *Noble* were applicable to the families of Tarquin, Collatinus, and Cincinnatus; but Lucretia was employed in domestic industry with her maids, and Cincinnatus followed the plough. The dignities, and even the offices, of civil society, were known many ages ago, in Europe, by their present appellations; but we find in the history of England, that a king and his court being assembled to solemnize a festival, an outlaw, who had subsisted by robbery, came to share in the feast. The king himself arose to force this unworthy guest from the company, a scuffle ensued between them, and the king was killed.* A chancellor and prime minister, whose magnificence and sumptuous furniture were the subject of admiration and envy, had his apartments covered every day in winter with clean straw and hay, and in summer with green rushes or boughs. Even the sovereign himself, in those ages, was provided with forage for his bed.† These picturesque features and characteristical strokes of the times, recal the imagination from the supposed distinction of monarch and subject, to that state of rough familiarity in which our ancestors lived, and under which they acted, with a view to objects, and on principles of conduct, which we seldom comprehend, when we are employed to record their transactions, or to study their characters.

Thucydides, notwithstanding the prejudice of his country against the name of *Barbarian*, understood that it was in the customs of barbarous nations he was to study the more ancient manners of Greece.

The Romans might have found an image of their own ancestors, in the representations they have given of ours: and if ever an Arab clan shall become a civilized nation, or any American tribe escape the poison which is administered by our traders of Europe, it may be from the relations of the present times, and the descriptions which are now given by travellers, that such a people, in after ages, may best collect the accounts of their origin. It is in their present condition, that we are to behold, as in a mirrour, the features of our own progenitors; and from thence we are to draw our conclusions with respect to the influence of situations, in which, we have reason to believe, our fathers were placed.

What should distinguish a German or a Briton, in the habits of his mind or his body, in his manners or apprehensions, from an American, who, like him, with his bow and his dart, is left to traverse the forest; and in a like severe or variable climate, is obliged to subsist by the chace?

---

* Hume's *History*, ch. 8, p. 278.   † *Ibid.*, p. 73.

If, in advanced years, we would form a just notion of our progress from the cradle, we must have recourse to the nursery, and from the example of those who are still in the period of life we mean to describe, take our representation of past manners, that cannot, in any other way, be recalled.

SECTION II.

Of Rude Nations prior to the Establishment of Property.

From one to the other extremity of America; from Kamschatka westward to the river Oby, and from the Northern sea, over that length of country, to the confines of China, of India, and Persia; from the Caspian to the Red sea, with little exception, and from thence over the inland continent and the western shores of Africa; we every where meet with nations on whom we bestow the appellations of barbarous or savage. That extensive tract of the earth, containing so great a variety of situation, climate, and soil, should, in the manners of its inhabitants, exhibit all the diversities which arise from the unequal influence of the sun, joined to a different nourishment and manner of life. Every question, however, on this subject is premature, till we have first endeavoured to form some general conception of our species in its rude state, and have learned to distinguish mere ignorance from dullness, and the want of arts from the want of capacity.

Of the nations who dwell in those, or any other of the less cultivated parts of the earth, some intrust their subsistence chiefly to hunting, fishing, or the natural produce of the soil. They have little attention to property, and scarcely any beginnings of subordination or government. Others having possessed themselves of herds, and depending for their provision on pasture, know what it is to be poor and rich. They know the relations of patron and client, of servant and master, and suffer themselves to be classed according to their measures of wealth. This distinction must create a material difference of character, and may furnish two separate heads, under which to consider the history of mankind in their rudest state; that of the savage, who is not yet acquainted with property; and that of the barbarian, to whom it is, although not ascertained by laws, a principal object of care and desire.

It must appear very evident, that property is a matter of progress. It requires, among other particulars which are the effects of time, some method of defining possession. The very desire of it proceeds from experience; and the industry by which it is gained, or improved, requires such a habit of acting with a view to distant objects, as may overcome the present disposition either to sloth or to enjoyment. This habit is slowly acquired, and is in reality a principal distinction of nations in the advanced state of mechanic and commercial arts.

In a tribe which subsists by hunting and fishing, the arms, the utensils, and the fur, which the individual carries, are to him the only subjects of property. The food of to-morrow is yet wild in the forest, or hid in the lake; it cannot be appropriated before it is caught; and even then, being the purchase of numbers, who fish or hunt in a body, it accrues to the community, and is applied to immediate use, or becomes an accession to the stores of the public.

Where savage nations, as in most parts of America, mix with the practice of hunting some species of rude agriculture, they still follow, with respect to the soil and the fruits of the earth, the analogy of their principal object. As the men hunt, so the women labour together; and, after they have shared the toils of the seed-time. they enjoy the fruits of the harvest in common. The field in which they have planted, like the district over which they are accustomed to hunt, is claimed as a property by the nation, but is not parcelled in lots to its members. They go forth in parties to prepare the ground, to plant, and to reap. The harvest is gathered into the public granary, and from thence, at stated times, is divided into shares for the maintenance of separate families.* Even the returns of the market, when they

* *History of the Caribbees.*

trade with foreigners, are brought home to the stock of the nation.*

As the fur and the bow pertain to the individual, the cabbin and its utensils are appropriated to the family; and as the domestic cares are committed to the women, so the property of the household seems likewise to be vested in them. The children are considered as pertaining to the mother, with little regard to descent on the father's side. The males, before they are married, remain in the cabbin in which they are born; but after they have formed a new connection with the other sex, they change their habitation, and become an accession to the family in which they have found their wives. The hunter and the warrior are numbered by the matron as a part of her treasure; they are reserved for perils and trying occasions; and in the recess of public councils, in the intervals of hunting or war, are maintained by the cares of the women, and loiter about in mere amusement or sloth.†

While one sex continue to value themselves chiefly on their courage, their talent for policy, and their warlike atchievements, this species of property which is bestowed on the other, is in reality a mark of subjection; not, as some writers alledge, of their having acquired an ascendant.‡ It is the care and trouble of a subject with which the warrior does not chuse to be embarrassed. It is a servitude, and a continual toil, where no honours are won; and they whose province it is, are in fact the slaves and the helots of their country. If in this destination of the sexes, while the men continue to indulge themselves in the contempt of sordid and mercenary arts, the cruel establishment of slavery is for some ages deferred; if in this tender, though unequal alliance, the affections of the heart prevent the severities practised on slaves; we have in the custom itself, as perhaps in many other instances, reason to prefer the first suggestions of nature, to many of her after refinements.

If mankind, in any instance, continue the article of property on the footing we have now represented, we may easily credit what is farther reported by travellers, that they admit of no distinctions of rank or condition; and that they have in fact no

---

* Charlevoix.   † Lafitau.   ‡ *Ibid.*

degree of subordination different from the distribution of function, which follows the differences of age, talents, and dispositions. Personal qualities give an ascendant in the midst of occasions which require their exertion; but in times of relaxation, leave no vestige of power or prerogative. A warrior who has led the youth of his nation to the slaughter of their enemies, or who has been foremost in the chace, returns upon a level with the rest of his tribe; and when the only business is to sleep, or to feed, can enjoy no pre-eminence; for he sleeps and he feeds no better than they.

Where no profit attends dominion, one party is as much averse to the trouble of perpetual command, as the other is to the mortification of perpetual submission: 'I love victory, I love great actions,' says Montesquieu in the character of Sylla; 'but have no relish for the languid detail of pacific government, or the pageantry of high station.' He has touched perhaps what is a prevailing sentiment in the simplest state of society, when the weakness of motives suggested by interest, and the ignorance of any elevation not founded on merit, supplies the place of disdain.

The character of the mind, however, in this state, is not founded on ignorance alone. Men are conscious of their equality, and are tenacious of its rights. Even when they follow a leader to the field, they cannot brook the pretensions to a formal command: they listen to no orders; and they come under no military engagements, but those of mutual fidelity, and equal ardour in the enterprise.*

This description, we may believe, is unequally applicable to different nations, who have made unequal advances in the establishment of property. Among the Caribbees, and the other natives of the warmer climates in America, the dignity of chieftain is hereditary, or elective, and continued for life: the unequal distribution of property creates a visible subordination.† But among the Iroquois, and other nations of the temperate zone, the titles of *magistrate* and *subject*, of *noble* and *mean*, are as little known as those of *rich* and *poor*. The old men, without being invested with any coercive power, employ their natural authority

* Charlevoix. † Wafer's account of the Isthmus of Darien.

in advising or in prompting the resolutions of their tribe: the military leader is pointed out by the superiority of his manhood and valour: the statesman is distinguished only by the attention with which his counsel is heard; the warrior by the confidence with which the youth of his nation follow him to the field: and if their concerts must be supposed to constitute a species of political government, it is one to which no language of ours can be applied. Power is no more than the natural ascendency of the mind; the discharge of office no more than a natural exercise of the personal character; and while the community acts with an appearance of order, there is no sense of disparity in the breast of any of its members.*

In these happy, though informal, proceedings, where age alone gives a place in the council; where youth, ardour, and valour in the field, give a title to the station of leader; where the whole community is assembled on any alarming occasion, we may venture to say, that we have found the origin of the senate, the executive power, and the assembly of the people; institutions for which ancient legislators have been so much renowned. The senate among the Greeks, as well as the Latins, appears, from the etymology of its name, to have been originally composed of elderly men. The military leader at Rome, in a manner not unlike to that of the American warrior, proclaimed his levies, and the citizen prepared for the field, in consequence of a voluntary engagement. The suggestions of nature, which directed the policy of nations in the wilds of America, were followed before on the banks of the Eurotas and the Tyber; and Lycurgus and Romulus found the model of their institutions where the members of every rude nation find the earliest mode of uniting their talents, and combining their forces.

Among the North-American nations, every individual is independent; but he is engaged by his affections and his habits in the cares of a family. Families, like so many separate tribes, are subject to no inspection or government from abroad; whatever passes at home, even bloodshed and murder, are only supposed to concern themselves. They are, in the mean time, the

* Colden's *History of the Five Nations.*

parts of a canton; the women assemble to plant their maize; the old men go to council; the huntsman and the warrior joins the youth of his village in the field. Many such cantons assemble to constitute a national council, or to execute a national enterprise. When the Europeans made their first settlements in America, six such nations had formed a league, had their amphyctiones or states-general, and, by the firmness of their union, and the ability of their councils, had obtained an ascendant from the mouth of the St Laurence to that of the Missisippi.* They appeared to understand the objects of the confederacy, as well as those of the separate nation; they studied a balance of power; the statesman of one country watched the designs and proceedings of another; and occasionally threw the weight of his tribe into a different scale. They had their alliances and their treaties, which, like the nations of Europe, they maintained, or they broke, upon reasons of state; and remained at peace from a sense of necessity or expediency, and went to war upon any emergence of provocation or jealousy.

Thus, without any settled form of government, or any bond of union, but what resembled more the suggestion of instinct, than the invention of reason, they conducted themselves with the concert, and the force, of nations. Foreigners, without being able to discover who is the magistrate, or in what manner the senate is composed, always find a council with whom they may treat, or a band of warriors with whom they may fight. Without police or compulsory laws, their domestic society is conducted with order, and the absence of vicious dispositions, is a better security than any public establishment for the suppression of crimes.

Disorders, however, sometimes occur, especially in times of debauch, when the immoderate use of intoxicating liquors, to which they are extremely addicted, suspends the ordinary caution of their demeanour, and inflaming their violent passions, engages them in quarrels and bloodshed. When a person is slain, his murderer is seldom called to an immediate account: but he has a quarrel to sustain with the family and the friends; or, if a stranger,

* Lafitau, Charlevoix, Colden, &c.

with the countrymen of the deceased; sometimes even with his own nation at home, if the injury committed be of a kind to alarm the society. The nation, the canton, or the family, endeavour, by presents, to atone for the offence of any of their members; and, by pacifying the parties aggrieved, endeavour to prevent what alarms the community more than the first disorder, the subsequent effects of revenge and animosity.* The shedding of blood, however, if the guilty person remain where he has committed the crime, seldom escapes unpunished: the friend of the deceased knows how to disguise, though not to suppress, his resentment; and even after many years have elapsed, is sure to repay the injury that was done to his kindred or his house.

These considerations render them cautious and circumspect, put them on their guard against their passions, and give to their ordinary deportment an air of phlegm and composure superior to what is possessed among polished nations. They are, in the mean time, affectionate in their carriage, and in their conversations pay a mutual attention and regard, says Charlevoix, more tender and more engaging, than what we profess in the ceremonial of polished societies.

This writer has observed, that the nations among whom he travelled in North America, never mentioned acts of generosity or kindness under the notion of duty. They acted from affection, as they acted from appetite, without regard to its consequences. When they had done a kindness, they had gratified a desire; the business was finished, and passed from the memory. When they received a favour, it might, or it might not, prove the occasion of friendship: if it did not, the parties appeared to have no apprehensions of gratitude, as a duty by which the one was bound to make a return, or the other intitled to reproach the person who had failed in his part. The spirit with which they give or receive presents, is the same which Tacitus observed among the ancient Germans: They delight in them, but do not consider them as matter of obligation.† Such gifts are of little consequence, except when employed as the seal of a bargain or treaty.

* Lafitau.
† Muneribus gaudent, sed nec data imputant, nec acceptis obligantur.

It was their favourite maxim, That no man is naturally indebted to another; that he is not, therefore, obliged to bear with any imposition, or unequal* treatment. Thus, in a principle apparently sullen and inhospitable, they have discovered the foundation of justice, and observe its rules, with a steadiness and candour which no cultivation has been found to improve. The freedom which they give in what relates to the supposed duties of kindness and friendship, serves only to engage the heart more entirely, where it is once possessed with affection. We love to chuse our object without any restraint, and we consider kindness itself as a task, when the duties of friendship are exacted by rule. We therefore, by our demand for attentions, rather corrupt than improve the system of morality; and by our exactions of gratitude, and our frequent proposals to inforce its observance, we only shew, that we have mistaken its nature; we only give symptoms of that growing sensibility to interest, from which we measure the expediency of friendship and generosity itself; and by which we would introduce the spirit of traffic into the commerce of affection. In consequence of this proceeding, we are often obliged to decline a favour with the same spirit that we throw off a servile engagement, or reject a bribe. To the unrefining savage every favour is welcome, and every present received without reserve or reflection.

The love of equality, and the love of justice, were originally the same: and although, by the constitution of different societies, unequal privileges are bestowed on their members; and although justice itself requires a proper regard to be paid to such privileges; yet he who has forgotten that men were originally equal, easily degenerates into a slave; or in the capacity of a master, is not to be trusted with the rights of his fellow-creatures. This happy principle gives to the mind its sense of independence, renders it indifferent to the favours which are in the power of other men, checks it in the commission of injuries, and leaves the heart open to the affections of generosity and kindness. It gives to the untutored American that air of candour, and of regard to the welfare of others, which, in some degree, softens the arrogant

* Charlevoix.

pride of his carriage, and in times of confidence and peace, without the assistance of government or law, renders the approach and commerce of strangers secure.

Among this people, the foundations of honour are eminent abilities and great fortitude; not the distinctions of equipage and fortune: The talents in esteem are such as their situation leads them to employ, the exact knowledge of a country, and stratagem in war. On these qualifications, a captain among the Caribbees underwent an examination. When a new leader was to be chosen, a scout was sent forth to traverse the forests which led to the enemy's country, and, upon his return, the candidate was desired to find the track in which he had travelled. A brook, or a fountain, was named to him on the frontier, and he was desired to find the nearest path to a particular station, and to plant a stake in the place.* They can, accordingly, trace a wild beast, or the human foot, over many leagues of a pathless forest, and find their way across a woody and uninhabited continent, by means of refined observations, which escape the traveller who has been accustomed to different aids. They steer in slender canoes, across stormy seas, with a dexterity equal to that of the most experienced pilot.† They carry a penetrating eye for the thoughts and intentions of those with whom they have to deal; and when they mean to deceive, they cover themselves with arts which the most subtile can seldom elude. They harangue in their public councils with a nervous and figurative elocution; and conduct themselves in the management of their treaties with a perfect discernment of their national interests.

Thus being able masters in the detail of their own affairs, and well qualified to acquit themselves on particular occasions, they study no science, and go in pursuit of no general principles. They even seem incapable of attending to any distant consequences, beyond those they have experienced in hunting or war. They intrust the provision of every season to itself; consume the fruits of the earth in summer; and, in winter, are driven in quest of their prey, through woods, and over deserts covered with snow. They do not form in one hour those maxims which may prevent

* Lafitau.   † Charlevoix.

the errors of the next; and they fail in those apprehensions, which, in the intervals of passion, produce ingenuous shame, compassion, remorse, or a command of appetite. They are seldom made to repent of any violence; nor is a person, indeed, thought accountable in his sober mood, for what he did in the heat of a passion, or in a time of debauch.

Their superstitions are groveling and mean: and did this happen among rude nations alone, we could not sufficiently admire the effects of politeness; but it is a subject on which few nations are intitled to censure their neighbours. When we have considered the supersitions of one people, we find little variety in those of another. They are but a repetition of similar weaknesses and absurdities, derived from a common source, a perplexed apprehension of invisible agents, that are supposed to guide all precarious events to which human foresight cannot extend.

In what depends on the known or the regular course of nature, the mind trusts to itself; but in strange and uncommon situations, it is the dupe of its own perplexity, and, instead of relying on its prudence or courage, has recourse to divination, and a variety of observances, that, for being irrational, are always the more revered. Superstition being founded in doubts and anxiety, is fostered by ignorance and mystery. Its maxims, in the mean time, are not always confounded with those of common life; nor does its weakness or folly always prevent the watchfulness, penetration, and courage, men are accustomed to employ in the management of common affairs. A Roman consulting futurity by the pecking of birds, or a King of Sparta inspecting the intrails of a beast, Mithridates consulting his women on the interpretation of his dreams, are examples sufficient to prove, that a childish imbecility on this subject is consistent with the greatest military and political talents.

Confidence in the effect of superstitious observances is not peculiar to any age or nation. Few, even of the accomplished Greeks and Romans, were able to shake off this weakness. In their case, it was not removed by the highest measures of civilization. It has yielded only to the light of true religion, or to the study of nature, by which we are led to substitute a wise providence operating by physical causes, in the place of phantoms that terrify or amuse the ignorant.

The principal point of honour among the rude nations of America, as indeed in every instance where mankind are not greatly corrupted, is fortitude. Yet their way of maintaining this point of honour, is very different from that of the nations of Europe. Their ordinary method of making war is by ambuscade; and they strive, by over-reaching an enemy, to commit the greatest slaughter, or to make the greatest number of prisoners, with the least hazard to themselves. They deem it a folly to expose their own persons in assaulting an enemy, and do not rejoice in victories which are stained with the blood of their own people. They do not value themselves, as in Europe, on defying their enemy upon equal terms. They even boast, that they approach like foxes, or that they fly like birds, not less than that they devour like lions. In Europe, to fall in battle is accounted an honour; among the natives of America, it is reckoned disgraceful.* They reserve their fortitude for the trials they abide when attacked by surprise, or when fallen into their enemies hands; and when they are obliged to maintain their own honour, and that of their nation, in the midst of torments that require efforts of patience more than of valour.

On these occasions, they are far from allowing it to be supposed that they wish to decline the conflict. It is held infamous to avoid it, even by a voluntary death; and the greatest affront which can be offered to a prisoner, is to refuse him the honours of a man, in the manner of his execution: 'With-hold,' says an old man, in the midst of his torture, 'the stabs of your knife; rather let me die by fire, that those dogs, your allies, from beyond the seas, may learn to suffer like men.'† With terms of defiance, the victim, in those solemn trials, commonly excites the animosity of his tormentors, as well as his own; and whilst we suffer for human nature, under the effect of its errors, we must admire its force.

The people with whom this practice prevailed, were commonly desirous of repairing their own losses, by adopting prisoners of

* Charlevoix.   † Colden.

war into their families: and even in the last moment, the hand which was raised to torment, frequently gave the sign of adoption, by which the prisoner became the child or the brother of his enemy, and came to share in all the privileges of a citizen. In their treatment of those who suffered, they did not appear to be guided by principles of hatred or revenge: they observed the point of honour in applying as well as in bearing their torments; and, by a strange kind of affection and tenderness, were directed to be most cruel where they intended the highest respect: the coward was put to immediate death by the hands of women: the valiant was supposed to be intitled to all the trials of fortitude that men could invent or employ: 'It gave me joy,' says an old man to his captive, 'that so gallant a youth was allotted to my share: I proposed to have placed you on the couch of my nephew, who was slain by your countrymen; to have transferred all my tenderness to you; and to have solaced my age in your company: but maimed and mutilated as you now appear, death is better than life: prepare yourself therefore to die like a man.'*

It is perhaps with a view to these exhibitions, or rather in admiration of fortitude, the principle from which they proceed, that the Americans are so attentive, in their earliest years, to harden their nerves.† The children are taught to vie with each other in bearing the sharpest torments; the youth are admitted into the class of manhood, after violent proofs of their patience; and leaders are put to the test, by famine, burning, and suffocation.‡

It might be apprehended, that among rude nations, where the means of subsistence are procured with so much difficulty, the mind could never raise itself above the consideration of this subject; and that man would, in this condition, give examples of the meanest and most mercenary spirit. The reverse, however, is true. Directed in this particular by the desires of nature, men, in their simplest state, attend to the objects of appetite no further

---

* Charlevoix.

† *Ibid.* This writer says, that he has seen a boy and a girl, having bound their naked arms together, place a burning coal between them, to try who would shake it off first.

‡ Lafitau.

than appetite requires; and their desires of fortune extend no further than the meal which gratifies their hunger: they apprehend no superiority of rank in the possession of wealth, such as might inspire any habitual principle of covetousness, vanity, or ambition: they can apply to no task that engages no immediate passion, and take pleasure in no occupation that affords no dangers to be braved, and no honours to be won.

It was not among the ancient Romans alone that commercial arts, or a sordid mind, were held in contempt. A like spirit prevails in every rude and independent society. 'I am a warrior, and not a merchant,' said an American to the governor of Canada, who proposed to give him goods in exchange for some prisoners he had taken; 'your cloaths and utensils do not tempt me; but my prisoners are now in your power, and you may seize them: if you do, I must go forth and take more prisoners, or perish in the attempt; and if that chance should befal me, I shall die like a man; but remember, that our nation will charge you as the cause of my death.'* With these apprehensions, they have an elevation, and a stateliness of carriage, which the pride of nobility, where it is most revered by polished nations, seldom bestows.

They are attentive to their persons, and employ much time, as well as endure great pain, in the methods they take to adorn their bodies, to give the permanent stains with which they are coloured, or preserve the paint, which they are perpetually repairing, in order to appear with advantage.

Their aversion to every sort of employment which they hold to be mean, makes them pass great part of their time in idleness or sleep; and a man who, in pursuit of a wild beast, or to surprise his enemy, will traverse a hundred leagues on snow, will not, to procure his food, submit to any species of ordinary labour. 'Strange,' says Tacitus, 'that the same person should be so much averse to repose, and so much addicted to sloth.'

Games of hazard are not the invention of polished ages; men of curiosity have looked for their origin, in vain, among the monuments of an obscure antiquity; and it is probable that they belonged to times too remote and too rude even for the conjec-

* Charlevoix.

tures of antiquarians to reach. The very savage brings his furs, his utensils, and his beads, to the hazard-table: he finds here the passions and agitations which the applications of a tedious industry could not excite: and while the throw is depending, he tears his hair, and beats his breast, with a rage which the more accomplished gamester has sometimes learned to repress: he often quits the party naked, and stripped of all his possessions; or where slavery is in use, stakes his freedom to have one chance more to recover his former loss.*

With all these infirmities, vices, or respectable qualities, belonging to the human species in its rudest state; the love of society, friendship, and public affection, penetration, eloquence, and courage, appear to have been its original properties, not the subsequent effects of device or invention. If mankind are qualified to improve their manners, the subject was furnished by nature; and the effect of cultivation is not to inspire the sentiments of tenderness and generosity, nor to bestow the principal constituents of a respectable character, but to obviate the casual abuses of passion; and to prevent a mind, which feels the best dispositions in their greatest force, from being at times likewise the sport of brutal appetite and ungovernable violence.

Were Lycurgus employed anew to operate on the materials we have described, he would find them, in many important particulars, prepared by nature herself for his use. His equality in matters of property being already established, he would have no faction to apprehend from the opposite interests of the poor and the rich; his senate, his assembly of the people, is constituted; his discipline is in some measure adopted; and the place of his helots is supplied by the task allotted to one of the sexes. With all these advantages, he would still have had a very important lesson for civil society to teach, that by which a few learn to command, and the many are taught to obey: he would have all his precautions to take against the future intrusion of mercenary arts, the admiration of luxury, and the passion for interest: he would still perhaps have a more difficult task than any of the former, in teaching his citizens the command of appetite, and an indiffer-

* Tacitus, Lafitau, Charlevoix.

ence to pleasure, as well as a contempt of pain; in teaching them to maintain, in the field, the formality of uniform precautions, and as much to avoid being themselves surprised, as they endeavour to surprise their enemy.

For want of these advantages, rude nations in general, though they are patient of hardship and fatigue, though they are addicted to war, and are qualified by their stratagem and valour to throw terror into the armies of a more regular enemy; yet, in the course of a continued struggle, always yield to the superior arts, and the discipline of more civilized nations. Hence the Romans were able to over-run the provinces of Gaul, Germany, and Britain; and hence the Europeans have a growing ascendency over the nations of Africa and America.

On the credit of a superiority which certain nations possess, they think that they have a claim to dominion; and even Caesar appears to have forgotten what were the passions, as well as the rights of mankind, when he complained, that the Britons, after having sent him a submissive message to Gaul, perhaps to prevent his invasion, still pretended to fight for their liberties, and to oppose his descent on their island.*

There is not, perhaps, in the whole description of mankind, a circumstance more remarkable than that mutual contempt and aversion which nations, under a different state of commercial arts, bestow on each other. Addicted to their own pursuits, and considering their own condition as the standard of human felicity, all nations pretend to the preference, and in their practice give sufficient proof of sincerity. Even the savage still less than the citizen, can be made to quit that manner of life in which he is trained: he loves that freedom of mind which will not be bound to any task, and which owns no superior: however tempted to mix with polished nations, and to better his fortune, the first moment of liberty brings him back to the woods again; he droops and he pines in the streets of the populous city; he wanders dissatisfied over the open and the cultivated field; he seeks the frontier and the forest, where, with a constitution prepared to

---

* Caesar questus, quod quum ultro in continentem legatis missis pacem a se petissent, bellum sine causa intulissent. *Lib.* 4.

undergo the hardships and the difficulties of the situation, he enjoys a delicious freedom from care, and a seducing society, where no rules of behaviour are prescribed, but the simple dictates of the heart.

SECTION III.

Of Rude Nations under the Impressions of Property and Interest.

It was a proverbial imprecation in use among the hunting nations on the confines of Siberia, That their enemy might be obliged to live like a Tartar, and be seized with the folly of breeding and attending his cattle.* Nature, it seems, in their apprehension, by storing the woods and the desert with game, rendered the task of the herdsman unnecessary, and left to man only the trouble of selecting and of seizing his prey.

The indolence of mankind, or rather their aversion to any application in which they are not engaged by immediate instinct and passion, retards their progress in extending the notion of property. It has been found, however, even while the means of subsistence are left in common, and the stock of the public is yet undivided, that this notion is already applied to different subjects; as the fur and the bow pertain to the individual, the cottage, with its furniture, are appropriated to the family.

When the parent begins to desire a better provision for his children than is found under the promiscuous management of many copartners, when he has applied his labour and his skill apart, he aims at an exclusive possession, and seeks the property of the soil, as well as the use of its fruits.

When the individual no longer finds among his associates the same inclination to commit every subject to public use, he is seized with concern for his personal fortune; and is alarmed by the cares which every person entertains for himself. He is urged as much by emulation and jealousy, as by the sense of necessity.

* Abulgaze's *Genealogical History of the Tartars.*

He suffers considerations of interest to rest on his mind, and when every present appetite is sufficiently gratified, he can act with a view to futurity, or rather finds an object of vanity in having amassed what is become a subject of competition, and a matter of universal esteem. Upon this motive, where violence is restrained, he can apply his hand to lucrative arts, confine himself to a tedious task, and wait with patience for the distant returns of his labour.

Thus mankind acquire industry by many and by slow degrees. They are taught to regard their interest; they are taught to abstain from unlawful profits; they are secured in the possession of what they fairly obtain; and by these methods the habits of the labourer, the mechanic, and the trader, are gradually formed. A hoard, collected from the simple productions of nature, or a herd of cattle, are, in every rude nation, the first species of wealth. The circumstances of the soil, and the climate, determine whether the inhabitant shall apply himself chiefly to agriculture or pasture; whether he shall fix his residence, or be moving continually about with all his possessions.

In the west of Europe; in America, from south to north, with a few exceptions; in the torrid zone, and every where within the warmer climates; mankind have generally applied themselves to some species of agriculture, and have been disposed to settlement. In the east and the north of Asia, they depended entirely on their herds, and were perpetually shifting their ground in search of new pasture. The arts which pertain to settlement have been practised, and variously cultivated, by the inhabitants of Europe. Those which are consistent with perpetual migration, have, from the earliest accounts of history, remained nearly the same with the Scythian or Tartar. The tent pitched on a moveable carriage, the horse applied to every purpose of labour, and of war, of the dairy, and of the butcher's stall, from the earliest to the latest accounts, have made up the riches and equipage of this wandering people.

But in whatever way rude nations subsist, there are certain points in which, under the first impressions of property, they nearly agree. Homer either lived with a people in this stage of their progress, or found himself engaged to exhibit their character.

Tacitus has made them the subject of a particular treatise; and if this be an aspect under which mankind deserve to be viewed, it must be confessed, that we have singular advantages in collecting their features. The portrait has already been drawn by the ablest hands, and gives, at one view, in the writings of these celebrated authors, whatever has been scattered in the relations of historians, or whatever we have opportunities to observe in the actual manners of men, who still remain in a similar state.

In passing from the condition we have described, to this we have at present in view, mankind still retain many parts of their earliest character. They are still averse to labour, addicted to war, admirers of fortitude, and, in the language of Tacitus, more lavish of their blood than of their sweat.* They are fond of fantastic ornaments in their dress, and endeavour to fill up the listless intervals of a life addicted to violence, with hazardous sports, and with games of chance. Every servile occupation they commit to women or slaves. But we may apprehend, that the individual having now found a separate interest, the bands of society must become less firm, and domestic disorders more frequent. The members of any community, being distinguished among themselves by unequal shares in the distribution of property, the ground of a permanent and palpable subordination is laid.

These particulars accordingly take place among mankind, in passing from the savage to what may be called the barbarous state. Members of the same community enter into quarrels of competition or revenge. They unite in following leaders, who are distinguished by their fortunes, and by the lustre of their birth. They join the desire of spoil with the love of glory; and from an opinion, that what is acquired by force, justly pertains to the victor, they become hunters of men, and bring every contest to the decision of the sword.

Every nation is a band of robbers, who prey without restraint, or remorse, on their neighbours. Cattle, says Achilles, may be seized in every field; and the coasts of the Aegean sea were

* Pigrum quin immo et iners videtur, sudore acquirere quod possis sanguine parare.

accordingly pillaged by the heroes of Homer, for no other reason, than because those heroes chose to possess themselves of the brass and iron, the cattle, the slaves, and the women, which were found among the nations around them.

A Tartar mounted on his horse, is an animal of prey, who only inquires where cattle are to be found, and how far he must go to possess them. The monk, who had fallen under the displeasure of Mangu Chan, made his peace, by promising, that the Pope, and the Christian princes, should make a surrender of all their herds.*

A similar spirit reigned, without exception, in all the barbarous nations of Europe, Asia, and Africa. The antiquities of Greece and Italy, and the fables of every ancient poet, contain examples of its force. It was this spirit that brought our ancestors first into the provinces of the Roman empire; and that afterward, more perhaps than their reverence for the cross, led them to the East, to share with the Tartars in the spoils of the Saracen empire.

From the descriptions contained in the last section, we may incline to believe, that mankind, in their simplest state, are on the eve of erecting republics. Their love of equality, their habit of assembling in public councils, and their zeal for the tribe to which they belong, are qualifications that fit them to act under that species of government; and they seem to have but a few steps to make, in order to reach its establishment. They have only to define the numbers of which their councils shall consist, and to settle the forms of their meeting: They have only to bestow a permanent authority for repressing disorders, and to enact a few rules in favour of that justice they have already acknowledged, and from inclination so strictly observe.

But these steps are far from being so easily made, as they appear on a slight or a transient view. The resolution of chusing, from among their equals, the magistrate to whom they give from thenceforward a right to controul their own actions, is far from the thoughts of simple men; and no eloquence, perhaps, could make them adopt this measure, or give them any sense of its use.

* Rubruquis.

Even after nations have chosen a military leader, they do not intrust him with any species of civil authority. The captain, among the Caribbees, did not pretend to decide in domestic disputes; the terms *jurisdiction* and *government* were unknown in their tongue.*

Before this important change is admitted, men must be accustomed to the distinction of ranks; and before they are sensible that subordination is matter of choice, must arrive at unequal conditions by chance. In desiring property, they only mean to secure their subsistence: but the brave who lead in war, have likewise the largest share in its spoils. The eminent are fond of devising hereditary honours; and the multitude, who admire the parent, are ready to extend their esteem to his offspring.

Possessions descend, and the lustre of family grows brighter with age. Hercules, who perhaps was an eminent warrior, became a god with posterity, and his race was set apart for royalty and sovereign power. When the distinctions of fortune and those of birth are conjoined, the chieftain enjoys a pre-eminence, as well at the feast as in the field. His followers take their place in subordinate stations; and instead of considering themselves as parts of a community, they rank as the followers of a chieftain, and take their designation from the name of their leader. They find a new object of public affection, in defending his person, and in supporting his station; they lend of their substance to form his estate; they are guided by his smiles and his frowns; and court, as the highest distinction, a share in the feast which their own contributions have furnished.

As the former state of mankind seemed to point at democracy, this seems to exhibit the rudiments of monarchical government. But it is yet far short of that establishment which is known in after ages by the name of *monarchy*. The distinction between the leader and the follower, the prince and the subject, is still but imperfectly marked: their pursuits and occupations are not different; their minds are not unequally cultivated; they feed from the same dish; they sleep together on the ground; the children of the king, as well as those of the subject, are employed in

* *History of the Caribbees.*

tending the flock; and the keeper of the swine was a prime counsellor at the court of Ulysses.

The chieftain, sufficiently distinguished from his tribe, to
excite their admiration, and to flatter their vanity by a supposed
affinity to his noble descent, is the object of their veneration, not
of their envy: he is considered as the common bond of connection,
not as their common ·master; is foremost in danger, and has a
principal share in their troubles: his glory is placed in the number of his attendants, in his superior magnanimity and valour; that
of his followers, in being ready to shed their blood in his service.*

The frequent practice of war tends to strengthen the bands of
society, and the practice of depredation itself engages men in
trials of mutual attachment and courage. What threatened to
ruin and overset every good disposition in the human breast,
what seemed to banish justice from the societies of men, tends
to unite the species in clans and fraternities; formidable, indeed, and
hostile to one another, but in the domestic society of each, faithful
disinterested, and generous. Frequent dangers, and the experience
of fidelity and valour, awaken the love of those virtues, render
them a subject of admiration, and endear their possessors.

Actuated by great passions, the love of glory, and the desire of
victory; roused by the menaces of an enemy, or stung with
revenge; in suspense between the prospects of ruin or conquest,
the barbarian spends every moment of relaxation in the indulgence of sloth. He cannot descend to the pursuits of industry or
mechanical labour: the beast of prey is a sluggard; the hunter and
the warrior sleeps, while women or slaves are made to toil for
his bread. But shew him a quarry at a distance, he is bold, im-
petuous, artful, and rapacious: no bar can withstand his violence,
and no fatigue can allay his activity.

Even under this description mankind are generous and hospitable to strangers, as well as kind, affectionate, and gentle, in
their domestic society.† Friendship and enmity are to them terms
of the greatest importance: they mingle not their functions
together; they have singled out their enemy, and they have

---

* Tacitus, *De moribus Germanorum.*
† Jean du Plan Carpen. Rubruquis, Caesar, Tacit.

chosen their friend. Even in depredation, the principal object is glory; and spoil is considered as a badge of victory. Nations and tribes are their prey: the solitary traveller, by whom they can acquire only the reputation of generosity, is suffered to pass unhurt, or is treated with splendid munificence.

Though distinguished into small cantons under their several chieftains, and for the most part separated by jealousy and animosity; yet when pressed by wars and formidable enemies, they sometimes unite in greater bodies. Like the Greeks in their expedition to Troy, they follow some remarkable leader, and compose a kingdom of many separate tribes. But such coalitions are merely occasional; and even during their continuance, more resemble republic than monarchy. The inferior chieftains reserve their importance, and intrude, with an air of equality, into the councils of their leader, as the people of their several clans commonly intrude upon them.* Upon what motive indeed could we suppose, that men who live together in the greatest familiarity, and amongst whom the distinctions of rank are so obscurely marked, would resign their personal sentiments and inclinations, or pay an implicit submission to a leader who can neither overawe nor corrupt?

Military force must be employed to extort, or the hire of the venal to buy, that engagement which the Tartar comes under to his prince, when he promises, 'That he will go where he shall be commanded; that he will come when he shall be called; that he will kill whoever is pointed out to him; and, for the future, that he will consider the voice of the King as a sword.'†

These are the terms to which even the stubborn heart of the barbarian has been reduced, in consequence of a despotism he himself had established; and men have, in that low state of the commercial arts, in Europe, as well as in Asia, tasted of political slavery. When interest prevails in every breast, the sovereign and his party cannot escape the infection: he employs the force with which he is intrusted, to turn his people into a property, and to command their possessions for his profit or his pleasure.

* Kolbe, *Description of the Cape of Good Hope.*
† Simon de St Quintin.

If riches are by any people made the standard of good and of evil, let them beware of the powers they intrust to their prince. 'With the Suiones,' says Tacitus, 'riches are in high esteem; and this people are accordingly disarmed, and reduced to slavery.'*

It is in this woful condition that mankind, being slavish, interested, insidious, deceitful, and bloody, bear marks, if not of the least curable, surely of the most lamentable, sort of corruption.† Among them, war is the mere practice of rapine, to enrich the individual; commerce is turned into a system of snares and impositions; and government by turns oppressive or weak.

It were happy for the human race, when guided by interest, and not governed by laws, that being split into nations of a moderate extent, they found in every canton some natural bar to its further enlargement, and met with occupation enough in maintaining their independence, without being able to extend their dominion.

There is not disparity of rank, among men in rude ages, sufficient to give their communities the form of legal monarchy; and in a territory of considerable extent, when united under one head, the warlike and turbulent spirit of its inhabitants seems to require the bridle of despotism and military force. Where any degree of freedom remains, the powers of the prince are, as they were in most of the rude monarchies of Europe, extremely precarious, and depend chiefly on his personal character: where, on the contrary, the powers of the prince are above the control of his people, they are likewise above the restrictions of law. Rapacity and terror become the predominant motives of conduct, and form the character of the only parties into which mankind are divided, that of the oppressor, and that of the oppressed.

This calamity threatened Europe for ages, under the conquest and settlement of its new inhabitants.‡ It has actually taken place in Asia, where similar conquests have been made; and

---

* *De moribus Germanorum.*
† Chardin's *Travels.*
‡ See Hume's *History of the Tudors.*—There seemed to be nothing wanting to establish a perfect despotism in that house, but a few regiments of troops under the command of the crown.

even without the ordinary opiates of effeminacy, or a servile weakness, founded on luxury, it has surprised the Tartar on his wain, in the rear of his herds. Among this people, in the heart of a great continent, bold and enterprising warriors arose: they subdued, by surprise, or superior abilities, the contiguous hords; they gained, in their progress, accessions of numbers and of strength; and, like a torrent increasing as it descends, became too strong for any bar that could be opposed to their passage. The conquering tribe, during a succession of ages, furnished the prince with his guards; and while they themselves were allowed to share in its spoils, were the voluntary tools of oppression. In this manner has despotism and corruption made their way into regions so much renowned for the wild freedom of nature: a power which was the terror of every effeminate province is disarmed, and the nursery of nations is itself gone to decay.*

Where rude nations escape this calamity, they require the exercise of foreign wars to maintain domestic peace: when no enemy appears from abroad, they have leisure for private feuds, and employ that courage in their dissensions at home, which, in time of war, is employed in defence of their country.

'Among the Gauls,' says Caesar, 'there are subdivisions, not only in every nation, and in every district and village, but almost in every house, everyone must fly to some patron for protection.'†
In this distribution of parties, not only the feuds of clans, but the quarrels of families, even the differences and competitions of individuals, are decided by force. The sovereign, when unassisted by superstition, endeavours in vain to employ his jurisdiction, or to procure a submission to the decisions of law. By a people who are accustomed to owe their possessions to violence, and who despise fortune itself without the reputation of courage, no umpire is admitted but the sword. Scipio offered his arbitration to terminate the competition of two Spaniards in a disputed succession: 'That,' said they, 'we have already refused to our relations: we do not submit our difference to the judgement of men; and even among the gods, we appeal to Mars alone.'‡

It is well known that the nations of Europe carried this mode

---

* See the *History of the Huns.*   † *De Bello Gallico*, lib. 6.   ‡ Livy.

of proceeding to a degree of formality unheard of in other parts of the world: the civil and criminal judge could, in most cases, do no more than appoint the lists, and leave the parties to decide their cause by the combat: they apprehended that the victor had a verdict of the gods in his favour: and when they dropped in any instance this extraordinary form of process, they substituted in its place some other more capricious appeal to chance; in which they likewise thought that the judgement of the gods was declared.

The fierce nations of Europe were even fond of the combat as an exercise and a sport. In the absence of real quarrels, companions challenged each other to a trial of skill, in which one of them frequently perished. When Scipio celebrated the funeral of his father and his uncle, the Spaniards came in pairs to fight, and, by a public exhibition of their duels, to increase the solemnity.*

In this wild and lawless state, where the effects of true religion would have been so desireable, and so salutary, superstition frequently disputes the ascendant even with the admiration of valour; and an order of men, like the Druids among the ancient Gauls and Britons,† or some pretender to divination, as at the Cape of Good Hope, finds, in the credit which is paid to his sorcery, a way to the possession of power: his magic wand comes in competition with the sword itself; and, in the manner of the Druids, gives the first rudiments of civil government to some, or, like the supposed descendent of the sun among the Natchez, and the Lama among the Tartars, to others, an early taste of despotism and absolute slavery.

We are generally at a loss to conceive how mankind can subsist under customs and manners extremely different from our own; and we are apt to exaggerate the misery of barbarous times, by an imagination of what we ourselves should suffer in a situation to which we are not accustomed. But every age hath its consolations, as well as its sufferings.‡ In the interval of occasional

---

* Livy, lib. 3.   † Caesar.

‡ Priscus, when employed on an embassy to Attila, was accosted in Greek, by a person who wore the dress of a Scythian. Having expressed surprise, and being desirous to know the cause of his stay in so wild a company, was told, that this Greek had been a captive, and for some time a slave, till he obtained

outrages, the friendly intercourses of men, even in their rudest condition, is affectionate and happy.* In rude ages, the persons and properties of individuals are secure; because each has a friend, as well as an enemy; and if the one is disposed to molest, the other is ready to protect; and the very admiration of valour, which in some instances tends to sanctify violence, inspires likewise certain maxims of generosity and honour, that tend to prevent the commission of wrongs.

Men bear with the defects of their policy, as they do with hardships and inconveniencies in their manner of living. The alarms and the fatigues of war become a necessary recreation to those who are accustomed to them, and who have the tone of their passions raised above less animating or trying occasions. Old men, among the courtiers of Attila, wept, when they heard of heroic deeds, which they themselves could no longer perform.† And among the Celtic nations, when age rendered the warrior unfit for his former toils, it was the custom, in order to abridge the languors of a listless and inactive life, to sue for death at the hands of his friends.‡

With all this ferocity of spirit, the rude nations of the West were subdued by the policy and more regular warfare of the Romans. The point of honour, which the barbarians of Europe adopted as individuals, exposed them to a peculiar disadvantage, by rendering them, even in their national wars, averse to assailing

* D'Arvieux's *History of the Wild Arabs.*   † *Ibid.*
‡ Ubi transcendit florentes viribus annos,
  Impatiens aevi spernit novisse senectam.
                              Silius, lib. i, 225.

his liberty in reward of some remarkable action. 'I live more happily here,' says he, 'than ever I did under the Roman government: for they who live with the Scythians, if they can endure the fatigues of war, have nothing else to molest them ; they enjoy their possessions undisturbed: whereas you are continually a prey to foreign enemies, or to bad government; you are forbid to carry arms in your own defence; you suffer from the remissness and ill conduct of those who are appointed to protect you; the evils of peace are even worse than those of war; no punishment is ever inflicted on the powerful or the rich; no mercy is shown to the poor; although your institutions were wisely devised, yet in the management of corrupted men, their effects are pernicious and cruel.' *Excerpta de legationibus.*

their enemy by surprise, or taking the benefit of stratagem; and though separately bold and intrepid, yet, like other rude nations, they were, when assembled in great bodies, addicted to superstition, and subject to panics.

They were, from a consciousness of their personal courage and force, sanguine on the eve of battle; they were, beyond the bounds of moderation, elated on success, and dejected in adversity; and being disposed to consider every event as a judgement of the gods, they were never qualified by an uniform application of prudence, to make the most of their forces, to repair their misfortunes, or to improve their advantages.

Resigned to the government of affection and passion, they were generous and faithful where they had fixed an attachment; implacable, froward, and cruel, where they had conceived a dislike: addicted to debauchery, and the immoderate use of intoxicating liquors, they deliberated on the affairs of state in the heat of their riot; and in the same dangerous moments, conceived the designs of military enterprise, or terminated their domestic dissensions by the dagger or the sword.

In their wars they preferred death to captivity. The victorious armies of the Romans, in entering a town by assault, or inforcing an incampment, have found the mother in the act of destroying her children, that they might not be taken; and the dagger of the parent, red with the blood of his family, ready to be plunged at last into his own breast.*

In all these particulars we perceive that vigour of spirit, which renders disorder itself respectable, and which qualifies men, if fortunate in their situation, to lay the basis of domestic liberty, as well as to maintain against foreign enemies their national independence and freedom.

* Liv. lib. xli. ii. Dio. Cass.

PART THIRD.
Of the History of Policy and Arts.

SECTION I.
Of the Influences of Climate and Situation.

What we have hitherto observed on the condition and manners of nations, though chiefly derived from what has passed in the temperate climates, may, in some measure, be applied to the rude state of mankind in every part of the earth: but if we intend to pursue the history of our species in its further attainments, we may soon enter on subjects which will confine our observation to more narrow limits. The genius of political wisdom and civil arts appears to have chosen his seats in particular tracts of the earth, and to have selected his favourites in particular races of men.

Man, in his animal capacity, is qualified to subsist in every climate. He reigns with the lion and the tyger under the equatorial heats of the sun, or he associates with the bear and the raindeer beyond the polar circle. His versatile disposition fits him to assume the habits of either condition, or his talent for arts enables him to supply its defects. The intermediate climates, however, appear most to favour his nature; and in whatever manner we account for the fact, it cannot be doubted, that this animal has always attained to the principal honours of his species within the temperate zone. The arts, which he has on this scene repeatedly invented, the extent of his reason, the fertility of his fancy, and the force of his genius in literature, commerce, policy, and war, sufficiently declare either a distinguished advantage of situation, or a natural superiority of mind.

The most remarkable races of men, it is true, have been rude before they were polished. They have in some cases returned to rudeness again: and it is not from the actual possession of arts, science, or policy, that we are to pronounce of their genius.

There is a vigour, a reach of capacity, and a sensibility of mind, which may characterise as well the savage as the citizen, the slave as well as the master; and the same powers of the mind may be turned to a variety of purposes. A modern Greek, perhaps, is mischievous, slavish, and cunning, from the same animated temperament that made his ancestor ardent, ingenious, and bold, in the camp, or in the council of his nation. A modern Italian is distinguished by sensibility, quickness, and art, while he employs on trifles the capacity of an ancient Roman; and exhibits now, in the scene of amusement, and in the search of a frivolous applause, that fire, and those passions, with which Gracchus burned in the forum, and shook the assemblies of a severer people.

The commercial and lucrative arts have been, in some climates, the principal object of mankind, and have been retained through every disaster; in others, even under all the fluctuations of fortune, they have still been neglected; while in the temperate climates of Europe and Asia, they have had their ages of admiration as well as contempt.

In one state of society, arts are slighted, from that very ardour of mind, and principle of activity, by which, in another, they are practised with the greatest success. While men are ingrossed by their passions, heated and roused by the struggles and dangers of their country; while the trumpet sounds, or the alarm of social engagement is rung, and the heart beats high, it were a mark of dullness, or of an abject spirit, to find leisure for the study of ease, or the pursuit of improvements, which have mere convenience or ease for their object.

The frequent vicissitudes and reverses of fortune, which nations have experienced on that very ground where the arts have prospered, are probably the effects of a busy, inventive, and versatile spirit, by which men have carried every national pursuit to extremes. They have raised the fabric of despotic empire to its greatest height, where they had best understood the foundations of freedom. They perished in the flames which they themselves had kindled; and they only, perhaps, were capable of displaying, by turns, the greatest improvements, or the lowest corruptions, to which the human mind can be brought.

On this scene, mankind have twice, within the compass of history, ascended from rude beginnings to very high degrees of refinement. In every age, whether destined by its temporary disposition to build or to destroy, they have left the vestiges of an active and vehement spirit. The pavement and the ruins of Rome are buried in dust, shaken from the feet of barbarians, who trod with contempt on the refinements of luxury, and spurned those arts, the use of which it was reserved for the posterity of the same people to discover and to admire. The tents of the wild Arab are even now pitched among the ruins of magnificent cities; and the waste fields which border on Palestine and Syria, are perhaps become again the nursery of infant nations. The chieftain of an Arab tribe, like the founder of Rome, may have already fixed the roots of a plant that is to flourish in some future period, or laid the foundations of a fabric, that will attain to its grandeur in some distant age.

Great part of Africa has been always unknown; but the silence of fame, on the subject of its revolutions, is an argument, where no other proof can be found, of weakness in the genius of its people. The torrid zone, every where round the globe, however known to the geographer, has furnished few materials for history; and though in many places supplied with the arts of life in no contemptible degree, has no where matured the more important projects of political wisdom, nor inspired the virtues which are connected with freedom, and required in the conduct of civil affairs.

It was indeed in the torrid zone that mere arts of mechanism and manufacture were found, among the inhabitants of the new world, to have made the greatest advance: it is in India, and in the regions of this hemisphere, which are visited by the vertical sun, that the arts of manufacture, and the practice of commerce, are of the greatest antiquity, and have survived, with the smallest diminution, the ruins of time, and the revolutions of empire.

The sun, it seems, which ripens the pine-apple and the tamarind, inspires a degree of mildness than can even assuage the rigours of despotical government: and such is the effect of a gentle and pacific disposition in the natives of the East, that no conquest, no irruption of barbarians, terminates, as they did among the stubborn natives of Europe, by a total destruction of what the love of ease and of pleasure had produced.

Transferred, without any great struggle, from one master to another, the natives of India are ready, upon every change, to pursue their industry, to acquiesce in the enjoyment of life, and the hopes of animal pleasure: the wars of conquest are not prolonged to exasperate the parties engaged in them, or to desolate the land for which those parties contend: even the barbarous invader leaves untouched the commercial settlement which has not provoked his rage: though master of opulent cities, he only incamps in their neighbourhood, and leaves to his heirs the option of entering, by degrees, on the pleasures, the vices, and the pageantries his acquisitions afford: his successors, still more than himself, are disposed to foster the hive, in proportion as they taste more of its sweets; and they spare the inhabitant, together with his dwelling, as they spare the herd or the stall, of which they are become the proprietors.

The modern description of India is a repetition of the ancient, and the present state of China is derived from a distant antiquity, to which there is no parallel in the history of mankind. The succession of monarchs has been changed; but no revolutions have affected the state. The African and the Samoiede are not more uniform in their ignorance and barbarity, than the Chinese and the Indian, if we may credit their own story, have been in the practice of manufacture, and in the observance of a certain police, which was calculated only to regulate their traffic, and to protect them in their application to servile or lucrative arts.

If we pass from these general representations of what mankind have done, to the more minute description of the animal himself, as he has occupied different climates, and is diversified in his temper, complexion, and character, we shall find a variety of genius corresponding to the effects of his conduct, and the result of his story.

Man, in the perfection of his natural faculties, is quick and delicate in his sensibility; extensive and various in his imaginations and reflections; attentive, penetrating, and subtile, in what relates to his fellow-creatures; firm and ardent in his purposes; devoted to friendship or to enmity; jealous of his independence and his honour, which he will not relinquish for safety or for profit: under all his corruptions or improvements, he retains his natural sensibility, if not his force; and his commerce is a blessing or a curse, according to the direction his mind has received.

But under the extremes of heat or of cold, the active range of the human soul appears to be limited; and men are of inferior importance, either as friends, or as enemies. In the one extreme, they are dull and slow, moderate in their desires, regular and pacific in their manner of life; in the other, they are feverish in their passions, weak in their judgements, and addicted by temperament to animal pleasure. In both the heart is mercenary, and makes important concessions for childish bribes: in both the spirit is prepared for servitude: in the one it is subdued by fear of the future; in the other it is not roused even by its sense of the present.

The nations of Europe who would settle or conquer on the south or the north of their own happier climates, find little resistance: they extend their dominion at pleasure, and find no where a limit but in the ocean, and in the satiety of conquest. With few of the pangs and the struggles that precede the reduction of nations, mighty provinces have been successively annexed to the territory of Russia; and its sovereign, who accounts within his domain, entire tribes, with whom perhaps none of his emissaries have ever conversed, dispatched a few geometers to extend his empire, and thus to execute a project, in which the Romans were obliged to employ their consuls and their legions.* These modern conquerors complain of rebellion, where they meet with

* See Russian Atlas.

repugnance; and are surprised at being treated as enemies, where they come to impose their tribute.

It appears, however, that on the shores of the Eastern sea, they have met with nations* who have questioned their title to reign, and who have considered the requisition of a tax as the demand of effects for nothing. Here perhaps may be found the genius of ancient Europe, and under its name of ferocity, the spirit of national independence†; that spirit which disputed its ground in the West with the victorious armies of Rome, and baffled the attempts of the Persian monarchs to comprehend the villages of Greece within the bounds of their extensive domnion.

The great and striking diversities which obtain betwixt the inhabitants of climates far removed from each other, are, like the varieties of other animals in different regions, easily observed. The horse and the raindeer are just emblems of the Arab and the Laplander: the native of Arabia, like the animal for whose race his country is famed, whether wild in the woods, or tutored by art, is lively, active, and fervent in the exercise on which he is bent. This race of men, in their rude state, fly to the desert for freedom, and in roving bands alarm the frontiers of empire, and strike a terror in the province to which their moving encampments advance.‡ When roused by the prospect of conquest, or disposed to act on a plan, they spread their dominion, and their system of imagination, over mighty tracts of the earth: when possessed of property and of settlement, they set the example of a lively invention, and superior ingenuity, in the practice of arts, and the study of science. The Laplander, on the contrary, like the associate of his climate, is hardy, indefatigable, and patient of famine; dull rather than tame; serviceable in a particular tract; and incapable of change. Whole nations continue from age to age in the same condition, and, with immoveable phlegm, submit to the appellations of *Dane*, of *Swede*, or of *Muscovite*, according to the land they inhabit; and suffer their country to

* The Tchutzi.
† Notes to the *Genealogical History of the Tartars*.
‡ D'Arvieux.

be severed like a common, by the line on which those nations have traced their limits of empire.

It is not in the extremes alone that these varieties of genius may be clearly distinguished. Their continual change keeps pace with the variations of climate with which we suppose them connected: and though certain degrees of capacity, penetration, and ardour, are not the lot of entire nations, nor the vulgar properties of any people; yet their unequal frequency, and unequal measure, in different countries, are sufficiently manifest from the manners, the tone of conversation, the talent for business, amusement, and literary composition, which predominate in each.

It is to the Southern nations of Europe, both ancient and modern, that we owe the invention and the embellishment of that mythology, and those early traditions, which continue to furnish the materials of fancy, and the field of poetic allusion. To them we owe the romantic tales of chivalry, as well as the subsequent models of a more rational style, by which the heart and the imagination are kindled, and the understanding informed.

The fruits of industry have abounded most in the North, and the study of science has here received its most solid improvements: the efforts of imagination and sentiment were most frequent and most successful in the South. While the shores of the Baltic became famed for the studies of Copernicus, Tycho Brahe, and Kepler, those of the Mediterranean were celebrated for giving birth to men of genius in all its variety, and for having abounded with poets and historians, as well as with men of science.

On one side, learning took its rise from the heart and the fancy; on the other, it is still confined to the judgement and the memory. A faithful detail of public transactions, with little discernment of their comparative importance; the treaties and the claims of nations, the births and genealogies of princes, are, in the literature of Northern nations, amply preserved; while the lights of the understanding, and the feelings of the heart, are suffered to perish. The history of the human character; the interesting memoir, founded no less on the careless proceedings of a private life, than on the formal transactions of a public station; the ingenious pleasantry, the piercing ridicule, the tender, pathetic, or the elevated strain of elocution, have been confined in modern as well as ancient times, with a few exceptions, to the same latitudes with the fig and the vine.

These diversities of natural genius, if real, must have great part of their foundation in the animal frame: and it has been often observed, that the vine flourishes, where, to quicken the ferments of the human blood, its aids are the least required. While spirituous liquors are, among Southern nations, from a sense of their ruinous effects, prohibited; or from a love of decency, and the possession of a temperament sufficiently warm, not greatly desired; they carry in the North a peculiar charm, while they awaken the mind, and give a taste of that lively fancy and ardour of passion, which the climate is found to deny.

The melting desires, or the fiery passions, which in one climate take place between the sexes, are in another changed into a sober consideration, or a patience of mutual disgust. This change is remarked in crossing the Mediterranean, in following the course of the Missisippi, in ascending the mountains of Caucasus, and in passing from the Alps and the Pyrenees to the shores of the Baltic.

The female sex domineers on the frontier of Louisiana, by the double engine of superstition, and of passion. They are slaves among the native inhabitants of Canada, and chiefly valued for the toils they endure, and the domestic service they yield.*

The burning ardours, and the torturing jealousies, of the seraglio and the haram, which have reigned so long in Asia and Africa, and which, in the Southern parts of Europe, have scarcely given way to the difference of religion and civil establishments, are found, however, with an abatement of heat in the climate, to be more easily changed, in one latitude, into a temporary passion which ingrosses the mind, without enfeebling it, and which excites to romantic atchievements: by a farther progress to the North, it is changed into a spirit of gallantry, which employs the wit and the fancy more than the heart; which prefers intrigue to enjoyment; and substitutes affectation and vanity, where senti-

* Charlevoix.

ment and desire have failed. As it departs from the sun, the same passion is further composed into a habit of domestic connection, or frozen into a state of insensibility, under which the sexes at freedom scarcely chuse to unite their society.

These variations of temperament and character, do not indeed correspond with the number of degrees that are measured from the equator to the pole; nor does the temperature of the air itself depend on the latitude. Varieties of soil and position, the distance or neighbourhood of the sea, are known to affect the atmosphere, and may have signal effects in composing the animal frame.

The climates of America, though taken under the same parallel, are observed to differ from those of Europe. There, extensive marshes, great lakes, aged, decayed, and crouded forests, with the other circumstances that mark an uncultivated country, are supposed to replenish the air with heavy and noxious vapours, that give a double asperity to the winter, and, during many months, by the frequency and continuance of fogs, snow, and frost, carry the inconveniencies of the frigid zone far into the temperate. The Samoiede and the Laplander, however, have their counterpart, though on a lower latitude, on the shores of America: the Canadian and the Iroquois bear a resemblance to the ancient inhabitants of the middling climates of Europe: the Mexican, like the Asiatic of India, being addicted to pleasure, was sunk in effeminacy; and in the neighbourhood of the wild and the free, had suffered to be raised on his weakness, a domineering superstition, and a permanent fabric of despotical government.

Great part of Tartary lies under the same parallels with Greece, Italy, and Spain; but the climates are found to be different; and while the shores, not only of the Mediterranean, but even those of the Atlantic, are favoured with a moderate change and vicissitude of seasons, the eastern parts of Europe, and the northern continent of Asia, are afflicted with all their extremes. In one season, we are told, that the plagues of an ardent summer reach almost to the frozen sea; and that the inhabitant is obliged to screen himself from noxious vermin in the same clouds of smoke in which he must, at a different time of the year, take shelter from the rigours of cold. When winter returns, the transition is rapid, and with an asperity almost equal in every latitude, lays waste the face of the earth, from the northern confines of Siberia, to the descents of Mount Caucasus and the frontier of India.

With this unequal distribution of climate, by which the lot, as well as the national character, of the Northern Asiatic may be deemed inferior to that of Europeans who lie under the same parallels, a similar gradation of temperament and spirit, however, has been observed, in following the meridian on either tract; and the Southern Tartar has over the Tonguses and the Samoiede, the same pre-eminence that certain nations of Europe are known to possess over their Northern neighbours, in situations more advantageous to both.

The Southern hemisphere scarcely offers a subject of like observation. The temperate zone is there still undiscovered, or is only known in two promontories, the Cape of Good Hope, and Cape Horn, which stretch into moderate latitudes on that side of the line. But the savage of South America, notwithstanding the interposition of the nations of Peru and of Mexico, is found to resemble his counterpart on the North; and the Hottentot, in many things, the barbarian of Europe: he is tenacious of freedom, has rudiments of policy, and a national vigour, which serve to distinguish his race from the other African tribes, who are exposed to the more vertical rays of the sun.

While we have, in these observations, only thrown out what must present itself on the most cursory view of the history of mankind, or what may be presumed from the mere obscurity of some nations, who inhabit great tracts of the earth, as well as from the lustre of others, we are still unable to explain the manner in which climate may affect the temperament, or foster the genius, of its inhabitant.

That the temper of the heart, and the intellectual operations of the mind, are, in some measure, dependent on the state of the animal organs, is well known from experience. Men differ from themselves in sickness and in health; under a change of diet, of air, and of exercise: but we are, even in these familiar instances, at a loss how to connect the cause with its supposed effect: and though climate, by including a variety of such causes, may, by some regular influence, affect the characters of men, we can never hope to explain the manner of those influences till we have understood what probably we shall never understand, the structure of those finer organs with which the operations of the soul are connected.

When we point out, in the situation of a people, circumstances which, by determining their pursuits, regulate their habits, and their manner of life; and when, instead of referring to the supposed physical source of their dispositions, we assign their inducements to a determinate conduct; in this we speak of effects and of causes whose connection is more familiarly known. We can understand, for instance, why a race of men like the Samoiede, confined, during great part of the year, to darkness, or retired into caverns, should differ, in their manners and apprehensions, from those who are at liberty in every season; or who, instead of seeking relief from the extremities of cold, are employed in search of precautions against the oppressions of a burning sun. Fire and exercise are the remedies of cold; repose and shade the securities from heat. The Hollander is laborious and industrious in Europe; he becomes more languid and slothful in India.*

Great extremities, either of heat or cold, are, perhaps, in a moral view, equally unfavourable to the active genius of mankind, and by presenting alike unsuperable difficulties to be overcome, or strong inducements to indolence and sloth, equally prevent the first applications of ingenuity, or limit their progress. Some intermediate degrees of inconvenience in the situation, at once excite the spirit, and, with the hopes of success, encourage its efforts. 'It is in the least favourable situations,' says Mr Rousseau, 'that arts have flourished the most. I could show them in Egypt, as they spread with the overflowing of the Nile; and in Africa, as they mounted up to the clouds, from a rocky soil

---

* The Dutch sailors who were employed in the siege of Malaco, tore or burnt the sail-cloth which was given them to make tents, that they might not have the trouble of making or pitching them. *Voy. de Matelief.*

and from barren sands; while on the fertile banks of the Eurotas, they were not able to fasten their roots.'

Where mankind from the first subsist by toil, and in the midst of difficulties, the defects of their situation are supplied by industry: and while dry, tempting, and healthful lands are left uncultivated,* the pestilent marsh is drained with great labour, and the sea is fenced off with mighty barriers, the materials and the costs of which, the soil to be gained can scarcely afford, or repay. Harbours are opened, and crouded with shipping, where vessels of burden, if they are not constructed with a view to the situation, have not water to float. Elegant and magnificent edifices are raised on foundations of slime; and all the conveniencies of human life are made to abound, where nature does not seem to have prepared a reception for men. It is in vain to expect, that the residence of arts and commerce should be determined by the possession of natural advantages. Men do more when they have certain difficulties to surmount, than when they have supposed blessings to enjoy: and the shade of the barren oak and the pine are more favourable to the genius of mankind, than that of the palm or the tamarind.

Among the advantages which enable nations to run the career of policy, as well as of arts, it may be expected, from the observations already made, that we should reckon every circumstance which enables them to divide and to maintain themselves in distinct and independent communities. The society and concourse of other men, are not more necessary to form the individual, than the rivalship and competition of nations are to invigorate the principles of political life in a state. Their wars, and their treaties, their mutual jealousies, and the establishments which they devise with a view to each other, constitute more than half the occupations of mankind, and furnish materials for their greatest and most improving exertions. For this reason, clusters of islands, a continent divided by many natural barriers, great rivers, ridges of mountains, and arms of the sea, are best fitted for becoming the nursery of independent and respectable nations. The distinction of states being clearly maintained, a principle

* Compare the state of Hungary with that of Holland.

of political life is established in every division, and the capital
of every district, like the heart in an animal body, communi-
cates with ease the vital blood and the national spirit to its
members.

The most respectable nations have always been found where at
least one part of the frontier has been washed by the sea. This
barrier, perhaps the strongest of all in the times of barbarity,
does not, however, even then supersede the cares of a national
defence; and in the advanced state of arts, gives the greatest
scope and facility to commerce.

Thriving and independent nations were accordingly scattered
on the shores of the Pacific and the Atlantic. They surrounded
the Red sea, the Mediterranean, and the Baltic; while, a few
tribes excepted, who retire among the mountains bordering on
India and Persia, or who have found some rude establishment
among the creeks and the shores of the Caspian and the Euxine,
there is scarcely a people in the vast continent of Asia who deserves the name of a nation. The unbounded plain is traversed
at large by hordes, who are in perpetual motion, or who are dis-
placed and harassed by their mutual hostilities. Although they are
never perhaps actually blended together in the course of hunting,
or in the search of pasture, they cannot bear one great distinction
of nations, which is taken from the territory, and which is deeply
impressed by an affection to the native seat. They move in troops,
without the arrangement or the concert of nations; they become
easy accessions to every new empire among themselves, or to the
Chinese and the Muscovite, with whom they hold a traffic for
the means of subsistence, and the materials of pleasure.

Where a happy system of nations is formed, they do not rely
for the continuance of their separate names, and for that of their
political independence, on the barriers erected by nature. Mutual
jealousies lead to the maintenance of a balance of power; and
this principle, more than the Rhine and the Ocean, than the
Alps and the Pyrenees in modern Europe; more than the straits
of Thermopylae, the mountains of Thrace, or the bays of
Salamine and Corinth in ancient Greece; tended to prolong the
separation, to which the inhabitants of these happy climates

have owed their felicity as nations, the lustre of their fame, and their civil accomplishments.

If we mean to pursue the history of civil society, our attention must be chiefly directed to such examples, and we must here bid farewel to those regions of the earth, on which our species, by the effects of situation or climate, appear to be restrained in their national pursuits, or inferior in the powers of the mind.

SECTION II.

The History of Subordination.

We have hitherto observed mankind, either united together on terms of equality, or disposed to admit of a subordination founded merely on the voluntary respect and attachment which they paid to their leaders; but, in both cases, without any concerted plan of government, or system of laws.

The savage, whose fortune is comprised in his cabin, his fur, and his arms, is satisfied with that provision, and with that degree of security, he himself can procure. He perceives, in treating with his equal, no subject of discussion that should be referred to the decision of a judge; nor does he find in any hand the badges of magistracy, or the ensigns of a perpetual command.

The barbarian, though induced by his admiration of personal qualities, the lustre of a heroic race, or a superiority of fortune, to follow the banners of a leader, and to act a subordinate part in his tribe, knows not, that what he performs from choice, is to be made a subject of obligation. He acts from affections unacquainted with forms; and when provoked, or when engaged in disputes, he recurs to the sword, as the ultimate means of decision, in all questions of right.

Human affairs, in the mean time, continue their progress. What was in one generation a propensity to herd with the species, becomes, in the ages which follow, a principle of national union. What was originally an alliance for common defence, becomes a concerted plan of political force; the care of subsistence becomes an anxiety for accumulating wealth, and the foundation of commercial arts.

Mankind, in following the present sense of their minds, in striving to remove inconveniencies, or to gain apparent and contiguous advantages, arrive at ends which even their imagination could not anticipate, and pass on, like other animals, in the track of their nature, without perceiving its end. He who first said, 'I will appropriate this field: I will leave it to my heirs;' did not perceive, that he was laying the foundation of civil laws and political establishments. He who first ranged himself under a leader, did not perceive, that he was setting the example of a permanent subordination, under the pretence of which, the rapacious were to seize his possessions, and the arrogant to lay claim to his service.

Men, in general, are sufficiently disposed to occupy themselves in forming projects and schemes: but he who would scheme and project for others, will find an opponent in every person who is disposed to scheme for himself. Like the winds, that come we know not whence, and blow whithersoever they list, the forms of society are derived from an obscure and distant origin; they arise, long before the date of philosophy, from the instincts, not from the speculations, of men. The croud of mankind, are directed in their establishments and measures, by the circumstances in which they are placed; and seldom are turned from their way, to follow the plan of any single projector.

Every step and every movement of the multitude, even in what are termed enlightened ages, are made with equal blindness to the future; and nations stumble upon establishments, which are indeed the result of human action, but not the execution of any human design.* If Cromwell said, That a man never mounts higher, than when he knows not whither he is going; it may with more reason be affirmed of communities, that they admit of the greatest revolutions where no change is intended, and that the most refined politicians do not always know whither they are leading the state by their projects.

If we listen to the testimony of modern history, and to that of

* De Retz *Memoirs.*

the most authentic parts of the ancient; if we attend to the practice of nations in every quarter of the world, and in every condition, whether that of the barbarian or the polished, we shall find very little reason to retract this assertion. No constitution is formed by concert, no government is copied from a plan. The members of a small state contend for equality; the members of a greater, find themselves classed in a certain manner that lays a foundation for monarchy. They proceed from one form of government to another, by easy transitions, and frequently under old names adopt a new constitution. The seeds of every form are lodged in human nature; they spring up and ripen with the season. The prevalence of a particular species is often derived from an imperceptible ingredient mingled in the soil.

We are therefore to receive, with caution, the traditionary histories of ancient legislators, and founders of states. Their names have long been celebrated; their supposed plans have been admired; and what were probably the consequences of an early situation, is, in every instance, considered as an effect of design. An author and a work, like cause and effect, are perpetually coupled together. This is the simplest form under which we can consider the establishment of nations: and we ascribe to a previous design, what came to be known only by experience, what no human wisdom could foresee, and what, without the concurring humour and disposition of his age, no authority could enable an individual to execute.

If men, during ages of extensive reflection, and employed in the search of improvement, are wedded to their institutions; and, labouring under many acknowledged inconveniencies, cannot break loose from the trammels of custom; what shall we suppose their humour to have been in the times of Romulus and Lycurgus? They were not surely more disposed to embrace the schemes of innovators, or to shake off the impressions of habit: they were not more pliant and ductile, when their knowledge was less; not more capable of refinement, when their minds were more circumscribed.

We imagine, perhaps, that rude nations must have so strong a sense of the defects under which they labour, and be so conscious that reformations are requisite in their manners, that they must be ready to adopt, with joy, every plan of improvement, and to receive every plausible proposal with implicit compliance. And we are thus inclined to believe, that the harp of Orpheus could effect, in one age, what the eloquence of Plato could not produce in another. We mistake, however, the characteristic of simple ages: mankind then appear to feel the fewest defects, and are then least desirous to enter on reformations.

The reality, in the mean time, of certain establishments at Rome and at Sparta, cannot be disputed: but it is probable, that the government of both these states took its rise from the situation and genius of the people, not from the projects of single men; that the celebrated warrior and statesman, who are considered as the founders of those nations, only acted a superior part among numbers who were disposed to the same institutions; and that they left to posterity a renown, pointing them out as the inventors of many practices which had been already in use, and which helped to form their own manners and genius, as well as those of their countrymen.

It has been formerly observed, that, in many particulars, the customs of simple nations coincide with what is ascribed to the invention of early statesmen; that the model of republican government, the senate, and the assembly of the people; that even the equality of property, or the community of goods, were not reserved to the invention or contrivance of singular men.

If we consider Romulus as the founder of the Roman state, certainly he who killed his brother that he might reign alone, did not desire to come under restraints from the controuling power of the senate, nor to refer the councils of his sovereignty to the decision of a collective body. Love of dominion is, by its nature, averse to constraint; and this chieftain, like every leader in a rude age, probably found a class of men ready to intrude on his councils, and without whom he could not proceed. He met with occasions, on which, as at the sound of a trumpet, the body of the people assembled, and took resolutions, which any individual might in vain dispute, or attempt to controul; and Rome, which commenced on the general plan of every artless society, found lasting improvements in the pursuit of temporary expedients, and digested her political frame in adjusting the pretensions of parties which arose in the state.

Mankind, in very early ages of society, learn to covet riches, and to admire distinction: they have avarice and ambition, and are occasionally led by them to depredation and conquest: but in their ordinary conduct, these motives are balanced or restrained by other habits and other pursuits; by sloth, or intemperance; by personal attachments, or personal animosities; which mislead from the attention to interest. These circumstances render mankind, at times, remiss or outrageous: they prove the source of civil peace or disorder, but disqualify those who are actuated by them, from maintaining any fixed usurpation; slavery and rapine are first threatened from abroad, and war, either offensive or defensive, is the great business of every tribe. The enemy occupy their thoughts; they have no leisure for domestic dissensions. It is the desire of every separate community, however, to secure itself; and in proportion as it gains this object, by strengthening its barrier, by weakening its enemy, or by procuring allies, the individual at home bethinks him of what he may gain or lose for himself: the leader is disposed to enlarge the advantages which belong to his station; the follower becomes jealous of rights which are open to incroachment; and parties who united before, from affection and habit, or from a regard to their common preservation, disagree in supporting their several claims to precedence or profit.

When the animosities of faction are thus awakened at home, and the pretensions of freedom are opposed to those of dominion, the members of every society find a new scene upon which to exert their activity. They had quarrelled, perhaps, on points of interest; they had balanced between different leaders; but they had never united as citizens, to withstand the encroachments of sovereignty, or to maintain their common rights as a people. If the prince, in this contest, finds numbers to support, as well as to oppose his pretensions, the sword which was whetted against foreign enemies, may be pointed at the bosom of fellow-subjects, and every interval of peace from abroad, be filled with domestic war. The sacred names of Liberty, Justice, and Civil Order, are made to resound in public assemblies; and, during the absence of other alarms, give a society, within itself, an abundant subject of ferment and animosity.

If what is related of the little principalities which, in ancient times, were formed in Greece, in Italy, and over all Europe, agrees with the character we have given of mankind under the first impressions of property, of interest, and of hereditary distinctions; the seditions and domestic wars which followed in those very states, the expulsion of their kings, or the questions which arose concerning the prerogatives of the sovereign, or privilege of the subject, are agreeable to the representation which we now give of the first step toward political establishment, and the desire of a legal constitution.

What this constitution may be in its earliest form, depends on a variety of circumstances in the condition of nations: It depends on the extent of the principality in its rude state; on the degree of disparity to which mankind had submitted before they began to dispute its abuses: it depends likewise on what we term *accidents*, the personal character of an individual, or the events of a war.

Every community is originally a small one. That propensity by which mankind at first unite, is not the principle from which they afterwards act in extending the limits of empire. Small tribes, where they are not assembled by common objects of conquest or safety, are even averse to a coalition. If, like the real or fabulous confederacy of the Greeks for the destruction of Troy, many nations combine in pursuit of a single object, they easily separate again, and act anew on the maxims of rival states.

There is, perhaps, a certain national extent, within which the passions of men are easily communicated from one, or a few, to the whole; and there are certain numbers of men who can be assembled, and act in a body. If, while the society is not enlarged beyond this dimension, and while its members are easily assembled, political contentions arise, the state seldom fails to proceed on republican maxims, and to establish democracy. In most rude principalities, the leader derived his prerogative from the lustre of his race, and from the voluntary attachment of his tribe: the people he commanded, were his friends, his subjects, and his troops. If we suppose, upon any change in their manners, that they cease to revere his dignity, that they pretend to equality among themselves, or are seized with a jealousy of his assuming too much, the foundations of his power are already withdrawn. When the voluntary subject becomes refractory; when considerable parties, or the collective body, chuse to act for themselves; the small kingdom, like that of Athens, becomes of course a republic.

The changes of condition, and of manners, which, in the progress of mankind, raise up to nations a leader and a prince, create, at the same time, a nobility, and a variety of ranks, who have, in a subordinate degree, their claim to distinction. Superstition, too, may create an order of men, who, under the title of priesthood, engage in the pursuit of a separate interest; who, by their union and firmness as a body, and by their incessant ambition, deserve to be reckoned in the list of pretenders to power. These different orders of men are the elements of whose mixture the political body is generally formed; each draws to its side some part from the mass of the people. The people themselves are a party upon occasion; and numbers of men, however classed and distinguished, become, by their jarring pretensions and separate views, mutual interruptions and checks; and have, by bringing to the national councils the maxims and apprehensions of a particular order, and by guarding a particular interest, a share in adjusting or preserving the political form of the state.

The pretensions of any particular order, if not checked by some collateral power, would terminate in tyranny; those of a prince, in despotism; those of a nobility or priesthood, in the abuses of aristocracy; of a populace, in the confusions of anarchy. These terminations, as they are never the professed, so are they seldom even the disguised, object of party: but the measures which any party pursues, if suffered to prevail, will lead, by degrees, to every extreme.

In their way to the ascendant they endeavour to gain, and in the midst of interruptions which opposite interests mutually give, liberty may have a permanent or a transient existence; and the constitution may bear a form and a character as various as the casual combination of such multiplied parts can effect.

To bestow on communities some degree of political freedom, it is perhaps sufficient, that their members, either singly, or as they are involved with their several orders, should insist on their rights; that under republics, the citizen should either maintain his own equality with firmness, or restrain the ambition of his fellow-citizen within moderate bounds: that under monarchy, men of every rank should maintain the honours of their private or their public stations; and sacrifice, neither to the impositions of a court, nor to the claims of a populace, those dignities which are destined, in some measure, independent of fortune, to give stability to the throne, and to procure a respect to the subject.

Amidst the contentions of party, the interests of the public, even the maxims of justice and candour, are sometimes forgotten; and yet those fatal consequences which such a measure of corruption seems to portend, do not unavoidably follow. The public interest is often secure, not because individuals are disposed to regard it as the end of their conduct, but because each, in his place, is determined to preserve his own. Liberty is maintained by the continued differences and oppositions of numbers, not by their concurring zeal in behalf of equitable government. In free states, therefore, the wisest laws are never, perhaps, dictated by the interest and spirit of any order of men: they are moved, they are opposed, or amended, by different hands; and come at last to express that medium and composition which contending parties have forced one another to adopt.

When we consider the history of mankind in this view, we cannot be at a loss for the causes which, in small communities, threw the balance on the side of democracy; which, in states more enlarged in respect to territory and numbers of people, gave the ascendant to monarchy; and which, in a variety of conditions and of different ages, enabled mankind to blend and unite the characters of different forms; and, instead of any of the simple constitutions we have mentioned,* to exhibit a medley of all.

* Part i, sect. 10.

In emerging from a state of rudeness and simplicity, men must be expected to act from that spirit of equality, or moderate subordination, to which they have been accustomed. When crouded together in cities, or within the compass of a small territory, they act by contagious passions, and every individual feels a degree of importance proportioned to his figure in the croud, and the smallness of its numbers. The pretenders to power and dominion appear in too familiar a light to impose upon the multitude, and they have no aids at their call, by which they can bridle the refractory humours of a people who resist their pretensions. Theseus, King of Attica, we are told, assembled the inhabitants of its twelve cantons into one city. In this he took an effectual method to unit into one democracy, what were before the separate members of his monarchy, and to hasten the downfall of the regal power.

The monarch of an extensive territory has many advantages in maintaining his station. Without any grievance to his subjects, he can support the magnificence of a royal estate, and dazzle the imagination of his people, by that very wealth which themselves have bestowed. He can employ the inhabitants of one district against those of another; and while the passions that lead to mutiny and rebellion, can at any one time seize only on a part of his subjects, he feels himself strong in the possession of a general authority. Even the distance at which he resides from many of those who receive his commands, augments the mysterious awe and respect which are paid to his government.

With these different tendencies, accident and corruption, however, joined to a variety of circumstances, may throw particular states from their bias, and produce exceptions to every general rule. This has actually happened in some of the later principalities of Greece, and modern Italy, in Sweden, Poland, and the German empire. But the united states of the Netherlands, and the Swiss cantons, are perhaps the most extensive communities, which maintaining the union of nations, have, for any considerable time, resisted the tendency to monarchical government; and Sweden is the only instance of a republic established in a great kingdom on the ruins of monarchy.

The sovereign of a petty district, or a single city, when not supported, as in modern Europe, by the contagion of monarchical manners, holds the sceptre by a precarious tenure, and is perpetually alarmed by the spirit of mutiny in his people, is guided by jealousy, and supports himself by severity, prevention, and force.

The popular and aristocratical powers in a great nation, as in the case of Germany and Poland, may meet with equal difficulty in maintaining their pretensions; and in order to avoid their danger on the side of kingly usurpation, are obliged to withhold from the supreme magistrate even the necessary trust of an executive power.

The states of Europe, in the manner of their first settlement, laid the foundations of monarchy, and were prepared to unite under regular and extensive governments. If the Greeks, whose progress at home terminated in the establishment of so many independent republics, had under Agamemnon effected a conquest and settlement in Asia, it is probable, that they might have furnished an example of the same kind. But the original inhabitants of any country, forming many separate cantons, come by slow degrees to that coalition and union into which conquering tribes are, in effecting their conquests, or in securing their possessions, hurried at once. Caesar encountered some hundreds of independent nations in Gaul, whom even their common danger did not sufficiently unite. The German invaders, who settled in the lands of the Romans, made, in the same district, a number of separate establishments, but far more extensive than what the ancient Gauls, by their conjunctions and treaties, or in the result of their wars, could after many ages have reached.

The seeds of great monarchies, and the roots of extensive dominion, were every where planted with the colonies that divided the Roman empire. We have no exact account of the numbers, who, with a seeming concert, continued, during some ages, to invade and to seize this tempting prize. Where they expected resistance, they endeavoured to muster up a proportionable force; and when they proposed to settle, entire nations removed to share in the spoil. Scattered over an extensive province, where they could not be secure, without maintaining their union, they continued to acknowledge the leader under whom they had fought; and, like an army sent by divisions into separate stations, were prepared to assemble whenever occasion should require their united operations or counsels.

Every separate party had its post assigned, and every subordinate chieftain his possessions, from which he was to provide his own subsistence, and that of his followers. The model of government was taken from that of a military subordination, and a fief was the temporary pay of an officer proportioned to his rank.[*] There was a class of the people destined to military service, another to labour, and to cultivate lands for the benefit of their masters. The officer improved his tenure by degrees, first changing a temporary grant into a tenure for his life; and this also, upon the observance of certain conditions, into a grant including his heirs.

The rank of the nobles became hereditary in every quarter, and formed a powerful and permanent order of men in every state. While they held the people in servitude, they disputed the claims of their sovereign; they withdrew their attendance upon occasion, or turned their arms against him. They formed a strong and insurmountable barrier against a general despotism in the state; but they were themselves, by means of their warlike retainers, the tyrants of every little district, and prevented the establishment of order, or any regular applications of law. They took the advantage of weak reigns or minorities, to push their incroachments on the sovereign; or having made the monarchy elective, they by successive treaties and stipulations, at every election, limited or undermined the monarchical power. The prerogatives of the prince have been, in some instances, as in that of the German empire in particular, reduced to a mere title; and the national union itself preserved in the observance only of a few insignificant formalities.

Where the contest of the sovereign, and of his vassals, under hereditary and ample prerogatives annexed to the crown, had a different issue, the feudal lordships were gradually stript of their powers, the nobles were reduced to the state of subjects,

* See Dr Robertson's *History of Scotland*, b. 1.

and obliged to hold their honours, and exercise their jurisdictions, in a dependence on the prince. It was his supposed interest to reduce them to a state of equal subjection with the people, and to extend his own authority, by rescuing the labourer and the dependent from the oppressions of their immediate superiors.

In this project the princes of Europe have variously succeeded. While they protected the people, and thereby encouraged the practice of commercial and lucrative arts, they paved the way for despotism in the state; and with the same policy by which they relieved the subject from many oppressions, they increased the powers of the crown.

But where the people had by the constitution a representative in the government, and a head, under which they could avail themselves of the wealth they acquired, and of the sense of their personal importance, this policy turned against the crown; it formed a new power to restrain the prerogative, to establish the government of law, and to exhibit a spectacle new in the history of mankind; monarchy mixed with republic, and extensive territory, governed, during some ages, without military force.

Such were the steps by which the nations of Europe have arrived at their present establishments: in some instances, they have come to the possession of legal constitutions; in others, to the exercise of a mitigated despotism; or continue to struggle with the tendency which they severally have to these different extremes.

The progress of empire, in the early ages of Europe, threatened to be rapid, and to bury the independent spirit of nations in that grave which the Ottoman conquerors found for themselves; and for the wretched race they had vanquished. The Romans were led by slow degrees to extend the limits of their empire; every new acquisition was the result of a tedious war, and required the sending of colonies, and a variety of measures, to secure any new possession. But the feudal superior being animated, from the moment he had gained an establishment, with a desire of extending his territory, and of enlarging the list of his vassals, made frequent annexation of new provinces, merely by bestowing investiture, and received independent states, without any material innovation in the form of their policy, as the subjects of his growing dominion.

Separate principalities were, like the parts of an engine, ready to be joined, and, like the materials of a building, ready to be erected. They were in the result of their struggles put together or taken asunder with facility. The independence of weak states was preserved only by the mutual jealousies of the strong, or by the general attention of all to maintain a balance of power.

The happy system of policy on which European states have proceeded in preserving this balance; the degree of moderation which is, in adjusting their treaties, become habitual even to victorious and powerful monarchies, does honour to mankind, and may give hopes of a lasting felicity to be derived from a pre-possession, never, perhaps, equally strong in any former period, or among any number of nations, that the first conquering people will ruin themselves, as well as their rivals.

It is in such states, perhaps, as in a fabric of a large dimension, that we can perceive most distinctly the several parts of which a political body consists; and observe that concurrence or opposition of interests, which serve to unite or to separate different orders of men, and lead them, by maintaining their several claims, to establish a variety of political forms. The smallest republics, however, consist of parts similar to these, and of members who are actuated by a similar spirit. They furnish examples of government diversified by the casual combinations of parties, and by the different advantages with which those parties engage in the conflict.

In every society there is a casual subordination, independent of its formal establishment, and frequently adverse to its constitution. While the administration and the people speak the language of a particular form, and seem to admit no pretensions to power, without a legal nomination in one instance, or without the advantage of hereditary honours in another, this casual subordination, possibly arising from the distribution of property, or from some other circumstance that bestows unequal degrees of influence, gives the state its tone, and fixes its character.

The plebeian order at Rome having been long considered as of an inferior condition, and excluded from the higher offices of magistracy, had sufficient force, as a body, to get this invidious distinction removed; but the individual still acting under the impressions of a subordinate rank, gave in every competition his suffrage to a patrician, whose protection he had experienced, and whose personal authority he felt. By this means, the ascendency of the patrician families was, for a certain period, as regular as it could be made by the avowed maxims of aristocracy; but the higher offices of state being gradually shared by plebeians, the effects of former distinctions were prevented or weakened. The laws that were made to adjust the pretensions of different orders were easily eluded. The populace became a faction, and their alliance was the surest road to dominion. Clodius, by a pretended adoption into a plebeian family, was qualified to become tribune of the people; and Caesar, by espousing the cause of this faction, made his way to usurpation and tyranny.

In such fleeting and transient scenes, forms of government are only modes of proceeding, in which every subsequent age may differ from the former. Faction is ever ready to seize all occasional advantages; and mankind, when in hazard from any party, seldom find a better protection than that of its rival. Cato united with Pompey in opposition to Caesar, and guarded against nothing so much as that reconciliation of parties, which was in effect to be a combination of different leaders against the freedom of the republic. This illustrious personage stood distinguished in his age like a man among children, and was raised above his opponents, as much by the justness of his understanding, and the extent of his penetration, as he was by the manly fortitude and disinterestedness with which he strove to baffle the designs of a vain and childish ambition, that was operating to the ruin of mankind.

Although free constitutions of government seldom or never take their rise from the scheme of any single projector, yet are they often preserved by the vigilance, activity, and zeal, of single men. Happy are they who understand and who chuse this object of care; and happy it is for mankind when it is not chosen too late. It has been reserved to signalize the lives of a Cato or a

Brutus, on the eve of fatal revolutions; to foster in secret the indignation of Thrasea and Helvidius; and to occupy the reflections of speculative men in time of corruption. But even in such late and ineffectual examples, it was happy to know, and to value, an object which is so important to mankind. The pursuit, and the love of it, however unsuccessful, has thrown a lustre on human nature.

SECTION III.

Of National Objects in general, and of Establishments and Manners relating to them.

While the mode of subordination is casual, and forms of government take their rise, chiefly from the manner in which the members of a state have been originally classed, and from a variety of circumstances that procure to particular orders of men a sway in their country, there are certain objects that claim the attention of every government, that lead the apprehensions and the reasonings of mankind in every society, and that not only furnish an employment to statesmen, but in some measure direct the community to those institutions, under the authority of which the magistrate holds his power. Such are the national defence, the distribution of justice, the preservation and internal prosperity of the state. If these objects be neglected, we must apprehend that the very scene in which parties contend for power, for privilege, or equality, must disappear, and society itself no longer exist.

The consideration due to these objects will be pleaded in every public assembly, and will produce, in every political contest, appeals to that common sense and opinion of mankind, which, struggling with the private views of individuals, and the claims of party, may be considered as the great legislator of nations.

The measures required for the attainment of most national objects, are connected together, and must be jointly pursued: they are often the same. The force which is prepared for defence against foreign enemies, may be likewise employed to keep the peace at home: the laws made to secure the rights and liberties of the people, may serve as encouragements to population and commerce: and every community, without considering how its objects may be classed or distinguished by speculative men, is, in every instance, obliged to assume or to retain that form which is best fitted to preserve its advantages, or to avert its misfortunes.

Nations, however, like private men, have their favourite ends, and their principal pursuits, which diversify their manners, as well as their establishments. They even attain to the same ends by different means; and, like men who make their fortune by different professions, retain the habits of their principal calling in every condition at which they arrive. The Romans became wealthy in pursuing their conquests; and probably, for a certain period, increased the numbers of mankind, while their disposition to war seemed to threaten the earth with desolation. Some modern nations proceed to dominion and enlargement on the maxims of commerce; and while they only intend to accumulate riches at home, continue to gain an imperial ascendant abroad.

The characters of the warlike and the commercial are variously combined: they are formed in different degrees by the influence of circumstances that more or less frequently give rise to war, and excite the desire of conquest; of circumstances that leave a people in quiet to improve their domestic resources, or to purchase, by the fruits of their industry, from foreigners, what their own soil and their climate deny.

The members of every community are more or less occupied with matters of state, in proportion as their constitution admits them to a share in the government, and summons up their attention to objects of a public nature. A people are cultivated or unimproved in their talents, in proportion as those talents are employed in the practice of arts, and in the affairs of society: they are improved or corrupted in their manners, in proportion as they are encouraged and directed to act on the maxims of freedom and justice, or as they are degraded into a state of meanness and servitude.

But whatever advantages are obtained, or whatever evils are avoided, by nations, in any of these important respects, are generally considered as mere occasional incidents: they are seldom admitted among the objects of policy, or entered among the reasons of state.

We hazard being treated with ridicule, when we require political establishments, merely to cultivate the talents of men, and to inspire the sentiments of a liberal mind: we must offer some motive of interest, or some hopes of external advantage, to animate the pursuits, or to direct the measures, of ordinary men. They would be brave, ingenious, and eloquent, only from necessity, or for the sake of profit: they magnify the uses of wealth, population, and the other resources of war; but often forget that these are of no consequence without the direction of able capacities, and without the supports of a national vigour. We may expect, therefore, to find among states the bias to a particular policy, taken from the regards to public safety; from the desire of securing personal freedom, or private property; seldom from the consideration of moral effects, or from a view to the genius of mankind.

SECTION IV.

Of Population and Wealth.

When we imagine what the Romans must have felt when the tidings came that the flower of their city had perished at Cannae; when we think of what the orator had in his mind when he said, 'That the youth among the people was like the spring among the seasons;' when we hear of the joy with which the huntsman and the warrior is adopted, in America, to sustain the honours of the family and the nation; we are made to feel the most powerful motives to regard the increase and preservation of our fellow-citizens. Interest, affection, and views of policy, combine to recommend this object; and it is treated with entire neglect only by the tyrant who mistakes his own advantage, by the statesman who trifles with the charge committed to his care, or by the people who are become corrupted, and who consider their fellow-subjects as rivals in interest, and competitors in their lucrative pursuits.

Among rude societies, and among small communities in general, who are engaged in frequent struggles and difficulties, the preservation and increase of their members is a most important object. The American rates his defeat from the numbers of men he has lost, or he estimates his victory from the prisoners he has made; not from his having remained the master of a field, or from his being driven from a ground on which he encountered his enemy. A man with whom he can associate in all his pursuits, whom he can embrace as his friend; in whom he finds an object to his affections, and an aid in his struggles, is to him the most precious accession of fortune.

Even where the friendship of particular men is out of the question, the society, being occupied in forming a party that may defend itself, and annoy its enemy, finds no object of greater moment than the increase of its numbers. Captives who may be adopted, or children of either sex who may be reared for the public, are accordingly considered as the richest spoil of an enemy. The practice of the Romans in admitting the vanquished to share in the privileges of their city, the rape of the Sabines, and the subsequent coalition with that people, were not singular or uncommon examples in the history of mankind. The same policy has been followed, and was natural and obvious where-ever the strength of a state consisted in the arms of a few, and where men were valued in themselves, distinct from the consideration of estate or of fortune.

In rude ages, therefore, while mankind subsist in small divisions, it should appear, that if the earth be thinly peopled, this defect does not arise from a disregard to numbers on the part of states. It is even probable, that the most effectual course that could be taken to increase the species, would be, to prevent the coalition of nations, and to oblige mankind to act in such small bodies as would make the preservation of their numbers a principal object of their care. This alone, it is true, would not be sufficient: we must probably add the encouragement for rearing families, which mankind enjoy under a favourable policy, and the means of subsistence which they owe to the practice of arts.

The mother is unwilling to increase her offspring, and is ill provided to rear them, where she herself is obliged to undergo great hardships in the search of her food. In North America, we are told, that she joins to the reserves of a cold or a moderate temperament, the abstinencies to which she submits from the consideration of this difficulty. In her apprehension, it is matter of prudence, and of conscience, to bring one child to the condition of feeding on venison, and of following on foot, before she will hazard a new burden in travelling the woods.

In warmer lattitudes, by the different temperament, perhaps, which the climate bestows, and by a greater facility in procuring subsistence, the numbers of mankind increase, while the object itself is neglected; and the commerce of the sexes, without any concern for population, is made a subject of mere debauch. In some places, we are told, it is even made the object of a barbarous policy, to defeat or to restrain the intentions of nature. In the island of Formosa, the males are prohibited to marry before the age of forty; and females, if pregnant before the age of thirty-six, have an abortion procured by order of the magistrate, who employs a violence that endangers the life of the mother, together with that of the child.*

In China, the permission given to parents to kill or to expose their children, was probably meant as a relief from the burden of a numerous offspring. But notwithstanding what we hear of a practice so repugnant to the human heart, it has not, probably, the effects in restraining population, which it seems to threaten; but, like many other institutions, has an influence the reverse of what it seemed to portend. The parents marry with this means of relief in their view, and the children are saved.

However important the object of population may be held by mankind, it will be difficult to find, in the history of civil policy, any wise or effectual establishments solely calculated to obtain it. The practice of rude or feeble nations is inadequate, or cannot

* *Collection of Dutch Voyages.*

surmount the obstacles which are found in their manner of life. The growth of industry, the endeavours of men to improve their arts, to extend their commerce, to secure their possessions, and to establish their rights, are indeed the most effectual means to promote population: but they arise from a different motive; they arise from regards to interest and personal safety. They are intended for the benefit of those who exist, not to procure the increase of their numbers.

It is, in the mean time, of importance to know, that where a people are fortunate in their political establishments, and successful in the pursuits of industry, their population is likely to grow in proportion. Most of the other devices thought of for this purpose, only serve to frustrate the expectations of mankind, or to mislead their attention.

In planting a colony, in striving to repair the occasional wastes of pestilence or war, the immediate contrivance of statesmen may be useful; but if in reasoning on the increase of mankind in general, we overlook their freedom, and their happiness, our aids to population become weak and ineffectual. They only lead us to work on the surface, or to pursue a shadow, while we neglect the substantial concern; and in a decaying state, make us tamper with palliatives, while the roots of an evil are suffered to remain. Octavius revived or inforced the laws that related to population at Rome: but it may be said of him, and of many sovereigns in a similar situation, that they administer the poison, while they are devising the remedy; and bring a damp and a palsy on the principles of life, while they endeavour, by external applications to the skin, to restore the bloom of a decayed and a sickly body.

It is indeed happy for mankind, that this important object is not always dependent on the wisdom of sovereigns, or the policy of single men. A people intent on freedom, find for themselves a condition in which they may follow the propensities of nature with a more signal effect, than any which the councils of state could devise. When sovereigns, or projectors, are the supposed masters of this subject, the best they can do, is to be cautious of hurting an interest they cannot greatly promote, and of making breaches they cannot repair.

'When nations were divided into small territories, and petty commonwealths, where each man had his house and his field to himself, and each county had its capital free and independent; what a happy situation for mankind,' says Mr Hume, 'how favourable to industry and agriculture, to marriage and to population!' Yet here were probably no schemes of the statesman for rewarding the married, or for punishing the single; for inviting foreigners to settle, or for prohibiting the departure of natives. Every citizen finding a possession secure, and a provision for his heirs, was not discouraged by the gloomy fears of oppression or want: and where every other function of nature was free, that which furnished the nursery could not be restrained. Nature has required the powerful to be just; but she has not otherwise intrusted the preservation of her works to their visionary plans. What fewel can the statesman add to the fires of youth? Let him only not smother it, and the effect is secure. Where we oppress or degrade mankind with one hand, it is vain, like Octavius, to hold out in the other, the baits of marriage, or the whip to barrenness. It is vain to invite new inhabitants from abroad, while those we already possess are made to hold their tenure with uncertainty; and to tremble, not only under the prospect of a numerous family, but even under that of a precarious and doubtful subsistence for themselves. The arbitrary sovereign, who has made this the condition of his subjects, owes the remains of his people to the powerful instincts of nature, not to any device of his own.

Men will croud where the situation is tempting, and, in a few generations, will people every country to the measure of its means of subsistence. They will even increase under circumstances that portend a decay. The frequent wars of the Romans, and of many a thriving community; even the pestilence, and the market for slaves, find their supply, if, without destroying the source, the drain become regular; and if an issue is made for the offspring, without unsettling the families from which they arise. Where a happier provision is made for mankind, the statesman, who by premiums to marriage, by allurements to foreigners, or by confining the natives at home, apprehends, that he has made the numbers of his people to grow, is often like the fly in the fable, who admired its success, in turning the wheel, and in moving the carriage: he has only accompanied what was already in motion; he has dashed with his oar, to hasten the cataract; and waved with his fan, to give speed to the winds.

Projects of mighty settlement, and of sudden population, however successful in the end, are always expensive to mankind. Above a hundred thousand peasants, we are told, were yearly driven, like so many cattle, to Petersburgh, in the first attempts to replenish that settlement, and yearly perished for want of subsistence.* The Indian only attempts to settle in the neighbourhood of the plantain,† and while his family increases, he adds a tree to the walk.

If the plantain, the cocoa, or the palm, were sufficient to maintain an inhabitant, the race of men in the warmer climates might become as numerous as the trees of the forest. But in many parts of the earth, from the nature of the climate, and the soil, the spontaneous produce being next to nothing; the means of subsistence are the fruits only of labour and skill. If a people, while they retain their frugality, increase their industry, and improve their arts, their numbers must grow in proportion. Hence it is, that the cultivated fields of Europe are more peopled than the wilds of America, or the plains of Tartary.

But even the increase of mankind which attends the accumulation of wealth, has its limits. The *necessary of life* is a vague and a relative term: it is one thing in the opinion of the savage; another in that of the polished citizen: it has a reference to the fancy, and to the habits of living. While arts improve, and riches increase; while the possessions of individuals, or their prospects of gain, come up to their opinion of what is required to settle a family, they enter on its cares with alacrity. But when the possession, however redundant, falls short of the standard, and a fortune supposed sufficient for marriage is attained with difficulty, population is checked, or begins to decline. The citizen, in his own apprehension, returns to the state of the savage; his children, he thinks, must perish for want; and he quits a scene overflowing

* Strahlenberg.   † Dampier.

with plenty, because he has not the fortune which his supposed rank, or his wishes, require. No ultimate remedy is applied to this evil, by merely accumulating wealth; for rare and costly materials, whatever these are, continue to be sought; and if silks and pearl are made common, men will begin to covet some new decorations, which the wealthy alone can procure. If they are indulged in their humour, their demands are repeated: For it is the continual increase of riches, not any measure attained, that keeps the craving imagination at ease.

Men are tempted to labour, and to practise lucrative arts, by motives of interest. Secure to the workman the fruit of his labour, give him the prospects of independence or freedom, the public has found a faithful minister in the acquisition of wealth, and a faithful steward in hoarding what he has gained. The statesman in this, as in the case of population itself, can do little more than avoid doing mischief. It is well, if, in the beginnings of commerce, he knows how to repress the frauds to which it is subject. Commerce, if continued, is the branch in which men committed to the effects of their own experience, are least apt to go wrong.

The trader, in rude ages, is short-sighted, fraudulent, and mercenary; but in the progress and advanced state of his art, his views are enlarged, his maxims are established: he becomes punctual, liberal, faithful, and enterprising; and in the period of general corruption, he alone has every virtue, except the force to defend his acquisitions. He needs no aid from the state, but its protection; and is often in himself its most intelligent and respectable member. Even in China, we are informed, where pilfering, fraud, and corruption, are the reigning practice with all the other orders of men, the great merchant is ready to give, and to procure confidence: while his countrymen act on the plans and under the restrictions of a police adjusted to knaves, he acts on the reasons of trade, and the maxims of mankind.

If population be connected with national wealth, liberty and personal security is the great foundation of both: and if this foundation be laid in the state, nature has secured the increase and the industry of its members; the one by desires the most ardent in the human frame; the other by a consideration the most uniform and constant of any that possesses the mind. The great object of policy, therefore, with respect to both, is, to secure to the family its means of subsistence and settlement; to protect the industrious in the pursuit of his occupation; to reconcile the restrictions of police, and the social affections of mankind, with their separate and interested pursuits.

In matters of particular profession, industry, and trade, the experienced practitioner is the master, and every general reasoner is a novice. The object in commerce is to make the individual rich; the more he gains for himself, the more he augments the wealth of his country. If a protection be required, it must be granted; if crimes and frauds be committed, they must be repressed; and government can pretend to no more. When the refined politician would lend an active hand, he only multiplies interruptions and grounds of complaint; when the merchant forgets his own interest to lay plans for his country, the period of vision and chimera is near, and the solid basis of commerce withdrawn. He might be told, perhaps, that while he pursues his advantage, and gives no cause of complaint, the interest of commerce is safe.

The general police of France, proceeding on a supposition that the exportation of corn must drain the country where it has grown, had, till of late, laid that branch of commerce under a severe prohibition. The English landholder and the farmer had credit enough to obtain a premium for exportation, to favour the sale of their commodity; and the event has shewn, that private interest is a better patron of commerce and plenty, than the refinements of state. One nation lays the refined plan of a settlement on the continent of North America, and trusts little to the conduct of traders and short-sighted men; another leaves men to find their own position in a state of freedom, and to think for themselves. The active industry and the limited views of the one, made a thriving settlement; the great projects of the other were still in idea.

But I willingly quit a subject in which I am not much conversant, and still less engaged by the views with which I write.

Speculations on commerce and wealth have been delivered by the ablest writers, who have left nothing so important to be offered on the subject, as the general caution, not to consider these articles as making the sum of national felicity, or the principal object of any state.

One nation, in search of gold and of precious metals, neglect the domestic sources of wealth, and become dependent on their neighbours for the necessaries of life: another so intent on improving their internal resources, and on increasing their commerce, that they become dependent on foreigners for the defence of what they acquire. It is even painful in conversation to find the interests of trade give the tone to our reasonings, and to find a subject perpetually offered as the great business of national councils, to which any interposition of government is seldom, with propriety, applied, or never beyond the protection it affords.

We complain of a want of public spirit; but whatever may be the effect of this error in practice, in speculation it is none of our faults: we reason perpetually for the public; but the want of national views were frequently better than the possession of those we express: we would have nations, like a company of merchants, think of nothing but the increase of their stock; assemble to deliberate on profit and loss; and, like them too, intrust their protection to a force which they do not possess in themselves.

Because men, like other animals, are maintained in multitudes, where the necessaries of life are amassed, and the store of wealth is enlarged, we drop our regards for the happiness, the moral and political character of a people; and anxious for the herd we would propagate, carry our views no farther than the stall and the pasture. We forget that the few have often made a prey of the many; that to the poor there is nothing so enticing as the coffers of the rich; and that when the price of freedom comes to be paid, the heavy sword of the victor may fall into the opposite scale.

Whatever be the actual conduct of nations in this matter, it is certain, that many of our arguments would hurry us, for the sake of wealth and of population, into a scene where mankind being exposed to corruption, are unable to defend their possessions; and where they are, in the end, subject to oppression and ruin.

We cut off the roots, while we would extend the branches, and thicken the foliage.

It is possibly from an opinion that the virtues of men are secure, that some who turn from their attention to public affairs, think of nothing but the numbers and wealth of a people: it is from a dread of corruption, that others think of nothing but how to preserve the national virtues. Human society has great obligations to both. They are opposed to one another only by mistake; and even when united, have not strength sufficient to combat the wretched party, that refers every object to personal interest, and that cares not for the safety or increase of any stock but its own.

SECTION V.

Of National Defence and Conquest.

It is impossible to ascertain how much of the policy of any state has a reference to war, or to national safety. 'Our legislator,' says the Cretan in Plato, 'thought that nations were by nature in a state of hostility: he took his measures accordingly; and observing that all the possessions of the vanquished pertain to the victor, he held it ridiculous to propose any benefit to his country, before he had provided that it should not be conquered.'

Crete, which is supposed to have been a model of military policy, is commonly considered as the original from which the celebrated laws of Lycurgus were copied. Mankind, it seems, in every instance, must have some palpable object to direct their proceedings, and must have a view to some point of external utility, even in the choice of their virtues. The discipline of Sparta was military; and a sense of its use in the field, more than the force of unwritten and traditionary laws, or the supposed engagement of the public faith obtained by the lawgiver, may have induced this people to persevere in the observance of many rules, which to other nations do not appear necessary, except in the presence of an enemy.

Every institution of this singular people gave a lesson of

obedience, of fortitude, and of zeal for the public: but it is remarkable that they chose to obtain, by their virtues alone, what
other nations are fain to buy with their treasure; and it is well
known, that, in the course of their history, they came to regard
their discipline merely on account of its moral effects. They had
experienced the happiness of a mind courageous, disinterested,
and devoted to its best affections; and they studied to preserve
this character in themselves, by resigning the interests of ambition, and the hopes of military glory, even by sacrificing the
numbers of their people.

It was the fate of Spartans who escaped from the field, not of
those who perished with Cleombrotus at Leuctra, that filled the
cottages of Lacedemon with mourning and serious reflection*: it
was the fear of having their citizens corrupted abroad, by intercourse with servile and mercenary men, that made them quit
the station of leaders in the Persian war, and leave Athens, during
fifty years, to pursue, unrivalled, that career of ambition and
profit, by which she made such acquisitions of power and of
wealth.†

We have had occasion to observe, that in every rude state, the
great business is war; and that in barbarous times, mankind,
being generally divided into small parties, are engaged in almost
perpetual hostilities. This circumstance gives the military leader
a continued ascendant in his country, and inclines every people,
during warlike ages, to monarchical government.

The conduct of an army can least of all subjects be divided:
and we may be justly surprised to find, that the Romans, after
many ages of military experience, and after having recently felt
the arms of Hannibal, in many encounters, associated two leaders
at the head of the same army, and left them to adjust their pretensions, by taking the command, each a day in his turn. The
same people, however, on other occasions, thought it expedient
to suspend the exercise of every subordinate magistracy, and in
the time of great alarms, to intrust all the authority of the state in
the hands of one person.

Republics have generally found it necessary, in the conduct of

* Xenophon.   † Thucydides, book I.

war, to place great confidence in the executive branch of their government. When a consul at Rome had proclaimed his levies, and administered the military oath, he became from that moment master of the public treasury, and of the lives of those who were under his command.* The axe and the rods were no longer a mere badge of magistracy, or an empty pageant, in the hands of the lictor: they were, at the command of the father, stained with the blood of his own children; and fell, without appeal, on the mutinous and the disobedient of every condition.

In every free state, there is a perpetual necessity to distinguish the maxims of martial law from those of the civil; and he who has not learned to give an implicit obedience, where the state has given him a military leader, and to resign his personal freedom in the field, from the same magnanimity with which he maintains it in the political deliberations of his country, has yet to learn the most important lesson of civil society, and is only fit to occupy a place in a rude, or in a corrupted state, where the principles of mutiny and of servility being joined, the one or the other is frequently adopted in the wrong place.

From a regard to what is necessary in war, nations inclined to popular or aristocratical government, have had recourse to establishments that bordered on monarchy. Even where the highest office of the state was in common times administered by a plurality of persons, the whole power and authority belonging to it was, on particular occasions, committed to one; and upon great alarms, when the political fabric was shaken or endangered, a monarchical power has been applied, like a prop, to secure the state against the rage of the tempest. Thus were the dictators occasionally named at Rome, and the stadtholders in the United Provinces; and thus, in mixed governments, the royal prerogative is occasionally enlarged, by the temporary suspension of laws,† and the barriers of liberty appear to be removed, in order to vest a dictatorial power in the hands of the king.

Had mankind, therefore, no view but to warfare, it is probable that they would continue to prefer monarchical government to

* Polybius.
† In Britain, by the suspension of the *Habeas corpus.*

any other; or at least that every nation, in order to procure secret and united councils, would intrust the executive power with unlimited authority. But, happily for civil society, men have objects of a different sort: and experience has taught, that although the conduct of armies requires an absolute and undivided command; yet a national force is best formed, where numbers of men are inured to equality; and where the meanest citizen may consider himself, upon occasion, as destined to command as well as to obey. It is here that the dictator finds a spirit and a force prepared to second his councils; it is here too that the dictator himself is formed, and that numbers of leaders are presented to the public choice; it is here that the prosperity of a state is independent of single men, and that a wisdom which never dies, with a system of military arrangements permanent and regular, can, even under the greatest misfortunes, prolong the national struggle. With this advantage, the Romans, finding a number of distinguished leaders arise in succession, were at all times almost equally prepared to contend with their enemies of Asia or Africa; while the fortune of those enemies, on the contrary, depended on the casual appearance of singular men, of a Mithridates, or of a Hannibal.

The soldier, we are told, has his point of honour, and a fashion of thinking, which he wears with his sword. This point of honour in free and uncorrupted states, is a zeal for the public; and war to them, is an operation of passions, not the mere pursuit of a calling. Its good and its ill effects are felt in extremes: the friend is made to experience the warmest proofs of attachment, the enemy the severest effects of animosity. On this system the celebrated nations of antiquity made war under their highest attainments of civility, and under their greatest degrees of refinement.

In small and rude societies, the individual finds himself attacked in every national war; and none can propose to devolve his defence on another. 'The King of Spain is a great prince,' said an American chief to the governor of Jamaica, who was preparing a body of troops to join in an enterprise against the Spaniards: 'do you propose to make war upon so great a king with so small a force?' Being told that the forces he saw were to be joined by troops from Europe, and that the governor could then command no more: 'Who are these then,' said the American, 'who form this croud of spectators? are they not your people? and why do you not all go forth to so great a war?' He was answered, That the spectators were merchants, and other inhabitants, who took no part in the service: 'Would they be merchants still,' continued this statesman, 'if the King of Spain was to attack you here? For my part, I do not think that merchants should be permitted to live in any country: when I go to war, I leave no body at home but the women.' It should seem that this simple warrior considered merchants as a kind of neutral persons, who took no part in the quarrels of their country; and that he did not know how much war itself may be made a subject of traffic; what mighty armies may be put in motion from behind the counter; how often human blood is, without any national animosity, bought and sold for bills of exchange; and how often the prince, the nobles, and the statesmen, in many a polished nation, might, in his account, be considered as merchants.

In the progress of arts and of policy, the members of every state are divided into classes; and in the commencement of this distribution, there is no distinction more serious than that of the warrior and the pacific inhabitant; no more is required to place men in the relation of master and slave. Even when the rigours of an established slavery abate, as they have done in modern Europe, in consequence of a protection, and a property, allowed to the mechanic and labourer, this distinction serves still to separate the noble from the base, and to point out that class of men who are destined to reign and to domineer in their country.

It was certainly never foreseen by mankind, that in the pursuit of refinement, they were to reverse this order; or even that they were to place the government, and the military force of nations, in different hands. But is it equally unforseen, that the former order may again take place? and that the pacific citizen, however distinguished by privilege and rank, must one day bow to the person with whom he has intrusted his sword. If such revolutions should actually follow, will this new master revive in his own order the spirit of the noble and the free? Will he renew the characters of the warrior and the statesman? Will he restore to his country the civil and military virtues? I am afraid to reply. Montesquieu observes, that the government of Rome, even under the emperors, became, in the hands of the troops, elective and republican: but the Fabii or the Bruti were heard of no more, after the praetorian bands became the republic.

We have enumerated some of the heads under which a people, as they emerge from barbarity, may come to be classed. Such are, the nobility, the people, the adherents of the prince; and even the priesthood have not been forgotten: when we arrive at times of refinement, the army must be joined to the list. The departments of civil government and of war being severed, and the pre-eminence being given to the statesman, the ambitious will naturally devolve the military service on those who are contented with a subordinate station. They who have the greatest share in the division of fortune, and the greatest interest in defending their country, having resigned the sword, must pay for what they have ceased to perform; and armies, not only at a distance from home, but in the very bosom of their country, are subsisted by pay. A discipline is invented to inure the soldier to perform, from habit, and from the fear of punishment, those hazardous duties, which the love of the public, or a national spirit, no longer inspire.

When we consider the breach that such an establishment makes in the system of national virtues, it is unpleasant to observe, that most nations who have run the career of civil arts, have, in some degree, adopted this measure. Not only states, which either have wars to maintain, or precarious possessions to defend at a distance; not only a prince jealous of his authority, or in haste to gain the advantage of discipline, are disposed to employ foreign troops, or to keep standing armies; but even republics, with little of the former occasion, and none of the motives which prevail in monarchy, have been found to tread in the same path.

If military arrangements occupy so considerable a place in the domestic policy of nations, the actual consequences of war are equally important in the history of mankind. Glory and spoil were the earliest subject of quarrels; a concession of superiority, or a ransom, were the prices of peace. The love of safety, and the desire of dominion, equally lead mankind to wish for accessions of strength. Whether as victors or as vanquished, they tend to a coalition; and powerful nations considering a province, or a fortress acquired on their frontier, as so much gained, are perpetually intent on extending their limits.

The maxims of conquest are not always to be distinguished from those of self-defence. If a neighbouring state be dangerous, if it be frequently troublesome, it is a maxim founded in the consideration of safety, as well as of conquest, That it ought to be weakened or disarmed: If, being once reduced, it be disposed to renew the contest, it must from thenceforward be governed in form. Rome never avowed any other maxims of conquest; and she every where sent her insolent armies, under the specious pretence of procuring to herself and her allies a lasting peace, which she alone would reserve the power to disturb.

The equality of those alliances which the Grecian states formed against each other, maintained, for a time, their independence and separation; and that time was the shining and the happy period of their story. It was prolonged more by vigilance and conduct which they severally applied, than by the moderation of their councils, or by any peculiarities of domestic policy which arrested their progress. The victors were sometimes contented, with merely changing to a resemblance, of their own forms the government of the states they subdued. What the next step might have been in the progress of impositions, is hard to determine. But when we consider, that one party fought for the imposition of tributes, another for the ascendant in war, it cannot be doubted, that the Athenians, from a national ambition, and from the desire of wealth, and the Spartans, though they originally only meant to defend themselves, and their allies, were both, at last, equally willing to become the masters of Greece; and were preparing for each other at home, that yoke, which both, together with their confederates, were obliged to receive from abroad.

In the conquests of Philip, the desire of self-preservation and security seemed to be blended with the ambition natural to princes. He turned his arms successively to the quarters on which he found himself hurt, from which he had been alarmed or provoked: and when he had subdued the Greeks, he proposed to lead them against their ancient enemy of Persia. In this he laid the plan which was carried into execution by his son.

The Romans, become the masters of Italy, and the conquerors of Carthage, had been alarmed on the side of Macedon, and were led to cross a new sea in search of a new field, on which to exercise their military force. In prosecution of their wars, from the earliest to the latest date of their history, without intending the very conquests they made, perhaps without foreseeing what advantage they were to reap from the subjection of distant provinces, or in what manner they were to govern their new acquisitions, they still proceeded to seize what came successively within their reach; and, stimulated by a policy which engaged them in perpetual wars, which led to perpetual victory and accessions of territory, they extended the frontier of a state, which, but a few centuries before, had been confined within the skirts of a village, to the Euphrates, the Danube, the Weser, the Forth, and the Ocean.

It is vain to affirm, that the genius of any nation is adverse to conquest. Its real interests indeed most commonly are so; but every state which is prepared to defend itself, and to obtain victories, is likewise in hazard of being tempted to conquer.

In Europe, where mercenary and disciplined armies are every where formed, and ready to traverse the earth, where, like a flood pent up by slender banks, they are only restrained by political forms, or a temporary balance of power; if the sluices should break, what inundations may we not expect to behold? Effeminate kingdoms and empires are spread from the sea of Corea to the Atlantic ocean. Every state, by the defeat of its troops, may be turned into a province; every army opposed in the field to-day may be hired to-morrow; and every victory gained, may give the accession of a new military force to the victor.

The Romans, with inferior arts of communication both by

sea and land, maintained their dominion in a considerable part of Europe, Asia, and Africa, over fierce and intractable nations: What may not the fleets and armies of Europe, with the access they have by commerce to every part of the world, and the facility of their conveyance, effect, if that ruinous maxim should prevail, That the grandeur of a nation is to be estimated from the extent of its territory; or, That the interest of any particular people consists in reducing their neighbours to servitude?

SECTION VI.
Of Civil Liberty.

If war, either for depredation or defence, were the principal object of nations, every tribe would, from its earliest state, aim at the condition of a Tartar horde; and in all its successes would hasten to the grandeur of a Tartar empire. The military leader would supersede the civil magistrate; and preparations to fly with all their possessions, or to pursue with all their forces, would, in every society, make the sum of their public arrangements.

He who first on the banks of the Wolga, or the Jenisca, had taught the Scythian to mount the horse, to move his cottage on wheels, to harass his enemy alike by his attacks and his flights, to handle at full speed the lance and the bow, and when beat from the field, to leave his arrows in the wind to meet his pursuer; he who had taught his countrymen to use the same animal for every purpose of the dairy, the shambles, and the field; would be esteemed the founder of his nation; or, like Ceres and Bacchus among the Greeks, would be invested with the honours of a god, as the reward of his useful inventions. Amidst such institutions, the names and atchievements of Hercules and Jason might have been transmitted to posterity; but those of Lycurgus or Solon, the heroes of political society, could have gained no reputation, either fabulous or real, in the records of fame.

Every tribe of warlike barbarians may entertain among themselves the strongest sentiments of affection and honour, while they

carry to the rest of mankind the aspect of banditti and robbers.*
They may be indifferent to interest, and superior to danger; but
our sense of humanity, our regard to the rights of nations, our
admiration of civil wisdom and justice, even our effeminacy
itself, make us turn away with contempt, or with horror, from
a scene which exhibits so few of our good qualities, and which
serve so much to reproach our weakness.

It is in conducting the affairs of civil society, that mankind
find the exercise of their best talents, as well as the object of
their best affections. It is in being grafted on the advantages of
civil society, that the art of war is brought to perfection; that
the resources of armies, and the complicated springs to be touched
in their conduct, are best understood. The most celebrated warriors were also citizens: opposed to a Roman, or a Greek, the
chieftain of Thrace, of Germany, or Gaul, was a novice. The
native of Pella learned the principles of his art from Epaminondas
and Pelopidas.

If nations, as hath been observed in the preceding section,
must adjust their policy on the prospect of war from abroad,
they are equally bound to provide for the attainment of peace at
home. But there is no peace in the absence of justice. It may
subsist with divisions, disputes, and contrary opinions; but not
with the commission of wrongs. The injurious, and the injured,
are, as implied in the very meaning of the terms, in a state of
hostility.

Where men enjoy peace, they owe it either to their mutual
regards and affections, or to the restraints of law. Those are the
happiest states which procure peace to their members by the first
of these methods: but it is sufficiently uncommon to procure it
even by the second. The first would with-hold the occasions of
war and of competition: the second adjusts the pretensions of
men by stipulations and treaties. Sparta taught her citizens not
to regard interest: other free nations secure the interest of
their members, and consider this as a principal part of their
rights.

Law is the treaty to which members of the same community

* D'Arvieux's *History of the Arabs.*

have agreed, and under which the magistrate and the subject continue to enjoy their rights, and to maintain the peace of society. The desire of lucre is the great motive to injuries: law therefore has a principal reference to property. It would ascertain the different methods by which property may be acquired, as by prescription, conveyance, and succession; and it makes the necessary provisions for rendering the possession of property secure.

Beside avarice, there are other motives from which men are unjust; such are pride, malice, envy, and revenge. The law would eradicate the principles themselves, or at least prevent their effects.

From whatever motive wrongs are committed, there are different particulars in which the injured may suffer. He may suffer in his goods, in his person, or in the freedom of his conduct. Nature has made him master of every action which is not injurious to others. The laws of his particular society intitle him perhaps to a determinate station, and bestow on him a certain share in the government of his country. An injury, therefore, which in this respect puts him under any unjust restraint, may be called an infringement of his political rights.

Where the citizen is supposed to have rights of property and of station, and is protected in the exercise of them, he is said to be free; and the very restraints by which he is hindered from the commission of crimes, are a part of his liberty. No person is free, where any person is suffered to do wrong with impunity. Even the despotic prince on his throne, is not an exception to this general rule. He himself is a slave, the moment he pretends that force should decide any contest. The disregard he throws on the rights of his people recoils on himself; and in the general uncertainty of all conditions, there is no tenure more precarious than his own.

From the different particulars to which men refer, in speaking of liberty, whether to the safety of the person and the goods, the dignity of rank, or the participation of political importance, as well as from the different methods by which their rights are secured, they are led to differ in the interpretation of the term;

and every people is apt to imagine, that its signification is to be found only among themselves.

Some having thought, that the unequal distribution of wealth is unjust, required a new division of property, as the foundation of freedom. This scheme is suited to democratical government; and in such only it has been admitted with any degree of effect.

New settlements, like that of the people of Israel, and singular establishments, like those of Sparta and Crete, have furnished examples of its actual execution; but in most other states, even the democratical spirit could attain no more than to prolong the struggle for Agrarian laws; to procure, on occasion, the expunging of debts; and to keep the people in mind, under all the distinctions of fortune, that they still had a claim to equality.

The citizen at Rome, at Athens, and in many republics, contended for himself, and his order. The Agrarian law was moved and debated for ages: it served to awaken the mind; it nourished the spirit of equality, and furnished a field on which to exert its force; but was never established with any of its other and more formal effects.

Many of the establishments which serve to defend the weak from oppression, contribute, by securing the possession of property, to favour its unequal division, and to increase the ascendant of those from whom the abuses of power may be feared. Those abuses were felt very early both at Athens and Rome.*

It has been proposed to prevent the excessive accumulation of wealth in particular hands, by limiting the increase of private fortunes, by prohibiting entails, and by with-holding the right of primogeniture in the succession of heirs. It has been proposed to prevent the ruin of moderate estates, and to restrain the use, and consequently the desire, of great ones, by sumptuary laws. These different methods are more or less consistent with the interests of commerce, and may be adopted, in different degrees, by a people whose national object is wealth: and they have their degree of effect, by inspiring moderation, or a sense of equality, and by stifling the passions by which mankind are prompted to mutual wrongs.

* Plutarch in the life of Solon.—Livy.

It appears to be, in a particular manner, the object of sumptuary laws, and of the equal division of wealth, to prevent the gratification of vanity, to check the ostentation of superior fortune, and, by this means, to weaken the desire of riches, and to preserve in the breast of the citizen, that moderation and equity which ought to regulate his conduct.

This end is never perfectly attained in any state where the unequal division of property is admitted, and where fortune is allowed to bestow distinction and rank. It is indeed difficult, by any methods whatever, to shut up this source of corruption. Of all the nations whose history is known with certainty, the design itself, and the manner of executing it, appear to have been understood in Sparta alone.

There property was indeed acknowledged by law; but in consequence of certain regulations and practices, the most effectual, it seems, that mankind have hitherto found out, the manners that prevail among simple nations before the establishment of property, were in some measure preserved*; the passion for riches was, during many ages, suppressed; and the citizen was made to consider himself as the property of his country, not as the owner of a private estate.

It was held ignominious either to buy or to sell the patrimony of a citizen. Slaves were, in every family, intrusted with the care of its effects, and freemen were strangers to lucrative arts; justice was established on a contempt of the ordinary allurement to crimes; and the preservatives of civil liberty applied by the state, were the dispositions that were made to prevail in the hearts of its members.

The individual was relieved from every solicitude that could arise on the head of his fortune; he was educated, and he was employed for life in the service of the public; he was fed at a place of common resort, to which he could carry no distinction but that of his talents and his virtues; his children were th: wards and the pupils of the state; he himself was taught to be a parent, and a director to the youth of his country, not the anxious father of a separate family.

* See part 2, sect. 2.

This people, we are told, bestowed some care in adorning their persons, and were known from afar by the red or the purple they wore; but could not make their equipage, their buildings, or their furniture, a subject of fancy, or of what we call *taste*. The carpenter and the house-builder were restricted to the use of the axe and the saw: their workmanship must have been simple, and probably, in respect to its form, continued for ages the same. The ingenuity of the artist was employed in cultivating his own nature, not in adorning the habitations of his fellow-citizens.

On this plan, they had senators, magistrates, leaders of armies, and ministers of state; but no men of fortune. Like the heroes of Homer, they distributed honours by the measure of the cup and the platter. A citizen, who, in his political capacity, was the arbiter of Greece, thought himself honoured by receiving a double portion of plain entertainment at supper. He was active, penetrating, brave, disinterested, and generous; but his estate, his table, and his furniture, might, in our esteem, have marred the lustre of all his virtues. Neighbouring nations, however, applied for commanders to this nursery of statesmen and warriors, as we apply for the practitioners of every art to the countries in which they excel; for cooks to France, and for musicians to Italy.

After all, we are, perhaps, not sufficiently instructed in the nature of the Spartan laws and institutions, to understand in what manner all the ends of this singular state were obtained; but the admiration paid to its people, and the constant reference of contemporary historians to their avowed superiority, will not allow us to question the facts. 'When I observed,' says Xenophon, 'that this nation, though not the most populous, was the most powerful state of Greece, I was seized with wonder, and with an earnest desire to know by what arts it attained its pre-eminence; but when I came to the knowledge of its institutions, my wonder ceased.—As one man excels another, and as he who is at pains to cultivate his mind, must surpass the person who neglects it; so the Spartans should excel every nation, being the only state in which virtue is studied as the object of government.'

The subjects of property, considered with a view to subsistence, or even to enjoyment, have little effect in corrupting mankind, or in awakening the spirit of competition and of jealousy; but considered with a view to distinction and honour, where fortune constitutes rank, they excite the most vehement passions, and absorb all the sentiments of the human soul: they reconcile avarice and meanness with ambition and vanity; and lead men through the practice of sordid and mercenary arts to the possession of a supposed elevation and dignity.

Where this source of corruption, on the contrary, is effectually stopped, the citizen is dutiful, and the magistrate upright; any form of government may be wisely administered; places of trust are likely to be well supplied; and by whatever rule office and power are bestowed, it is likely that all the capacity and force that subsists in the state will come to be employed in its service: for on this supposition, experience and abilities are the only guides and the only titles to public confidence; and if citizens be ranged into separate classes, they become mutual checks by the difference of their opinions, not by the opposition of their interested designs.

We may easily account for the censures bestowed on the government of Sparta, by those who considered it merely on the side of its forms. It was not calculated to prevent the practice of crimes, by balancing against each other the selfish and partial dispositions of men; but to inspire the virtues of the soul, to procure innocence by the absence of criminal inclinations, and to derive its internal peace from the indifference of its members to the ordinary motives of strife and disorder. It were trifling to seek for its analogy to any other constitution of state, in which its principal characteristic and distinguishing feature is not to be found. The collegiate sovereignty, the senate, and the ephori, had their counterparts in other republics, and a resemblance has been found in particular to the government of Carthage*: but what affinity of consequence can be found between a state whose sole object was virtue, and another whose principal object was wealth; between a people whose associated kings, being lodged in the same cottage, had no fortune but their daily food; and a

* Aristotle.

commercial republic, in which a proper estate was required as a necessary qualification for the higher offices of state?

Other petty commonwealths expelled kings, when they became jealous of their designs, or after having experienced their tyranny; here the hereditary succession of kings was preserved: other states were afraid of the intrigues and cabals of their members in competition for dignities; here solicitation was required as the only condition upon which a place in the senate was obtained. A supreme inquisitorial power was, in the persons of the ephori, safely committed to a few men, who were drawn by lot, and without distinction, from every order of the people: and if a contrast to this, as well as to many other articles of the Spartan policy, be required, it may be found in the general history of mankind.

But Sparta, under every supposed error of its form, prospered for ages, by the integrity of its manners, and by the character of its citizens. When that integrity was broken, this people did not languish in the weakness of nations sunk in effeminacy. They fell into the stream by which other states had been carried in the torrent of violent passions, and in the outrage of barbarous times. They ran the career of other nations, after that of ancient Sparta was finished: they built walls, and began to improve their possessions, after they ceased to improve their people; and on this new plan, in their struggle for political life, they survived the system of states that perished under the Macedonian dominion: they lived to act with another which arose in the Achaean league; and were the last community of Greece that became a village in the empire of Rome.

If it should be thought we have dwelt too long on the history of this singular people, it may be remembered, in excuse, that they alone, in the language of Xenophon, made virtue an object of state.

We must be contented to derive our freedom from a different source; to expect justice from the limits which are set to the powers of the magistrate, and to rely for protection on the laws which are made to secure the estate, and the person of the subject. We live in societies, where men must be rich, in order to be great; where pleasure itself is often pursued from vanity; where the desire of a supposed happiness serves to inflame the worst of passions, and is itself the foundation of misery; where public justice, like fetters applied to the body, may, without inspiring the sentiments of candour and equity, prevent the actual commission of crimes.

Mankind come under this description the moment they are seized with their passions for riches and power. But their description in every instance is mixed: in the best there is an alloy of evil; in the worst a mixture of good. Without any establishments to preserve their manners, besides penal laws, and the restraints of police, they derive, from instinctive feelings, a love of integrity and candour, and, from the very contagion of society itself, an esteem for what is honourable and praise-worthy. They derive, from their union, and joint opposition to foreign enemies, a zeal for their own community, and courage to maintain its rights. If the frequent neglect of virtue as a political object, tend to discredit the understandings of men, its lustre, and its frequency, as a spontaneous offspring of the heart, will restore the honours of our nature.

In every casual and mixed state of the national manners, the safety of every individual, and his political consequence, depends much on himself, but more on the party to which he is joined. For this reason, all who feel a common interest, are apt to unite in parties; and, as far as that interest requires, mutually support each other.

Where the citizens of any free community are of different orders, each order has a peculiar set of claims and pretensions: relatively to the other members of the state, it is a party; relatively to the differences of interest among its own members, it may admit of numberless subdivisions. But in every state there are two interests very readily apprehended; that of a prince and his adherents, that of a nobility, or of any temporary faction, opposed to the people.

Where the sovereign power is reserved by the collective body, it appears unnecessary to think of additional establishments for securing the rights of the citizen, But it is difficult, if not impossible, for the collective body to exercise this power in a manner that supersedes the necessity of every other political caution.

If popular assemblies assume every function of government; and if, in the same tumultuous manner in which they can, with great propriety, express their feelings, the sense of their rights, and their animosity to foreign or domestic enemies, they pretend to deliberate on points of national conduct, or to decide questions of equity and justice; the public is exposed to manifold inconveniencies; and popular governments would, of all others, be the most subject to errors in administration, and to weakness in the execution of public measures.

To avoid these disadvantages, the people are always contented to delegate part of their powers. They establish a senate to debate, and to prepare, if not to determine, questions that are brought to the collective body for a final resolution. They commit the executive power to some council of this sort, or to a magistrate who presides in their meetings. Under the use of this necessary and common expedient, even while democratical forms are most carefully guarded, there is one party of the few, another of the many. One attacks, the other defends; and they are both ready to assume in their turns. But though, in reality, a great danger to liberty arises on the part of the people themselves, who, in times of corruption, are easily made the instruments of usurpation and tyranny; yet, in the ordinary aspect of government, the executive carries an air of superiority, and the rights of the people seem always exposed to incroachment.

Though on the day that the Roman people assembled in their tribes, the senators mixed with the croud, and the consul was no more than the servant of the multitude; yet, when this awful meeting was dissolved, the senators met to prescribe business for their sovereign, and the consul went armed with the axe and the rods, to teach every Roman, in his separate capacity, the submission which he owed to the state.

Thus, even where the collective body is sovereign, they are assembled only occasionally: and though on such occasions they determine every question relative to their rights and their interests as a people, and can assert their freedom with irresistible force;

yet they do not think themselves, nor are they in reality, safe, without a more constant and more uniform power operating in their favour.

The multitude is every where strong; but requires, for the safety of its members, when separate as well as when assembled, a head to direct and to employ its strength. For this purpose, the ephori, we are told, were established at Sparta, the council of a hundred at Carthage, and the tribunes at Rome. So prepared, the popular party has, in many instances, been able to cope with its adversaries, and has even trampled on the powers, whether aristocratical or monarchical, with which it would have been otherwise unequally matched. The state, in such cases, commonly suffered by the delays, interruptions, and confusions, which popular leaders, from private envy, or a prevailing jealousy of the great, seldom failed to create in the proceedings of government.

Where the people, as in some larger communities, have only a share in the legislature, they cannot overwhelm the collateral powers, who having likewise a share, are in condition to defend themselves: where they act only by their representatives, their force may be uniformly employed. And they may make part in a constitution of government more lasting than any of those in which the people possessing or pretending to the entire legislature, are, when assembled, the tyrants, and, when dispersed, the slaves, of a distempered state. In governments properly mixed, the popular interest, finding a counterpoise in that of the prince or of the nobles, a balance is actually established between them, in which the public freedom and the public order are made to consist.

From some such casual arrangement of different interests, all the varieties of mixed government proceed; and on the degree of consideration which every separate interest can procure to itself, depends the equity of the laws they enact, and the necessity they are able to impose, of adhering strictly to the terms of law in its execution. States are accordingly unequally qualified to conduct the business of legislation, and unequally fortunate in the completeness, and regular observance, of their civil code.

In democratical establishments, citizens, feeling themselves possessed of the sovereignty, are not equally anxious, with the subject of other governments, to have their rights explained, or secured, by actual statute. They trust to personal vigour, to the support of party, and to the sense of the public.

If the collective body perform the office of judge, as well as of legislator, they seldom think of devising rules for their own direction, and are found more seldom to follow any determinate rule, after it is made. They dispense, at one time, with what they enacted at another; and in their judicative, perhaps even more than in their legislative, capacity, are guided by passions and partialities that arise from circumstances of the case before them.

But under the simplest governments of a different sort, whether aristocracy or monarchy, there is a necessity for law, and there are a variety of interests to be adjusted in framing every statute. The sovereign wishes to give stability and order to administration, by express and promulgated rules. The subject wishes to know the conditions and limits of his duty. He acquiesces, or he revolts, according as the terms on which he is made to live with the sovereign, or with his fellow-subjects, are, or are not, consistent with the sense of his rights.

Neither the monarch, nor the council of nobles, where either is possessed of the sovereignty, can pretend to govern, or to judge at discretion. No magistrate, whether temporary or hereditary, can with safety neglect that reputation for justice and equity, from which his authority, and the respect that is paid to his person, are in a great measure derived. Nations, however, have been fortunate in the tenor, and in the execution of their laws, in proportion as they have admitted every order of the people, by representation or otherwise, to an actual share of the legislature. Under establishments of this sort, law is literally a treaty, to which the parties concerned have agreed, and have given their opinion in settling its terms. The interests to be affected by a law, are likewise consulted in making it. Every class propounds an objection, suggests an addition or an amendment of its own. They proceed to adjust, by stature, every subject of controversy: and while they continue to enjoy their freedom, they continue to multiply laws, and to accumulate volumes, as if they could remove every possible ground of dispute, and were secure of their rights, merely by having put them in writing.

Rome and England, under their mixed governments, the one inclining to democracy, the other to monarchy, have proved the great legislators among nations. The first has left the foundation, and great part of the superstructure of its civil code, to the continent of Europe: the other, in its island, has carried the authority and government of law to a point of perfection, which they never before attained in the history of mankind.

Under such favourable establishments, known customs, the practice and decisions of courts, as well as positive statutes, acquire the authority of laws; and every proceeding is conducted by some fixed and determinate rule. The best and most effectual precautions are taken for the impartial application of rules to particular cases; and it is remarkable, that, in the two examples we have mentioned, a surprising coincidence is found in the singular methods of their jurisdiction. The people in both reserved in a manner the office of judgement to themselves, and brought the decision of civil rights, or of criminal questions, to the tribunal of peers, who, in judging of their fellow-citizens, prescribed a condition of life for themselves.

It is not in mere laws, after all, that we are to look for the securities to justice, but in the powers by which those laws have been obtained, and without whose constant support they must fall to disuse. Statutes serve to record the rights of a people, and speak the intention of parties to defend what the letter of the law has expressed: but without the vigour to maintain what is acknowledged as a right, the mere record, or the feeble intention, is of little avail.

A populace roused by oppression, or an order of men possessed of a temporary advantage, have obtained many charters, concessions, and stipulations, in favour of their claims; but where no adequate preparation was made to preserve them, the written articles were often forgotten, together with the occasion on which they were framed.

The history of England, and of every free country, abounds with the example of statutes enacted when the people or their representatives assembled, but never executed when the crown or the executive was left to itself. The most equitable laws on paper are consistent with the utmost despotism in administration, Even the form of trial by juries in England had its authority in law, while the proceedings of courts were arbitrary and oppressive.

We must admire, as the key-stone of civil liberty, the statute which forces the secrets of every prison to be revealed, the cause of every commitment to be declared, and the person of the accused to be produced, that he may claim his enlargement, or his trial, within a limited time. No wiser form was ever opposed to the abuses of power. But it requires a fabric no less than the whole political constitution of Great Britain, a spirit no less than the refractory and turbulent zeal of this fortunate people, to secure its effects.

If even the safety of the person, and the tenure of property, which may be so well defined in the words of a statute, depend, for their preservation, on the vigour and jealousy of a free people, and on the degree of consideration which every order of the state maintains for itself; it is still more evident, that what we have called the political freedom, or the right of the individual to act in his station for himself and the public, cannot be made to rest on any other foundation. The estate may be saved, and the person released, by the forms of a civil procedure; but the rights of the mind cannot be sustained by any other force but its own.

SECTION VII.
Of the History of Arts.

We have already observed, that art is natural to man; and that the skill he acquires after many ages of practice, is only the improvement of a talent he possessed at the first. Vitruvius finds the rudiments of architecture in the form of a Scythian cottage. The armourer may find the first productions of his calling in the sling and the bow; and the ship-wright of his in the canoe of the savage. Even the historian and the poet may find the original essays of their arts in the tale, and the song, which celebrate the wars, the loves, and the adventures of men in their rudest condition.

Destined to cultivate his own nature, or to mend his situation, man finds a continued subject of attention, ingenuity, and labour. Even where he does not propose any personal improvement, his faculties are strengthened by those very exercises in which he seems to forget himself: his reason and his affections are thus profitably engaged in the affairs of society; his invention and his skill are exercised in procuring his accommodations and his food; his particular pursuits are prescribed to him by circumstances of the age and of the country in which he lives: in one situation he is occupied with wars and political deliberations; in another, with the care of his interest, of his personal ease, or conveniency. He suits his means to the ends he has in view; and, by multiplying contrivances, proceeds, by degrees, to the perfection of his arts. In every step of his progress, if his skill be increased, his desire must likewise have time to extend: and it would be as vain to suggest a contrivance of which he slighted the use, as it would be to tell him of blessings which he could not command.

Ages are generally supposed to have borrowed from those who went before them, and nations to have derived their portion of learning or of art from abroad. The Romans are thought to have learned from the Greeks, and the moderns of Europe from both. In this imagination we frequently proceed so far as to admit of nothing original in the practice or manners of any people. The Greek was a copy of the Egyptian, and even the Egyptian was an imitator, though we have lost sight of the model on which he was formed.

It is known, that men improve by example and intercourse; but in the case of nations, whose members excite and direct each other, why seek from abroad the origin of arts, of which every society, having the principles in itself, only requires a favourable occasion to bring them to light? When such occasion presents itself to any people, they generally seize it; and while it continues, they improve the inventions to which it gave rise among themselves, or they willingly copy from others: but they never employ their own invention, nor look abroad, for instruction on subjects that do not lie in the way of their common pursuits; they never adopt a refinement of which they have not discovered the use.

Inventions, we frequently observe, are accidental; but it is probable, that an accident which escapes the artist in one age, may be seized by one who succeeds him, and who is better apprised of its use. Where circumstances are favourable, and where a people is intent on the objects of any art, every invention is preserved, by being brought into general practice; every model is studied, and every accident is turned to account. If nations actually borrow from their neighbours, they probably borrow only what they are nearly in a condition to have invented themselves.

Any singular practice of one country, therefore, is seldom transferred to another, till the way be prepared by the introduction of similar circumstances. Hence our frequent complaints of the dullness or obstinacy of mankind, and of the dilatory communication of arts, from one place to another. While the Romans adopted the arts of Greece, the Thracians and Illyrians continued to behold them with indifference. Those arts were, during one period, confined to the Greek colonies, and during another, to the Roman. Even where they were spread by a visible intercourse, they were still received by independent nations with the slowness of invention. They made a progress not more rapid at Rome than they had done at Athens; and they passed to the extremities of the Roman empire, only in company with new colonies, and joined to Italian policy.

The modern race, who came abroad to the possession of cultivated provinces, retained the arts they had practised at home: the new master hunted the boar, or pastured his herds, where he might have raised a plentiful harvest: he built a cottage in the view of a palace: he buried, in one common ruin, the edifices, sculptures, paintings, and libraries, of the former inhabitant: he made a settlement upon a plan of his own, and opened anew the source of inventions, without perceiving from a distance to what length their progress might lead his posterity. The cottage of the present race, like that of the former, by degrees enlarged its dimensions; public buildings acquired a magnificence in a new taste. Even this taste came, in a course of ages, to be exploded, and the people of Europe recurred to the models which their fathers destroyed, and wept over the ruins which they could not restore.

The literary remains of antiquity were studied and imitated, after the original genius of modern nations had broke forth: the rude efforts of poetry in Italy and Provence, resembled those of the Greeks and the ancient Romans. How far the merit of our works might, without the aid of their models, have risen by successive improvements, or whether we have gained more by imitation than we have lost by quitting our native system of thinking, and our vein of fable, must be left to conjecture. We are certainly indebted to them for the materials, as well as the form, of many of our compositions; and without their example, the strain of our literature, together with that of our manners and policy, would have been different from what they at present are. This much however may be said with assurance, that although the Roman and the modern literature savour alike of the Greek original, yet mankind in either instance would not have drank of this fountain, unless they had been hastening to open springs of their own.

Sentiment and fancy, the use of the hand or the head, are not inventions of particular men; and the flourishing of arts that depend on them, are, in the case of any people, a proof rather of political felicity at home, than of any instruction received from abroad, or of any natural superiority in point of industry or talents.

When the attentions of men are turned toward particular subjects, when the acquisitions of one age are left entire to the next, when every individual is protected in his place, and left to pursue the suggestion of his wants, devices accumulate; and it is difficult to find the original of any art. The steps which lead to perfection are many; and we are at a loss on whom to bestow the greatest share of our praise; on the first or on the last who may have bore a part in the progress.

SECTION VIII.

Of the History of Literature.

If we may rely on the general observations contained in the last section, the literary, as well as mechanical arts, being a natural produce of the human mind, will rise spontaneously where-ever men are happily placed; and in certain nations it is not more necessary to look abroad for the origin of literature, than it is for the suggestion of any of the pleasures or exercises in which mankind, under a state of prosperity and freedom, are sufficiently inclined to indulge themselves.

We are apt to consider arts as foreign and adventitious to the nature of man: but there is no art that did not find its occasion in human life, and that was not, in some one or other of the situations in which our species is found, suggested as a means for the attainment of some useful end. The mechanic and commercial arts took their rise from the love of property, and were encouraged by the prospects of safety and of gain: the literary and liberal arts took their rise from the understanding, the fancy, and the heart. They are mere exercises of the mind in search of its peculiar pleasures and occupations; and are promoted by circumstances that suffer the mind to enjoy itself.

Men are equally engaged by the past, the present, and the future, and are prepared for every occupation that gives scope to their powers. Productions therefore, whether of narration, fiction, or reasoning, that tend to employ the imagination, or move the heart, continue for ages a subject of attention, and a source of delight. The memory of human transactions being preserved in tradition or writing, is the natural gratification of a passion that consists of curiosity, admiration, and the love of amusement.

Before many books are written, and before science is greatly advanced, the productions of mere genius are sometimes complete: the performer requires not the aid of learning where his description or story relates to near and contiguous objects; where it relates to the conduct and characters of men with whom he himself has acted, and in whose occupations and fortunes he himself has borne a part.

With this advantage, the poet is the first to offer the fruits of his genius, and to lead in the career of those arts by which the mind is destined to exhibit its imaginations, and to express its passions. Every tribe of barbarians have their passionate or historic rhymes, which contain the superstition, the enthusiasm, and the admiration of glory, with which the breasts of men, in the earliest state of society, are possessed. They delight in verse-compositions, either because the cadence of numbers is natural to the language of sentiment, or because, not having the advantage of writing, they are obliged to bring the ear in aid of the memory, in order to facilitate the repetition, and insure the preservation of their works.

When we attend to the language which savages employ on any solemn occasion, it appears that man is a poet by nature. Whether at first obliged by the mere defects of his tongue, and the scantiness of proper expressions, or seduced by a pleasure of the fancy in stating the analogy of its objects, he clothes every conception in image and metaphor. 'We have planted the tree of peace,' says an American orator; 'we have buried the axe under its roots: we will henceforth repose under its shade; we will join to brighten the chain that binds our nations together.' Such are the collections of metaphor which those nations employ in their public harangues. They have likewise already adopted those lively figures, and that daring freedom of language, which the learned have afterwards found so well fitted to express the rapid transitions of the imagination, and the ardours of a passionate mind.

If we are required to explain, how men could be poets, or orators, before they were aided by the learning of the scholar and the critic? we may inquire, in our turn, how bodies could fall by their weight, before the laws of gravitation were recorded in books? Mind, as well as body, has laws, which are exemplified in the practice of men, and which the critic collects only after the example has shewn what they are.

Occasioned, probably, by the physical connection we have mentioned, between the emotions of a heated imagination, and the impressions received from music and pathetic sounds, every tale among rude nations is repeated in verse, and is made to take the form of a song The early history of all nations is uniform in this particular. Priests, statesmen, and philosophers, in the first ages of Greece, delivered their instructions in poetry, and mixed with the dealers in music and heroic fable.

It is not so surprising, however, that poetry should be the first species of composition in every nation, as it is, that a style apparently so difficult, and so far removed from ordinary use, should be almost as universally the first to attain its maturity. The most admired of all poets lived beyond the reach of history, almost of tradition. The artless song of the savage, the heroic legend of the bard, have sometimes a magnificent beauty, which no change of language can improve, and no refinements of the critic reform.

Under the supposed disadvantage of a limited knowledge, and a rude apprehension, the simple poet has impressions that more than compensate the defects of his skill. The best subjects of poetry, the characters of the violent and the brave, the generous and the intrepid, great dangers, trials of fortitude and fidelity, are exhibited within his view, or are delivered in traditions which animate like truth, because they are equally believed. He is not engaged in recalling, like Virgil or Tasso, the sentiments or scenery of an age remote from his own: he needs not be told by the critic,* to recollect what another would have thought, or in what manner another would have expressed his conception. The simple passions, friendship, resentment, and love, are the movements of his own mind, and he has no occasion to copy. Simple and vehement in his conceptions and feelings, he knows no diversity of thought, or of style, to mislead or to exercise his judgement. He delivers the emotions of the heart, in words suggested by the heart: for he knows no other. And hence it is, that while we admire the judgement and invention of Virgil, and of other later poets, these terms appear misapplied to Homer.

* See Longinus.

Though intelligent, as well as sublime, in his conceptions, we cannot anticipate the lights of his understanding, nor the movements of his heart: he appears to speak from inspiration, not from invention; and to be guided in the choice of his thoughts and expressions by a supernatural instinct, not by reflection.

The language of early ages, is in one respect, simple and confined; in another, it is varied and free: it allows liberties, which, to the poet of after times, are denied.

In rude ages men are not separated by distinctions of rank or profession. They live in one manner, and speak one dialect. The bard is not to chuse his expression among the singular accents of different conditions. He has not to guard his language from the peculiar errors of the mechanic, the peasant, the scholar, or the courtier, in order to find that elegant propriety, and just elevation, which is free from the vulgar of one class, the pedantic of the second, or the flippant of the third. The name of every object, and of every sentiment, is fixed; and if his conception has the dignity of nature, his expression will have a purity which does not depend on his choice.

With this apparent confinement in the choice of his words, he is at liberty to break through the ordinary modes of construction; and in the form of a language not established by rules, may find for himself a cadence agreeable to the tone of his mind. The liberty he takes, while his meaning is striking, and his language is raised, appears an improvement, not a trespass on grammar. He delivers a style to the ages that follow, and becomes a model from which his posterity judge.

But whatever may be the early disposition of mankind to poetry, or the advantage they possess in cultivating this species of literature; whether the early maturity of poetical compositions arise from their being the first studied, or from their having a charm to engage persons of the liveliest genius, who are best qualified to improve the eloquence of their native tongue; it is a remarkable fact, that, not only in countries where every vein of composition was original, and was opened in the order of natural succession; but even at Rome, and in modern Europe, where the learned began early to practise on foreign models, we have poets of every nation, who are perused with pleasure, while the prose writers of the same ages are neglected.

As Sophocles and Euripides preceded the historians and moralists of Greece, not only Naevius and Ennius, who wrote the Roman history in verse, but Lucilius, Plautus, Terence, and we may add Lucretius, were prior to Cicero, Sallust, or Caesar. Dante and Petrarch went before any good prose writer in Italy; Corneille and Racine brought on the fine age of prose compositions in France; and we had in England, not only Chaucer and Spenser, but Shakespear and Milton, while our attempts in history or science were yet in their infancy; and deserve our attention, only for the sake of the matter they treat.

Hillanicus, who is reckoned among the first prose writers in Greece, and who immediately preceded, or was the contemporary of Herodotus, set out with declaring his intention to remove from history the wild representations, and extravagant fictions, with which it had been disgraced by the poets*. The want of records or authorities, relating to any distant transactions, may have hindered him, as it did his immediate successor, from giving truth all the advantage it might have reaped from this transition to prose. There are, however, ages in the progress of society, when such a proposition must be favourably received. When men become occupied on the subjects of policy, or commercial arts, they wish to be informed and instructed, as well as moved. They are interested by what was real in past transactions. They build on this foundation, the reflections and reasonings they apply to present affairs, and wish to receive information on the subject of different pursuits, and of projects in which they begin to be engaged. The manners of men, the practice of ordinary life, and the form of society, furnish their subjects to the moral and political writer. Mere ingenuity, justness of sentiment, and correct representation, though conveyed in ordinary language, are understood to constitute literary merit, and by applying to reason more than to the imagination and passions, meet with a reception that is due to the instruction they bring.

The talents of men come to be employed in a variety of affairs,

* Quoted by Demetrius Phalerius.

and their inquiries directed to different subjects. Knowledge is important in every department of civil society, and requisite to the practice of every art. The science of nature, morals, politics, and history, find their several admirers; and even poetry itself, which retains its former station in the region of warm imagination and enthusiastic passion, appears in a growing variety of forms.

Matters have proceeded so far, without the aid of foreign examples, or the direction of schools. The cart of Thespis was changed into a theatre, not to gratify the learned, but to please the Athenian populace: and the prize of poetical merit was decided by this populace equally before and after the invention of rules. The Greeks were unacquainted with every language but their own; and if they became learned, it was only by studying what they themselves had produced: the childish mythology, which they are said to have copied from Asia, was equally of little avail in promoting their love of arts, or their success in the practice of them.

When the historian is struck with the events he has witnessed, or heard; when he is excited to relate them by his reflections or his passions; when the statesman, who is required to speak in public, is obliged to prepare for every remarkable appearance in studied harangues; when conversation becomes extensive and refined; and when the social feelings and reflections of men are committed to writing, a system of learning may arise from the bustle of an active life. Society itself is the school, and its lessons are delivered in the practice of real affairs. An author writes from observations he has made on his subject, not from the suggestion of books; and every production carries the mark of his character as a man, not of his mere proficiency as a student or scholar. It may be made a question, whether the trouble of seeking for distant models, and of wading for instruction, through dark allusions and languages unknown, might not have quenched his fire, and rendered him a writer of a very inferior class.

If society may thus be considered as a school for letters, it is probable that its lessons are varied in every separate state, and in every age. For a certain period, the severe applications of the Roman people to policy and war suppressed the literary arts, and appear to have stifled the genius even of the historian and the poet. The institutions of Sparta gave a professed contempt for whatever was not connected with the practical virtues of a vigorous and resolute spirit: the charms of imagination, and the parade of language, were by this people classed with the arts of the cook and the perfumer: their songs in praise of fortitude are mentioned by some writers; and collections of their witty sayings and repartees are still preserved: they indicate the virtues and the abilities of an active people, not their proficiency in science or literary taste. Possessed of what was essential to happiness in the virtues of the heart, they had a discernment of its value, unimbarrassed by the numberless objects on which mankind in general are so much at a loss to adjust their esteem: fixed in their own apprehension, they turned a sharp edge on the follies of mankind. 'When will you begin to practise it?' was the question of a Spartan to a person who, in an advanced age of life, was still occupied with questions on the nature of virtue.

While this people confined their studies to one question, How to improve and to preserve the courage and the disinterested affections of the human heart? their rivals the Athenians gave a scope to refinement on every object of reflection or passion. By the rewards, either of profit or of reputation, which they bestowed on every effort of ingenuity employed in ministering to the pleasure, the decoration, or the conveniency of life; by the variety of conditions in which their citizens were placed; by their inequalities of fortune, and their several pursuits in war, politics, commerce, and lucrative arts, they awakened whatever was either good or bad in the natural dispositions of men. Every road to eminence was opened: eloquence, fortitude, military skill, envy, detraction, faction, and treason, even the muse herself, was courted to bestow importance among a busy, acute, and turbulent people.

From this example, we may safely conclude, that although business is sometimes a rival to study, retirement and leisure are not the principal requisites to the improvement, perhaps not even to the exercise, of literary talents. The most striking exertions of imagination and sentiment have a reference to mankind:

they are excited by the presence and intercourse of men: they have most vigour when actuated in the mind by the operation of its principal springs, by the emulations, the friendships, and the oppositions, which subsist among a forward and aspiring people. Amidst the great occasions which put a free, and even a licentious, society in motion, its members become capable of every exertion; and the same scenes which gave employment to Themistocles and Thrasybulus, inspired, by contagion, the genius of Sophocles and Plato. The petulant and the ingenuous find an equal scope to their talents; and literary monuments become the repositories of envy and folly, as well as of wisdom and virtue.

Greece, divided into many little states, and agitated, beyond any spot on the globe, by domestic contentions and foreign wars, set the example in every species of literature. The fire was communicated to Rome; not when the state ceased to be warlike, and had discontinued her political agitations, but when she mixed the love of refinement and of pleasure with her national pursuits, and indulged an inclination to study in the midst of ferments, occasioned by the wars and pretensions of opposite factions. It was revived in modern Europe among the turbulent states of Italy, and spread to the North, together with the spirit which shook the fabric of the Gothic policy: it rose while men were divided into parties, under civil or religious denominations, and when they were at variance on subjects held the most important and sacred.

We may be satisfied, from the example of many ages, that liberal endowments bestowed on learned societies, and the leisure with which they were furnished for study, are not the likeliest means to excite the exertions of genius: even science itself, the supposed offspring of leisure, pined in the shade of monastic retirement. Men at a distance from the objects of useful knowledge, untouched by the motives that animate an active and a vigorous mind, could produce only the jargon of a technical language, and accumulate the impertinence of academical forms.

To speak or to write justly from an observation of nature, it is necessary to have felt the sentiments of nature. He who is penetrating and ardent in the conduct of life, will probably exert a proportional force and ingenuity in the exercise of his literary talents: and although writing may become a trade, and require all the application and study which are bestowed on any other calling; yet the principal requisites in this calling are, the spirit and sensibility of a vigorous mind.

In one period, the school may take its light and direction from active life; in another, it is true, the remains of an active spirit are greatly supported by literary monuments, and by the history of transactions that preserve the examples and the experience of former and of better times. But in whatever manner men are formed for great efforts of elocution or conduct, it appears the most glaring of all other deceptions, to look for the accomplishments of a human character in the mere attainments of speculation, whilst we neglect the qualities of fortitude and public affection, which are so necessary to render our knowledge an article of happiness or of use.

PART FOURTH.

Of Consequences that result from the Advancement of Civil and Commercial Arts.

SECTION I.

Of the Separation of Arts and Professions.

It is evident, that, however urged by a sense of necessity, and a desire of convenience, or favoured by any advantages of situation and policy, a people can make no great progress in cultivating the arts of life, until they have separated, and committed to different persons, the several tasks, which require a peculiar skill and attention. The savage, or the barbarian, who must build and plant, and fabricate for himself, prefers, in the interval of great alarms and fatigues, the enjoyments of sloth to the improvement of his fortune: he is, perhaps, by the diversity of his wants, discouraged from industry; or, by his divided attention, prevented from acquiring skill in the management of any particular subject.

The enjoyment of peace, however, and the prospect of being able to exchange one commodity for another, turns, by degrees, the hunter and the warrior into a tradesman and a merchant. The accidents which distribute the means of subsistence unequally, inclination, and favourable opportunities, assign the different occupations of men; and a sense of utility leads them, without end, to subdivide their professions.

The artist finds, that the more he can confine his attention to a particular part of any work, his productions are the more perfect, and grow under his hands in the greater quantities. Every undertaker in manufacture finds, that the more he can subdivide the tasks of his workmen, and the more hands he can employ on separate articles, the more are his expences diminished, and his profits increased. The consumer too requires, in every kind of commodity, a workmanship more perfect than hands employed on a variety of subjects can produce; and the progress of commerce is but a continued subdivision of the mechanical arts.

Every craft may ingross the whole of a man's attention, and has a mystery which must be studied or learned by a regular apprenticeship. Nations of tradesmen come to consist of members who, beyond their own particular trade, are ignorant of all human affairs, and who may contribute to the preservation and enlargement of their commonwealth, without making its interest an object of their regard or attention. Every individual is distinguished by his calling, and has a place to which he is fitted. The savage, who knows no distinction but that of his merit, of his sex, or of his species, and to whom his community is the sovereign object of affection, is astonished to find, that in a scene of this nature, his being a man does not qualify him for any station whatever: he flies to the woods with amazement, distaste, and aversion.

By the separation of arts and professions, the sources of wealth are laid open; every species of material is wrought up to the greatest perfection, and every commodity is produced in the greatest abundance. The state may estimate its profits and its revenues by the number of its people. It may procure, by its treasure, that national consideration and power, which the savage maintains at the expence of his blood.

The advantage gained in the inferior branches of manufacture by the separation of their parts, seem to be equalled by those which arise from a similar device in the higher departments of policy and war. The soldier is relieved from every care but that of his service; statesmen divide the business of civil government into shares; and the servants of the public, in every office, without being skilful in the affairs of state, may succeed, by observing forms which are already established on the experience of others. They are made, like the parts of an engine, to concur to a purpose, without any concert of their own: and, equally blind with the trader to any general combination, they unite with him, in furnishing to the state its resources, its conduct, and its force.

The artifices of the beaver, the ant, and the bee, are ascribed to the wisdom of nature. Those of polished nations are ascribed to themselves, and are supposed to indicate a capacity superior to that of rude minds. But the establishments of men, like those of every animal, are suggested by nature, and are the result of instinct, directed by the variety of situations in which mankind are placed. Those establishments arose from successive improvements that were made, without any sense of their general effect; and they bring human affairs to a state of complication, which the greatest reach of capacity with which human nature was ever adorned, could not have projected; nor even when the whole is carried into execution, can it be comprehended in its full extent.

Who could anticipate, or even enumerate, the separate occupations and professions by which the members of any commercial state are distinguished; the variety of devices which are practised in separate cells, and which the artist, attentive to his own affair, has invented, to abridge or to facilitate his separate task? In coming to this mighty end, every generation, compared to its predecessors, may have appeared to be ingenious; compared to its followers, may have appeared to be dull: and human ingenuity, whatever heights it may have gained in a succession of ages, continues to move with an equal pace, and to creep in making the last as well as the first step of commercial or civil improvement.

It may even be doubted, whether the measure of national capacity increases with the advancement of arts. Many mechanical arts, indeed, require no capacity; they succeed best under a total suppression of sentiment and reason; and ignorance is the mother of industry as well as of superstition. Reflection and fancy are subject to err; but a habit of moving the hand, or the foot, is independent of either. Manufactures, accordingly, prosper most, where the mind is least consulted, and where the workshop may, without any great effort of imagination, be considered as an engine, the parts of which are men.

The forest has been felled by the savage without the use of the axe, and weights have been raised without the aid of the mechanical powers. The merit of the inventor, in every branch, probably deserves a preference to that of the performer; and he who invented a tool, or could work without its assistance, deserved the praise of ingenuity in a much higher degree than the mere artist, who, by its assistance, produced a superior work.

But if many parts in the practice of every art, and in the detail of every department, require no abilities, or actually tend to contract and to limit the views of the mind, there are others which lead to general reflections, and to enlargement of thought. Even in manufacture, the genius of the master, perhaps, is cultivated, while that of the inferior workman lies waste. The statesman may have a wide comprehension of human affairs, while the tools he employs are ignorant of the system in which they are themselves combined. The general officer may be a great proficient in the knowledge of war, while the soldier is confined to a few motions of the hand and the foot. The former may have gained, what the latter has lost; and being occupied in the conduct of disciplined armies, may practise on a larger scale, all the arts of preservation, of deception, and of stratagem, which the savage exerts in leading a small party, or merely in defending himself.

The practitioner of every art and profession may afford matter of general speculation to the man of science; and thinking itself, in this age of separations, may become a peculiar craft. In the bustle of civil pursuits and occupations, men appear in a variety of lights, and suggest matter of inquiry and fancy, by which conversation is enlivened, and greatly enlarged. The productions of ingenuity are brought to the market; and men are willing to pay for whatever has a tendency to inform or amuse. By this means the idle, as well as the busy, contribute to forward the progress of arts, and bestow on polished nations that air of superior ingenuity, under which they appear to have gained the ends that were pursued by the savage in his forest, knowledge, order, and wealth.

SECTION II.

Of the Subordination consequent to the Separation of Arts and Professions.

There is one ground of subordination in the difference of natural talents and dispositions; a second in the unequal division of property; and a third, not less sensible, in the habits which are acquired by the practice of different arts.

Some employments are liberal, others mechanic. They require different talents, and inspire different sentiments; and whether or not this be the cause of the preference we actually give, it is certainly reasonable to form our opinion of the rank that is due to men of certain professions and stations, from the influence of their manner of life in cultivating the powers of the mind, or in preserving the sentiments of the heart.

There is an elevation natural to man, by which he would be thought, in his rudest state, however urged by necessity, to rise above the consideration of mere subsistence, and the regards of interest: He would appear to act only from the heart, in its engagements of friendship, or opposition; he would shew himself only upon occasions of danger or difficulty, and leave ordinary cares to the weak or the servile.

The same apprehensions, in every situation, regulate his notions of meanness or of dignity. In that of polished society, his desire to avoid the character of sordid, makes him conceal his regard for what relates merely to his preservation or his livelihood. In his estimation, the beggar, who depends upon charity; the labourer, who toils that he may eat; the mechanic, whose art requires no exertion of genius, are degraded by the object they pursue, and by the means they employ to attain it. Professions requiring more knowledge and study; proceeding on the exercise of fancy, and the love of perfection; leading to applause as well as to profit, place the artist in a superior class, and bring him nearer to that station in which men are supposed to be highest; because in it they are bound to no task; because they are left to follow the disposition of the mind, and to take that part in society, to which they are led by the sentiments of the heart, or by the calls of the public.

This last was the station, which, in the distinction betwixt freemen and slaves, the citizens of every ancient republic strove to gain, and to maintain for themselves. Women, or slaves, in the earliest ages, had been set apart for the purposes of domestic care, or bodily labour; and in the progress of lucrative arts, the latter were bred to mechanical professions, and were even intrusted with merchandise for the benefit of their masters. Freemen would be understood to have no object beside those of politics and war. In this manner, the honours of one half of the species were sacrificed to those of the other; as stones from the same quarry are buried in the foundation, to sustain the blocks which happen to be hewn for the superior parts of the pile. In the midst of our encomiums bestowed on the Greeks and the Romans, we are, by this circumstance, made to remember, that no human institution is perfect.

In many of the Grecian states, the benefits arising to the free from this cruel distinction, were not conferred equally on all the citizens. Wealth being unequally divided, the rich alone were exempted from labour; the poor were reduced to work for their own subsistence: interest was a reigning passion in both, and the possession of slaves, like that of any other lucrative property, became an object of avarice, not an exemption from sordid attentions. The entire effects of the institution were obtained, or continued to be enjoyed for any considerable time, at Sparta alone. We feel its injustice; we suffer for the helot, under the severities and unequal treatment to which he was exposed: but when we think only of the superior order of men in this state; when we attend to that elevation and magnanimity of spirit, for which danger had no terror, interest no means to corrupt; when we consider them as friends, or as citizens, we are apt to forget, like themselves, that slaves have a title to be treated like men.

We look for elevation of sentiment, and liberality of mind, among those orders of citizens, who, by their condition, and their fortunes, are relieved from sordid cares and attentions. This was the description of a free man at Sparta; and if the lot of a slave among the ancients was really more wretched than that of the indigent labourer and the mechanic among the moderns, it may be doubted, whether the superior orders, who are in possession of consideration and honours, do not proportionally fail in the dignity which befits their condition. If the pretensions to equal justice and freedom should terminate in rendering every class equally servile and mercenary, we make a nation of helots, and have no free citizens.

In every commercial state, notwithstanding any pretension to equal rights, the exaltation of a few must depress the many. In this arrangement, we think that the extreme meanness of some classes must arise chiefly from the defect of knowledge, and of liberal education; and we refer to such classes, as to an image of what our species must have been in its rude and uncultivated state. But we forget how many circumstances, especially in populous cities, tend to corrupt the lowest orders of men. Ignorance is the least of their failings. An admiration of wealth unpossessed, becoming a principle of envy, or of servility; a habit of acting perpetually with a view to profit, and under a sense of subjection; the crimes to which they are allured, in order to feed their debauch, or to gratify their avarice, are examples, not of ignorance, but of corruption and baseness. If the savage has not received our instructions, he is likewise unacquainted with our vices. He knows no superior, and cannot be servile; he knows no distinctions of fortune, and cannot be envious; he acts from his talents in the highest station which human society can offer, that of the counsellor, and the soldier of his country. Toward forming his sentiments, he knows all that the heart requires to be known; he can distinguish the friend whom he loves, and the public interest which awakens his zeal.

The principal objections to democratical or popular government, are taken from the inequalities which arise among men in the result of commercial arts. And it must be confessed, that popular assemblies, when composed of men whose dispositions are sordid, and whose ordinary applications are illiberal, however they may be intrusted with the choice of their masters and leaders, are certainly, in their own persons, unfit to command. How can he who has confined his views to his own subsistence or preservation, be intrusted with the conduct of nations? Such men, when admitted to deliberate on matters of state, bring to its councils confusion and tumult, or servility and corruption; and seldom suffer it to repose from ruinous factions, or the effect of resolutions ill formed or ill conducted.

The Athenians retained their popular government under all these defects. The mechanic was obliged, under a penalty, to appear in the public market-place, and to hear debates on the subjects of war, and of peace. He was tempted by pecuniary rewards, to attend on the trial of civil and criminal causes. But notwithstanding an exercise tending so much to cultivate their talents, the indigent came always with minds intent upon profit, or with the habits of an illiberal calling. Sunk under the sense of their personal disparity and weakness, they were ready to resign themselves entirely to the influence of some popular leader, who flattered their passions, and wrought on their fears; or, actuated by envy, they were ready to banish from the state whomsoever was respectable and eminent in the superior order of citizens: and whether from their neglect of the public at one time, or their male-administration at another, the sovereignty was every moment ready to drop from their hands.

The people, in this case, are, in fact, frequently governed by one, or a few, who know how to conduct them. Pericles possessed a species of princely authority at Athens; Crassus, Pompey, and Caesar, either jointly or successively, possessed for a considerable period the sovereign direction at Rome.

Whether in great or in small states, democracy is preserved with difficulty, under the disparities of condition, and the unequal cultivation of the mind, which attend the variety of pursuits, and applications, that separate mankind in the advanced state of commercial arts. In this, however, we do but plead against the form of democracy, after the principle is removed; and see the absurdity of pretensions to equal influence and consideration, after the characters of men have ceased to be similar.

SECTION III.

Of the Manners of Polished and Commercial Nations.

Mankind, when in their rude state, have a great uniformity of manners; but when civilized, they are engaged in a variety of pursuits; they tread on a larger field, and separate to a greater distance. If they be guided, however, by similar dispositions, and by like suggestions of nature, they will probably, in the end, as well as in the beginning of their progress, continue to agree in many particulars; and while communities admit, in their members, that diversity of ranks and professions which we have already described, as the consequence or the foundation of commerce, they will resemble each other in many effects of this distribution, and of other circumstances in which they nearly concur.

Under every form of government, statesmen endeavour to remove the dangers by which they are threatened from abroad, and the disturbances which molest them at home. By this conduct, if successful, they in a few ages gain an ascendant for their country; establish a frontier at a distance from its capital; they find, in the mutual desires of tranquillity, which come to possess mankind, and in those public establishments which tend to keep the peace of society, a respite from foreign wars, and a relief from domestic disorders. They learn to decide every contest without tumult, and to secure, by the authority of law, every citizen in the possession of his personal rights.

In this condition, to which thriving nations aspire, and which they in some measure attain, mankind having laid the basis of safety, proceed to erect a superstructure suitable to their views. The consequence is various in different states; even in different orders of men of the same community; and the effect to every individual corresponds with his station. It enables the statesman and the soldier to settle the forms of their different procedure; it enables the practitioner in every profession to pursue his separate advantage; it affords the man of pleasure a time for refinement, and the speculative, leisure for literary conversation or study.

In this scene, matters that have little reference to the active pursuits of mankind, are made subjects of inquiry, and the exercise of sentiment and reason itself becomes a profession. The songs of the bard, the harangues of the statesman and the warrior, the tradition and the story of ancient times, are considered as the models, or the earliest production, of so many arts, which it becomes the object of different professions to copy or to improve. The works of fancy, like the subjects of natural history, are distinguished into classes and species; the rules of every particular kind are distinctly collected; and the library is stored, like the warehouse, with the finished manufacture of different arts, who, with the aids of the grammarian and the critic, aspire, each in his particular way, to instruct the head, or to move the heart.

Every nation is a motley assemblage of different characters, and contains, under any political form, some examples of that variety, which the humours, tempers, and apprehensions of men, so differently employed, are likely to furnish. Every profession has its point of honour, and its system of manners; the merchant his punctuality and fair dealing; the statesman his capacity and address; the man of society, his good-breeding and wit. Every station has a carriage, a dress, a ceremonial, by which it is distinguished, and by which it suppresses the national character under that of the rank, or of the individual.

This description may be applied equally to Athens and Rome, to London and Paris. The rude or the simple observer would remark the variety he saw in the dwellings and in the occupations of different men, not in the aspect of different nations. He would find, in the streets of the same city, as great a diversity, as in the territory of a separate people. He could not pierce through the cloud that was gathered before him, nor see how the tradesman, mechanic, or scholar, of one country, should differ from those of another. But the native of every province can distinguish the foreigner; and when he himself travels, is struck with the aspect of a strange country, the moment he passes the bounds of his own. The air of the person, the tone of the voice, the idiom of language, and the strain of conversation, whether pathetic or languid, gay or severe, are no longer the same.

Many such differences may arise among polished nations, from the effects of climate, or from sources of fashion, that are still more unaccountable and obscure; but the principal distinctions on which we can rest, are derived from the part a people are obliged to act in their national capacity; from the objects placed in their view by the state; or from the constitution of government, which prescribing the terms of society to its subjects, has a great influence in forming their apprehensions and habits.

The Roman people, destined to acquire wealth by conquest, and by the spoil of provinces; the Carthaginians, intent on the returns of merchandise, and the produce of commercial settlements, must have filled the streets of their several capitals with men of a different disposition and aspect. The Roman laid hold of his sword when he wished to be great, and the state found her armies prepared in the dwellings of her people. The Carthaginian retired to his counter on a similar project; and, when the state was alarmed, or had resolved on a war, lent of his profits to purchase an army abroad.

The member of a republic, and the subject of a monarchy, must differ, because they have different parts assigned to them by the forms of their country: the one destined to live with his equals, or, by his personal talents and character, to contend for pre-eminence; the other, born to a determinate station, where any pretence to equality creates a confusion, and where nought but precedence is studied. Each, when the institutions of his country are mature, may find in the laws a protection to his personal rights; but those rights themselves are differently understood, and with a different set of opinions, give rise to a different temper of mind. The republican must act in the state, to sustain his pretensions; he must join a party, in order to be safe; he must form one, in order to be great. The subject of monarchy refers to his birth for the honour he claims; he waits on a court, to shew his importance; and holds out the ensigns of dependence and favour, to gain him esteem with the public.

If national institutions, calculated for the preservation of liberty, instead of calling upon the citizen to act for himself, and to maintain his rights, should give a security, requiring, on his part, no personal attention or effort; this seeming perfection of government might weaken the bands of society, and, upon maxims of independence, separate and estrange the different ranks it was meant to reconcile. Neither the parties formed in republics, nor the courtly assemblies which meet in monarchical governments, could take place, where the sense of a mutual dependence should cease to summon their members together. The resorts for commerce might be frequented, and mere amusement might be pursued in the croud, while the private dwelling became a retreat for reserve, averse to the trouble arising from regards and attentions, which it might be part of the political creed to believe of no consequence, and a point of honour to hold in contempt.

This humour is not likely to grow either in republics or monarchies: it belongs more properly to a mixture of both; where the administration of justice may be better secured; where the subject is tempted to look for equality, but where he finds only independence in its place; and where he learns, from a spirit of equality, to hate the very distinctions to which, on account of their real importance, he pays a remarkable deference.

In either of the separate forms of republic or monarchy, or in acting on the principles of either, men are obliged to court their fellow-citizens, and to employ parts and address to improve their fortunes, or even to be safe. They find in both a school for discernment and penetration; but in the one, are taught to overlook the merits of a private character, for the sake of abilities that have weight with the public; and in the other, to overlook great and respectable talents, for the sake of qualities engaging or pleasant in the scene of entertainment, and private society. They are obliged, in both, to adapt themselves with care to the fashion and manners of their country. They find no place for caprice or singular humours. The republican must be popular, and the courtier polite. The first must think himself well placed in every company; the other must chuse his resorts, and desire to be distinguished only where the society itself is esteemed. With his inferiors, he takes an air of protection; and suffers, in his turn, the same air to be taken with himself. It did not, perhaps, require in a Spartan, who feared nothing but a failure in his duty, who loved nothing but his friend and the state, so constant a guard on himself to support his character, as it frequently does in the subject of a monarchy, to adjust his expence and his fortune to the desires of his vanity, and to appear in a rank as high as his birth, or ambition, can possibly reach.

There is no particular, in the mean time, in which we are more frequently unjust, than in applying to the individual the supposed character of his country; or more frequently misled, than in taking our notion of a people from the example of one, or a few of their members. It belonged to the constitution of Athens, to have produced a Cleon, and a Pericles; but all the Athenians were not, therefore, like Cleon, or Pericles. Themistocles and Aristides lived in the same age; the one advised what was profitable; the other told his country what was just.

SECTION IV.

The same subject continued.

The law of Nature, with respect to nations, is the same that it is with respect to individuals: it gives to the collective body a right to preserve themselves; to employ, undisturbed, the means of life; to retain the fruits of labour; to demand the observance of stipulations and contracts. In the case of violence, it condemns the aggressor, and establishes, on the part of the injured, the right of defence, and a claim to retribution. Its applications, however, admit of disputes, and give rise to variety in the apprehension, as well as the practice of mankind.

Nations have agreed universally, in distinguishing right from wrong; in exacting the reparation of injuries by consent or by force. They have always reposed, in a certain degree, on the faith of treaties; but have acted as if force were the ultimate, arbiter in all their disputes, and the power to defend themselves, the surest pledge of their safety. Guided by these common apprehensions, they have differed from one another, not merely in points of form, but in points of the greatest importance, respecting the usage of war, the effects of captivity, and the rights of conquest and victory.

When a number of independent communities have been frequently involved in wars, and have had their stated alliances and oppositions, they adopt customs which they make the foundation of rules, or of laws, to be observed, or alledged, in all their mutual transactions. Even in war itself, they would follow a system, and plead for the observance of forms in their very operations for mutual destruction.

The ancient states of Greece and Italy derived their manners in war from the nature of their republican government; those of modern Europe, from the influence of monarchy, which, by its prevalence in this part of the world, has a great effect on nations, even where it is not the form established, Upon the maxims of this government, we apprehend a distinction between the state and its members, as that between the King and the people, which renders war an operation of policy, not of popular animosity. While we strike at the public interest, we would spare the private; and we carry a respect and consideration for individuals, which often stops the issues of blood in the ardour of victory, and procures to the prisoner of war a hospitable reception in the very city which he came to destroy. These practices are so well established, that scarcely any provocation on the part of an enemy, or any exigence of service, can excuse a trespass on the supposed rules of humanity, or save the leader who commits it from becoming an object of detestation and horror.

To this, the general practice of the Greeks and the Romans was opposite. They endeavoured to wound the state by destroying its members, by desolating its territory, and by ruining the possessions of its subjects. They granted quarter only to inslave, or to bring the prisoner to a more solemn execution; and an enemy, when disarmed, was, for the most part, either sold in the market, or killed, that he might never return to strengthen his party. When this was the issue of war, it was no wonder, that battles were fought with desperation, and that every fortress was defended to the last extremity. The game of human life went upon a high stake, and was played with a proportional zeal.

The term *barbarian*, in this state of manners, could not be employed by the Greeks or the Romans in that sense in which we use it; to characterise a people regardless of commercial arts; profuse of their own lives, and of those of others; vehement in their attachment to one society, and implacable in their antipathy to another. This, in a great and shining part of their history, was their own character, as well as that of some other nations, whom, upon this very account, we distinguish by the appellations of *barbarous* or *rude*.

It has been observed, that those celebrated nations are indebted, for a great part of their estimation, not to the matter of their history, but to the manner in which it has been delivered, and to the capacity of their historians, and other writers. Their story has been told by men who knew how to draw our attention on the proceedings of the understanding and of the heart, more than on the detail of facts; and who could exhibit characters to be admired and loved, in the midst of actions which we should now universally hate or condemn. Like Homer, the model of Grecian literature, they could make us forget the horrors of a vindictive, cruel, and remorseless proceeding towards an enemy, in behalf of the strenuous conduct, the courage, and vehement affections, with which the hero maintained the cause of his friend and of his country.

Our manners are so different, and the system upon which we regulate our apprehensions, in many things, so opposite, that no less could make us endure the practice of ancient nations. Were that practice recorded by the mere journalist, who retains only the detail of events, without throwing any light on the character of the actors; who, like the Tartar historian, tells only what blood was spilt in the field, and how many inhabitants were massacred in the city; we should never have distinguished the Greeks from their barbarous neighbours, nor have thought, that the character of civility pertained even to the Romans, till very late in their history, and in the decline of their empire.

It would, no doubt, be pleasant to see the remarks of such a traveller as we sometimes send abroad to inspect the manners of mankind, left, unassisted by history, to collect the character of the Greeks from the state of their country, or from their practice in war. 'This country,' he might say, 'compared to ours, has an air of barrenness and desolation. I saw upon the road troops of labourers, who were employed in the fields; but no where the habitations of the master and the landlord. It was unsafe, I was told, to reside in the country; and the people of every district crouded intb towns to find a place of defence. It is indeed impossible, that they can be more civilized, till they have established some regular government, and have courts of justice to hear their complaints. At present, every town, nay, I may say, every village, acts for itself, and the greatest disorders prevail. I was not indeed molested; for you must know, that they call themselves nations, and do all their mischief under the pretence of war.

'I do not mean to take any of the liberties of travellers, nor to vie with the celebrated author of the voyage to Lilliput; but cannot help endeavouring to communicate what I felt on hearing them speak of their territory, their armies, their revenue, treaties, and alliances. Only imagine the church-wardens and constables of Highgate or Hampstead turned statesmen and generals, and you will have a tolerable conception of this singular country. I passed through one state, where the best house in the capital would not lodge the meanest of your labourers, and where your very beggars would not chuse to dine with the King; and yet they are thought a great nation, and have no less than two kings. I saw one of them; but such a potentate! he had scarcely cloaths to his back; and for his Majesty's table, he was obliged to go to the eating-house with his subjects. They have not a single farthing of money; and I was obliged to get food at the public expence, there being none to be had in the market. You will imagine, that there must have been a service of plate, and great attendance, to wait upon the illustrious stranger; but my fare was a mess of sorry pottage, brought me by a naked slave, who left me

to deal with it as I thought proper: and even this I was in continual danger of having stoln from me by the children, who are as
vigilant to seize opportunities, and as dextrous in snatching their
food, as any starved greyhound you ever saw. The misery of the
whole people, in short, as well as my own, while I staid there, was
beyond description. You would think that their whole attention
were to torment themselves as much as they can: they are even
displeased with one of their kings for being well liked. He had
made a present, while I was there, of a cow to one favourite, and of
a waistcoat to another*; and it was publicly said, that this method
of gaining friends was robbing the public. My landlord told me
very gravely, that a man should come under no obligation that
might weaken the love which he owes to his country; nor form
any personal attachment beyond the mere habit of living with
his friend, and of doing him a kindness when he can.

'I asked him once, Why they did not, for their own sakes,
enable their kings to assume a little more state? Because, says he,
we intend them the happiness of living with men. When I found
fault with their houses, and said in particular, that I was surprised
they did not build better churches; What would you be then,
says he, if you found religion in stone walls? This will suffice for
a sample of our conversation; and sententious as it was, you may
believe I did not stay long to profit by it.

'The people of this place are not quite so stupid. There is a
pretty large square of a market-place, and some tolerable buildings;
and, I am told, they have some barks and lighters employed in
trade, which they likewise, upon occasion, muster into a fleet,
like my Lord Mayor's shew. But what pleases me most, is, that
I am likely to get a passage from hence, and bid farewell to this
wretched country. I have been at some pains to observe their
ceremonies of religion, and to pick up curiosities. I have copied
some inscriptions, as you will see when you come to peruse my
journal, and will then judge, whether I have met with enough to
compensate the fatigues and bad entertainment to which I have
submitted. As for the people, you will believe, from the specimen
I have given you, that they could not be very engaging company:

     * Plutarch, in the *Life of Agesilaus*.

though poor and dirty, they still pretend to be proud; and a fellow who is not worth a groat, is above working for his livelihood. They come abroad barefooted, and without any cover to the head, wrapt up in the coverlets under which you would imagine they had slept. They throw all off, and appear like so many naked cannibals, when they go to violent sports and exercises; at which they highly value feats of dexterity and strength. Brawny limbs, and muscular arms, the faculty of sleeping out all nights, of fasting long, and of putting up with any kind of food, are thought genteel accomplishments. They have no settled government that I could learn; sometimes the mob, and sometimes the better sort, do what they please: they meet in great crouds in the open air, and seldom agree about any thing. If a fellow has presumption enough, and a loud voice, he can make a great figure. There was a tanner here, some time ago, who, for a while, carried every thing before him. He censured so loudly what others had done, and talked so big of what might be performed, that he was sent out at last to make good his words, and to curry the enemy instead of his leather.* You will imagine, perhaps, that he was pressed for a recruit; no;—he was sent to command the army. They are indeed seldom long of one mind, except in their readiness to harass their neighbours. They go out in bodies, and rob, pillage, and murder where-ever they come.' So far may we suppose our traveller to have written; and upon a recollection of the reputation which those nations have acquired at a distance, he might have added, perhaps, 'That he could not understand how scholars, fine gentlemen, and even women, should combine to admire a people, who so little resemble themselves.'

To form a judgement of the character from which they acted in the field, and in their competitions with neighbouring nations, we must observe them at home. They were bold and fearless in their civil dissensions; ready to proceed to extremities, and to carry their debates to the decision of force. Individuals stood distinguished by their personal spirit and vigour, not by the valuation of their estates, or the rank of their birth. They had

* Thucydides, lib. 4.—Aristophanes.

a personal elevation founded on the sense of equality, not of precedence. The general of one campaign was, during the next, a private soldier, and served in the ranks. They were solicitous to acquire bodily strength; because, in the use of their weapons, battles were a trial of the soldier's strength, as well as of the leader's conduct. The remains of their statuary, shews a manly grace, an air of simplicity and ease, which being frequent in nature, were familiar to the artist. The mind, perhaps, borrowed a confidence and force, from the vigour and address of the body; their eloquence and style bore a resemblance to the carriage of the person. The understanding was chiefly cultivated in the practice of affairs. The most respectable personages were obliged to mix with the croud, and derived their degree of ascendency, only from their conduct, their eloquence, and personal vigour. They had no forms of expression, to mark a ceremonious and guarded respect. Invective proceeded to railing, and the grossest terms were often employed by the most admired and accomplished orators. Quarrelling had no rules but the immediate dictates of passion, which ended in words of reproach, in violence, and blows. They fortunately went always unarmed; and to wear a sword in times of peace, was among them the mark of a barbarian. When they took arms in the divisions of faction, the prevailing party supported itself by expelling their opponents, by proscriptions, and bloodshed. The usurper endeavoured to maintain his station by the most violent and prompt executions. He was opposed, in his turn, by conspiracies and assassinations, in which the most respectable citizens were ready to use the dagger.

Such was the character of their spirit, in its occasional ferments at home; and it burst commonly with a suitable violence and force, against their foreign rivals and enemies. The amiable plea of humanity was little regarded by them in the operations of war. Cities were razed, or inslaved; the captive sold, mutilated, or condemned to die.

When viewed on this side, the ancient nations have but a sorry plea for esteem with the inhabitants of modern Europe, who profess to carry the civilities of peace into the practice of war; and who value the praise of indiscriminate lenity at a higher rate than even that of military prowess, or the love of their country. And yet they have, in other respects, merited and obtained our praise. Their ardent attachment to their country; their contempt of suffering, and of death, in its cause; their manly apprehensions of personal independence, which rendered every individual, even under tottering establishments, and imperfect laws, the guardian of freedom to his fellow-citizens; their activity of mind; in short, their penetration, the ability of their conduct, and force of their spirit, have gained them the first rank among nations.

If their animosities were great, their affections were proportionate: they, perhaps, loved, where we only pity; and were stern and inexorable, where we are not merciful, but only irresolute. After all, the merit of a man is determined by his candour and generosity to his associates, by his zeal for national objects, and by his vigour in maintaining political rights; not by moderation alone, which proceeds frequently from indifference to national and public interests, and which serves to relax the nerves on which the force of a private as well as a public character depends.

When under the Macedonian and the Roman monarchies, a nation came to be considered as the estate of a prince, and the inhabitants of a province to be regarded as a lucrative property, the possession of territory, not the destruction of its people, became the object of conquest. The pacific citizen had little concern in the quarrels of sovereigns; the violence of the soldier was restrained by discipline. He fought, because he was taught to carry arms, and to obey: he sometimes shed unnecessary blood in the ardour of victory; but, except in the case of civil wars, had no passions to excite his animosity beyond the field and the day of battle. Leaders judged of the objects of an enterprise, and they arrested the sword when these were obtained.

In the modern nations of Europe, where extent of territory admits of a distinction between the state and its subjects, we are accustomed to think of the individual with compassion, seldom of the public with zeal. We have improved on the laws of war, and on the lenitives which have been devised to soften its rigours; we have mingled politeness with the use of the sword; we have learned to make war under the stipulations of treaties and cartels, and trust to the faith of an enemy whose ruin we meditate. Glory is more successfully obtained by saving and protecting, than by destroying the vanquished: and the most amiable of all objects is, in appearance, attained; the employing of force, only for the obtaining of justice, and for the preservation of national rights.

This is, perhaps, the principal characteristic, on which, among modern nations, we bestow the epithets of *civilized* or of *polished*. But we have seen, that it did not accompany the progress of arts among the Greeks, nor keep pace with the advancement of policy, literature, and philosophy. It did not await the returns of learning and politeness among the moderns; it was found in early periods of our history, and distinguished, perhaps, more than at present, the manners of ages otherwise rude and undisciplined. A King of France, prisoner in the hands of his enemies, was treated, about four hundred years ago, with as much distinction and courtesy, as a crowned head, in the like circumstances, could possibly expect in this age of politeness.* The Prince of Conde, defeated and taken in the battle of Dreux, slept at night in the same bed with his enemy the Duke of Guise.†

If the moral of popular traditions, and the taste of fabulous legends, which are the production or entertainment of particular ages, are likewise sure indications of their notions and characters, we may presume, that the foundation of what is now held to be the law of war, and of nations, was laid in the manners of Europe, together with the sentiments which are expressed in the tales of chivalry, and of gallantry. Our system of war differs not more from that of the Greeks, than the favourite characters of our early romance differed from those of the Iliad, and of every ancient poem. The hero of the Greek fable, endued with superior force, courage, and address, takes every advantage of an enemy, to kill with safety to himself; and actuated by a desire of spoil, or by a principle of revenge, is never stayed in his progress by interruptions of remorse or compassion. Homer, who, of all poets, knew best how to exhibit the emotions of a vehement affection, seldom attempts to excite commiseration. Hector falls unpitied, and his body is insulted by every Greek.

    * Hume's *History of England*.   † Davila.

Our modern fable, or romance, on the contrary, generally couples an object of pity, weak, oppressed, and defenceless, with an object of admiration, brave, generous, and victorious; or sends the hero abroad in search of mere danger, and of occasions to prove his valour. Charged with the maxims of a refined courtesy, to be observed even towards an enemy; and of a scrupulous honour, which will not suffer him to take any advantages by artifice or surprise; indifferent to spoil, he contends only for renown, and employs his valour to rescue the distressed, and to protect the innocent. If victorious, he is made to rise above nature as much in his generosity and gentleness, as in his military prowess and valour.

It may be difficult, upon stating this contrast between the system of ancient and modern fable, to assign, among nations equally rude, equally addicted to war, and equally fond of military glory, the origin of apprehensions on the point of honour, so different, and so opposite. The hero of Greek poetry proceeds on the maxims of animosity and hostile passion. His maxims in war are like those which prevail in the woods of America. They require him to be brave, but they allow him to practise against his enemy every sort of deception. The hero of modern romance professes a contempt of stratagem, as well as of danger, and unites in the same person, characters and dispositions seemingly opposite; ferocity with gentleness, and the love of blood with sentiments of tenderness and pity.

The system of chivalry, when completely formed, proceeded on a marvellous respect and veneration to the fair sex, on forms of combat established, and on a supposed junction of the heroic and sanctified character. The formalities of the duel, and a kind of judicial challenge, were known among the ancient Celtic nations of Europe. The Germans, even in their native forests, paid a kind of devotion to the female sex. The Christian religion injoined meekness and compassion to barbarous ages. These different principles combined together, may have served as the foundation of a system, in which courage was directed by religion and love, and the warlike and gentle were united together. When the characters of the hero and the saint were mixed, the mild spirit of Christianity, though often turned into venom by the bigotry of opposite parties, though it could not always subdue the ferocity of the warrior, nor suppress the admiration of courage and force, may have confirmed the apprehensions of men in what was to be held meritorious and splendid in the conduct of their quarrels.

In the early and traditionary history of the Greeks and the Romans, rapes were assigned as the most frequent occasions of war; and the sexes were, no doubt, at all times, equally important to each other. The enthusiasm of love is most powerful in the neighbourhood of Asia and Africa; and beauty, as a possession, was probably more valued by the countrymen of Homer, than it was by those of Amadis de Gaul, or by the authors of modern gallantry. 'What wonder,' says the old Priam, when Helen appeared, 'that nations should contend for the possession of so much beauty?' This beauty, indeed, was possessed by different lovers; a subject on which the modern hero had many refinements, and seemed to soar in the clouds. He adored at a respectful distance, and employed his valour to captivate the admiration, not to gain the possession of his mistress. A cold and unconquerable chastity was set up, as an idol to be worshipped, in the toils, the sufferings, and the combats of the hero and the lover.

The feudal establishments, by the high rank to which they elevated certain families, no doubt greatly favoured this romantic system. Not only the lustre of a noble descent, but the stately castle beset with battlements and towers, served to inflame the imagination, and create a veneration for the daughter and the sister of gallant chiefs, whose point of honour it was to be inaccessible and chaste, and who could perceive no merit but that of the high-minded and the brave, nor be approached in any other accents than those of gentleness and respect.

What was originally singular in these apprehensions, was, by the writer of romance, turned to extravagance; and under the title of chivalry was offered as a model of conduct, even in common affairs: the fortunes of nations were directed by gallantry; and human life, on its greatest occasions, became a scene of affectation and folly. Warriors went forth to realize the legends they had studied; princes and leaders of armies dedicated their most serious exploits to a real or to a fancied mistress.

But whatever was the origin of notions, often so lofty and so ridiculous, we cannot doubt of their lasting effects on our manners. The point of honour, the prevalence of gallantry in our conversations, and on our theatres, many of the opinions which the vulgar apply even to the conduct of war; their notion, that the leader of an army, being offered battle upon equal terms, is dishonoured by declining it, are undoubtedly remains of this antiquated system: and chivalry, uniting with the genius of our policy, has probably suggested those peculiarities in the law of nations, by which modern states are distinguished from the ancient. And if our rule in measuring degrees of politeness and civilization is to be taken from hence, or from the advancement of commercial arts, we shall be found to have greatly excelled any of the celebrated nations of antiquity.

PART FIFTH.

Of the Decline of Nations.

SECTION I.

Of supposed National Eminence, and of the Vicissitudes of Human Affairs.

No nation is so unfortunate as to think itself inferior to the rest of mankind: few are even willing to put up with the claim to equality. The greater part having chosen themselves, as at once, the judges and the models of what is excellent in their kind, are first in their own opinion, and give to others consideration or eminence, so far only as they approach to their own condition. One nation is vain of the personal character, or of the learning, of a few of its members; another, of its policy, its wealth, its tradesmen, its gardens, and its buildings; and they who have nothing to boast, are vain, because they are ignorant. The Russians, before the reign of Peter the Great, thought themselves possessed of every national honour, and held the *Nenei*, or *dumb nations*, (the name which they bestowed on their western neighbours of Europe), in a proportional degree of contempt.* The map of the world, in China, was a square plate, the greater part of which was occupied by the provinces of this great empire, leaving on its skirts a few obscure corners, into which the wretched remainder of mankind were supposed to be driven. 'If you have not the use of our letters, nor the knowledge of our books,' said the learned Chinese to the European missionary, 'what literature, or what science, can you have.?†

* Strahlenberg.   † Gemelli Carceri.

The term *polished*, if we may judge from its etymology, originally referred to the state of nations in respect to their laws and government. In its later applications, it refers no less to their proficiency in the liberal and mechanical arts, in literature, and in commerce. But whatever may be its application, it appears, that if there were a name still more respectable than this, every nation, even the most barbarous, or the most corrupted, would assume it; and bestow its reverse where they conceived a dislike, or apprehended a difference. The names of *alien*, or *foreigner*, are seldom pronounced without some degree of intended reproach. That of *barbarian*, in use with one arrogant people, and that of *gentil*, with another, only served to distinguish the stranger, whose language and pedigree differed from theirs.

Even where we pretend to found our opinions on reason, and to justify our preference of one nation to another, we frequently bestow our esteem on circumstances which do not relate to national character, and which have little tendency to promote the welfare of mankind. Conquest, or great extent of territory, however peopled, and great wealth, however distributed or employed, are titles upon which we indulge our own, and the vanity of other nations, as we do that of private men on the score of their fortunes and honours. We even sometimes contend, whose capital is the most overgrown; whose king has the most absolute power; and at whose court the bread of the subject is consumed in the most senseless riot. These indeed are the notions of vulgar minds; but it is impossible to determine, how far the notions of vulgar minds may lead mankind.

There have certainly been very few examples of states, who have, by arts or policy, improved the original dispositions of human nature, or endeavoured, by wise and effectual precautions, to prevent its corruption. Affection, and force of mind, which are the band and the strength of communities, were the inspiration of God, and original attributes in the nature of man. The wisest policy of nations, except in a very few instances, has tended, we may suspect, rather to maintain the peace of society, and to repress the external effects of bad passions, than to strengthen the disposition of the heart itself to justice and goodness. It has tended, by introducing a variety of arts, to exercise the ingenuity of men, and by engaging them in a variety of pursuits, inquiries, and studies, to inform, but frequently to corrupt the mind. It has tended to furnish matter of distinction and vanity; and by incumbering the individual with new subjects of personal care, to substitute the anxiety he entertains for himself, instead of the confidence and the affection he should entertain for his fellow-creatures.

Whether this suspicion be just or no, we are come to point at circumstances tending to verify, or to disprove it: and if to understand the real felicity of nations be of importance, it is certainly so likewise, to know what are those weaknesses, and those vices, by which men not only mar this felicity, but in one age forfeit all the external advantages they had gained in a former.

The wealth, the aggrandizement and power of nations, are commonly the effects of virtue; the loss of these advantages, is often a consequence of vice.

Were we to suppose men to have succeeded in the discovery and application of every art by which states are preserved, and governed; to have attained, by efforts of wisdom and magnanimity, the admired establishments and advantages of a civilized and flourishing people; the subsequent part of their history, containing, according to vulgar apprehension, a full display of those fruits in maturity, of which they had till then carried only the blossom, and the first formation, should, still more than the former, merit our attention, and excite our admiration.

The event, however, has not corresponded to this expectation. The virtues of men have shone most during their struggles, not after the attainment of their ends. Those ends themselves, though attained by virtue, are frequently the causes of corruption and vice. Mankind, in aspiring to national felicity, have substituted arts which increase their riches, instead of those which improve their nature. They have entertained admiration of themselves, under the titles of *civilized* and of *polished*, where they should have been affected with shame; and even where they have for a while acted on maxims tending to raise, to invigorate, and to preserve the national character, they have, sooner or later, been diverted from their object, and fallen a prey to misfortune, or to the neglects which prosperity itself had encouraged.

War, which furnishes mankind with a principal occupation of their restless spirit, serves, by the variety of its events, to diversify their fortunes. While it opens to one tribe or society, the way to eminence, and leads to dominion, it brings another to subjection, and closes the scene of their national efforts. The celebrated rivalship of Carthage and Rome was, in both parties, the natural exercise of an ambitious spirit, impatient of opposition, or even of equality. The conduct and the fortune of leaders, held the balance for some time in suspense; but to whichever side it had inclined, a great nation was to fall; a seat of empire, and of policy, was to be removed from its place; and it was then to be determined, whether the Syriac or the Latin should contain the erudition that was, in future ages, to occupy the studies of the learned.

States have been thus conquered from abroad, before they gave any signs of internal decay, even in the midst of prosperity, and in the period of their greatest ardour for national objects. Athens, in the height of her ambition, and of her glory, received a fatal wound, in striving to extend her maritime power beyond the Grecian seas. And nations of every description, formidable by their rude ferocity, respected for their discipline and military experience, when advancing, as well as when declining, in their strength, fell a prey, by turns, to the ambition and arrogant spirit of the Romans. Such examples may excite and alarm the jealousy and caution of states; the presence of similar dangers may exercise the talents of politicians and statesmen; but mere reverses of fortune are the common materials of history, and must long since have ceased to create our surprise.

Did we find, that nations advancing from small beginnings, and arrived at the possession of arts which lead to dominion, became secure of their advantages, in proportion as they were qualified to gain them; that they proceeded in a course of uninterrupted felicity, till they were broke by external calamities; and that they retained their force, till a more fortunate or vigorous power arose to depress them; the subject in speculation could not be attended with many difficulties, nor give rise to many reflections. But when we observe among nations a kind of spontaneous return to obscurity and weakness; when, in spite of perpetual admonitions of the danger they run, they suffer themselves to be subdued, in one period, by powers which could not have entered into competition with them in a former, and by forces which they had often baffled and despised; the subject becomes more curious, and its explanation more difficult.

The fact itself is known in a variety of different examples. The empire of Asia was, more than once, transferred from the greater to the inferior power. The states of Greece, once so warlike, felt a relaxation of their vigour, and yielded the ascendant they had disputed with the monarchs of the east, to the forces of an obscure principality, become formidable in a few years, and raised to eminence under the conduct of a single man. The Roman empire, which stood alone for ages; which had brought every rival under subjection, and saw no power from whom a competition could be feared, sunk at last before an artless and contemptible enemy. Abandoned to inroad, to pillage, and at last to conquest, on her frontier, she decayed in all her extremities, and shrunk on every side. Her territory was dismembered, and whole provinces gave way, like branches fallen down with age, not violently torn by superior force. The spirit with which Marius had baffled and repelled the attacks of barbarians in a former age, the civil and military force with which the consul and his legions had extended this empire, were now no more. The Roman greatness, doomed to sink as it rose, by slow degrees, was impaired in every encounter. It was reduced to its original dimensions, within the compass of a single city; and depending for its preservation on the fortune of a siege, it was extinguished at a blow; and the brand, which had filled the world with its flames, sunk like a taper in the socket.

Such appearances have given rise to a general apprehension, that the progress of societies to what we call the heights of national greatness, is not more natural, than their return to weakness and obscurity is necessary and unavoidable. The images of youth, and of old age, are applied to nations; and communities, like single men, are supposed to have a period of life, and a length of thread, which is spun by the fates in one part uniform and strong, in another weakened and shattered by use; to be cut, when the destined æra is come, and to make way for a renewal of the emblem in the case of those who arise in succession. Carthage, being so much older than Rome, had felt her decay, says Polybius, so much the sooner: and the survivor too, he foresaw, carried in her bosom the seeds of mortality.

The image indeed is apposite, and the history of mankind renders the application familiar. But it must be obvious, that the case of nations, and that of individuals, are very different. The human frame has a general course; it has, in every individual, a frail contexture, and a limited duration; it is worn by exercise, and exhausted by a repetition of its functions: But in a society, whose constituent members are renewed in every generation, where the race seems to enjoy perpetuated youth, and accumulating advantages, we cannot, by any parity of reason, expect to find imbecilities connected with mere age and length of days.

The subject is not new, and reflections will croud upon every reader. The notions, in the mean time, which we entertain, even in speculation, upon a subject so important, cannot be entirely fruitless to mankind; and however little the labours of the speculative may influence the conduct of men, one of the most pardonable errors a writer can commit, is to believe that he is about to do a great deal of good. But leaving the care of effects to others, we proceed to consider the grounds of inconstancy among mankind, the sources of internal decay, and the ruinous corruptions to which nations are liable, in the supposed condition of accomplished civility.

SECTION II.

Of the Temporary Efforts and Relaxations of the National Spirit.

From what we have already observed on the general characteristics of human nature, it has appeared, that man is not made for repose. In him, every amiable and respectable quality is an active power, and every subject of commendation an effort. If his errors and his crimes are the movements of an active being, his virtues and his happiness consist likewise in the employment of his mind; and all the lustre which he casts around him, to captivate or engage the attention of his fellow-creatures, like the flame of a meteor, shines only while his motion continues: the moments of rest and of obscurity are the same. We know, that the talks assigned him frequently may exceed, as well as come short of his powers; that he may be agitated too much, as well as too little; but cannot ascertain a precise medium between the situations in which he would be harassed, and those in which he would fall into languor. We know, that he may be employed on a great variety of subjects, which occupy different passions; and that, in consequence of habit, he becomes reconciled to very different scenes. All we can determine in general is, that whatever be the subjects with which he is engaged, the frame of his nature requires him to be occupied, and his happiness requires him to be just.

We are now to inquire, why nations cease to be eminent; and why societies which have drawn the attention of mankind by great examples of magnanimity, conduct, and national success, should sink from the height of their honours, and yield, in one age, the palm which they had won in a former. Many reasons will probably occur. One may be taken from the fickleness and inconstancy of mankind, who become tired of their pursuits and exertions, even while the occasions that gave rise to those pursuits, in some measure continue: Another, from the change of situations, and the removal of objects which served to excite their spirit.

The public safety, and the relative interests of states; political establishments, the pretensions of party, commerce, and arts, are subjects which engage the attention of nations. The advantages gained in some of these particulars, determine the degree of national prosperity. The ardour and vigour with which they are at any one time pursued, is the measure of a national spirit. When those objects cease to animate, nations may be said to languish; when they are during any considerable time neglected, states must decline, and their people degenerate.

In the most forward, enterprising, inventive, and industrious nations, this spirit is fluctuating; and they who continue longest to gain advantages, or to preserve them, have periods of remissness, as well as of ardour. The desire of public safety, is, at all times, a powerful motive of conduct; but it operates most, when combined with occasional passions, when provocations inflame, when successes encourage, or mortifications exasperate.

A whole people, like the individuals of whom they are composed, act under the influence of temporary humours, sanguine hopes, or vehement animosities. They are disposed, at one time, to enter on national struggles with vehemence; at another, to drop them from mere lassitude and disgust. In their civil debates and contentions at home, they are occasionally ardent or remiss. Epidemical passions arise or subside, on trivial, as well as important, grounds. Parties are ready, at one time, to take their names, and the pretence of their oppositions, from mere caprice or accident; at another time, they suffer the most serious occasions to pass in silence. If a vein of literary genius be casually opened, or a new subject of disquisition be started, real or pretended discoveries suddenly multiply, and every conversation is inquisitive and animated. If a new source of wealth be found, or a prospect of conquest be offered, the imaginations of men are inflamed, and whole quarters of the globe are suddenly engaged in ruinous or in successful adventures.

Could we recall the spirit that was exerted, or enter into the views that were entertained, by our ancestors, when they burst, like a deluge, from their ancient seats, and poured into the Roman empire, we should probably, after their first successes, at least, find a ferment in the minds of men, for which no attempt was too arduous, no difficulties insurmountable.

The subsequent ages of enterprise in Europe, were those in which the alarm of enthusiasm was rung, and the followers of the cross invaded the East, to plunder a country, and to recover a sepulchre; those in which the people in different states contended for freedom, and assaulted the fabric of civil or religious usurpation; that in which having found means to cross the Atlantic, and to double the cape of Good Hope, the inhabitants of one half the world were let loose on the other, and parties from every quarter, wading in blood, and at the expence of every crime, and of every danger, traversed the earth in search of gold.

Even the weak and the remiss are roused to enterprise, by the contagion of such remarkable ages; and states which have not in their form the principles of a continued exertion, either favourable or adverse to the welfare of mankind, may have paroxysms of ardour, and a temporary appearance of national vigour. In the case of such nations, indeed, the returns of moderation are but a relapse to obscurity, and the presumption of one age is turned to dejection in that which succeeds.

But in the case of states that are fortunate in their domestic policy, even madness itself may, in the result of violent convulsions, subside into wisdom; and a people return to their ordinary mood, cured of their follies, and wiser by experience: or, with talents improved, in conducting the very scenes which frenzy had opened, they may then appear best qualified to pursue with success the object of nations. Like the ancient republics, immediately after some alarming sedition, or like the kingdom of Great Britain, at the close of its civil wars, they retain the spirit of activity, which was recently awakened, and are equally vigorous in every pursuit, whether of policy, learning, or arts. From having appeared on the brink of ruin, they pass to the greatest prosperity.

Men engage in pursuits with degrees of ardour not proportioned to the importance of their object. When they are stated in opposition, or joined in confederacy, they only wish for pretences to act. They forget, in the heat of their animosities, the subject of their controversy; or they seek, in their formal reasonings concerning it, only a disguise for their passions. When the heart is inflamed, no consideration can repress its ardour; when its fervour subsides, no reasoning can excite, and no eloquence awaken, its former emotions.

The continuance of emulation among states, must depend on the degree of equality by which their forces are balanced; or on the incentives by which either party, or all, are urged to continue their struggles. Long intermissions of war, suffer, equally in every period of civil society, the military spirit to languish. The reduction of Athens by Lysander, struck a fatal blow at the institutions of Lycurgus; and the quiet possession of Italy, happily, perhaps, for mankind, had almost put an end to the military progress of the Romans. After some years of repose, Hannibal found Italy unprepared for his onset, and the Romans in a disposition likely to drop, on the banks of the Po, that martial ambition, which, being roused by the sense of a new danger, afterwards carried them to the Euphrates and the Rhine.

States even distinguished for military prowess, sometimes lay down their arms from lassitude, and are weary of fruitless contentions: but if they maintain the station of independent communities, they will have frequent occasions to recall, and exert their vigour. Even under popular governments, men sometimes drop the consideration of their political rights, and appear at times remiss or supine; but if they have reserved the power to defend themselves, the intermission of its exercise cannot be of long duration. Political rights, when neglected, are always invaded; and alarms from this quarter must frequently come to renew the attention of parties. The love of learning, and of arts, may change its pursuits, or droop for a season; but while men are possessed of freedom, and while the exercises of ingenuity are not superseded, the public may proceed, at different times, with unequal fervour; but its progress is seldom altogether discontinued, or the advantages gained in one age are seldom entirely lost to the following.

If we would find the causes of final corruption, we must

examine those revolutions of state that remove or with-hold the objects of every ingenious study, or liberal pursuit; that deprive the citizen of occasions to act as the member of a public; that crush his spirit; that debase his sentiments, and disqualify his mind for affairs.

SECTION III.

Of Relaxations in the National Spirit incident to Polished Nations.

Improving nations, in the course of their advancement, have to struggle with foreign enemies, to whom they bear an extreme animosity, and with whom, in many conflicts, they contend for their existence as a people. In certain periods too, they feel in their domestic policy inconveniencies and grievances, which beget an eager impatience; and they apprehend reformations and new establishments, from which they have sanguine hopes of national happiness. In early ages, every art is imperfect, and susceptible of many improvements. The first principles of every science are yet secrets to be discovered, and to be successively published with applause and triumph.

We may fancy to ourselves, that in ages of progress, the human race, like scouts gone abroad on the discovery of fertile lands, having the world open before them, are presented at every step with the appearance of novelty. They enter on every new ground with expectation and joy: They engage in every enterprise with the ardour of men, who believe they are going to arrive at national felicity, and permanent glory; and forget past disappointments amidst the hopes of future success. From mere ignorance, rude minds are intoxicated with every passion; and partial to their own condition, and to their own pursuits, they think that every scene is inferior to that in which they are placed. Roused alike by success, and by misfortune, they are sanguine, ardent, and precipitant; and leave to the more knowing ages which succeed them, monuments of imperfect skill, and of rude execution in every art; but they leave likewise the marks of a vigorous and ardent spirit, which their successors are not always qualified to sustain, or to imitate.

This may be admitted, perhaps, as a fair description of prosperous societies, at least during certain periods of their progress. The spirit with which they advance may be unequal, in different ages, and may have its paroxysms, and intermissions, arising from the inconstancy of human passions, and from the casual appearance or removal of occasions that excite them. But does this spirit, which for a time continues to carry on the project of civil and commercial arts, find a natural pause in the termination of its own pursuits? May the business of civil society be accomplished, and may the occasion of farther exertion be removed? Do continued disappointments reduce sanguine hopes, and familiarity with objects blunt the edge of novelty? Does experience itself cool the ardour of the mind? May the society be again compared to the individual? And may it be suspected, although the vigour of a nation, like that of a natural body, does not waste by a physical decay, that yet it may sicken for want of exercise, and die in the close of its own exertions? May societies, in the completion of all their designs, like men in years, who disregard the amusements, and are insensible to the passions, of youth, become cold and indifferent to objects that used to animate in a ruder age? And may a polished community be compared to a man, who having executed his plan, built his house, and made his settlement; who having, in short, exhausted the charms of every subject, and wasted all his ardour, sinks into languor and listless indifference? If so, we have found at least another simile to our purpose. But it is probable, that here too, the resemblance is imperfect; and the inference that would follow, like that of most arguments drawn from analogy, tends rather to amuse the fancy, than to give any real information on the subject to which it refers.

The materials of human art are never entirely exhausted, and the applications of industry are never at an end. The national ardour is not, at any particular time, proportioned to the occasion there is for activity; nor curiosity, to the extent of subject that remains to be studied.

The ignorant and the artless, to whom objects of science are new, and who are worst furnished with the conveniencies of life, instead of being more active, and more curious, are commonly more quiescent, and less inquisitive, than the knowing and the polished. When we compare the particulars which occupy mankind in their rude and in their polished condition, they will be found greatly multiplied and enlarged in the last. The questions we have put, however, deserve to be answered; and if, in the advanced ages of society, we do not find the objects of human pursuit removed, or greatly diminished, we may find them at least changed; and in estimating the national spirit, we may find a negligence in one part, but ill compensated by the growing attention which is paid to another.

It is true, in general, that in all our pursuits, there is a termination of trouble, and a point of repose to which we aspire. We would remove this inconvenience, or gain that advantage, that our labours may cease. When I have conquered Italy and Sicily, says Pyrrhus, I shall then enjoy my repose. This termination is proposed in our national as well as in our personal exertions; and in spite of frequent experience to the contrary, is considered at a distance as the height of felicity. But nature has wisely, in most particulars, baffled our project; and placed no where within our reach this visionary blessing of absolute ease. The attainment of one end is but the beginning of a new pursuit; and the discovery of one art is but a prolongation of the thread by which we are conducted to further inquiries, and only hope to escape from the labyrinth.

Among the occupations that may be enumerated, as tending to exercise the invention, and to cultivate the talents of men, are the pursuits of accommodation and wealth, including all the different contrivances which serve to increase manufactures, and to perfect the mechanical arts. But it must be owned, that as the materials of commerce may continue to be accumulated without any determinate limit, so the arts which are applied to improve them, may admit of perpetual refinements. No measure of fortune, or degree of skill, is found to diminish the supposed necessities of human life; refinement and plenty foster new desires, while they furnish the means, or practise the methods, to gratify them.

In the result of commercial arts, inequalities of fortune are greatly increased, and the majority of every people are obliged by necessity, or at least strongly incited by ambition and avarice, to employ every talent they possess. After a history of some thousand years employed in manufacture and commerce, the inhabitants of China are still the most laborious and industrious of any people on the surface of the earth.

Some part of this observation may be extended to the elegant and literary arts. They too have their materials, which cannot be exhausted, and proceed from desires which cannot be satiated. But the respect paid to literary merit is fluctuating, and matter of transient fashion. When learned productions accumulate, the acquisition of knowledge occupies the time that might be bestowed on invention. The object of mere learning is attained with moderate or inferior talents, and the growing list of pretenders diminishes the lustre of the few who are eminent. When we only mean to learn what others have taught, it is probable, that even our knowledge will be less than that of our masters. Great names continue to be repeated with admiration, after we have ceased to examine the foundations of our praise: and new pretenders are rejected, not because they fall short of their predecessors, but because they do not excel them; or because, in reality, we have, without examination, taken for granted the merit of the first, and cannot judge of either.

After libraries are furnished, and every path of ingenuity is occupied, we are, in proportion to our admiration of what is already done, prepossessed against farther attempts. We become students and admirers, instead of rivals; and substitute the knowledge of books, instead of the inquisitive or animated spirit in which they were written.

The commercial and lucrative arts may continue to prosper, but they gain an ascendant at the expence of other pursuits. The desire of profit stifles the love of perfection. Interest cools the imagination, and hardens the heart; and, recommending employments in proportion as they are lucrative, and certain in their gains, it drives ingenuity, and ambition itself, to the counter and the workshop.

But apart from these considerations, the separation of professions, while it seems to promise improvement of skill, and is actually the cause why the productions of every art become more perfect as commerce advances; yet in its termination, and ultimate effects, serves, in some measure, to break the bands of society, to substitute form in place of ingenuity, and to withdraw individuals from the common scene of occupation, on which the sentiments of the heart, and the mind, are most happily employed.

Under the *distinction* of callings, by which the members of polished society are separated from each other, every individual is supposed to possess his species of talent, or his peculiar skill, in which the others are confessedly ignorant; and society is made to consist of parts, of which none is animated with the spirit of society itself. 'We see in the same persons,' said Pericles, 'an equal attention to private and to public affairs; and in men who have turned to separate professions, a competent knowledge of what relates to the community; for we alone consider those who are inattentive to the state, as perfectly insignificant.' This encomium on the Athenians, was probably offered under an apprehension, that the contrary was likely to be charged by their enemies, or might soon take place. It happened accordingly, that the business of state, as well as of war, came to be worse administered at Athens, when these, as well as other applications, became the objects of separate professions; and the history of this people abundantly shewed, that men ceased to be citizens, even to be good poets and orators, in proportion as they came to be distinguished by the profession of these, and other separate crafts.

Animals less honoured than we, have sagacity enough to procure their food, and to find the means of their solitary pleasures; but it is reserved for man to consult, to persuade, to oppose, to kindle in the society of his fellow-creatures, and to lose the sense of his personal interest or safety, in the ardour of his friendships and his oppositions.

When we are involved in any of the divisions into which mankind are separated, under the denominations of a country, a tribe, or an order of men any way affected by common interests, and guided by communicating passions, the mind recognises its natural station; the sentiments of the heart, and the talents of the understanding, find their natural exercise. Wisdom, vigilance, fidelity, and fortitude, are the characters requisite in such a scene, and the qualities which it tends to improve.

In simple or barbarous ages, when nations are weak, and beset with enemies, the love of a country, of a party, or a faction, are the same. The public is a knot of friends, and its enemies are the rest of mankind. Death, or slavery, are the ordinary evils which they are concerned to ward off; victory and dominion, the objects to which they aspire. Under the sense of what they may suffer from foreign invasions, it is one object, in every prosperous society, to increase its force, and to extend its limits. In proportion as this object is gained, security increases. They who possess the interior districts, remote from the frontier, are unused to alarms from abroad. They who are placed on the extremities, remote from the seats of government, are unused to hear of political interests; and the public becomes an object perhaps too extensive, for the conceptions of either. They enjoy the protection of its laws, or of its armies; and they boast of its splendor, and its power; but the glowing sentiments of public affection, which, in small states, mingle with the tenderness of the parent and the lover, of the friend and the companion, merely by having their object enlarged, lose great part of their force.

The manners of rude nations require to be reformed. Their foreign quarrels, and domestic dissensions, are the operations of extreme and sanguinary passions. A state of greater tranquillity hath many happy effects. But if nations pursue the plan of enlargement and pacification, till their members can no longer apprehend the common ties of society, nor be engaged by affection in the cause of their country, they must err on the opposite side, and by leaving too little to agitate the spirits of men, bring on ages of languor, if not of decay.

The members of a community may, in this manner, like the inhabitants of a conquered province, be made to lose the sense of every connection, but that of kindred or neighbourhood; and have no common affairs to transact, but those of trade: Connections, indeed, or transactions, in which probity and friendship may still take place; but in which the national spirit, whose ebbs and flows we are now considering, cannot be exerted.

What we observe, however, on the tendency of enlargement to loosen the bands of political union, cannot be applied to nations who, being originally narrow, never greatly extended their limits, nor to those who, in a rude state, had already the extension of a great kingdom.

In territories of considerable extent, subject to one government, and possessed of freedom, the national union, in rude ages, is extremely imperfect. Every district forms a separate party; and the descendents of different families are opposed to one another, under the denomination of *tribes* or of *clans*: they are seldom brought to act with a steady concert; their feuds and animosities give more frequently the appearance of so many nations at war, than of a people united by connections of policy. They acquire a spirit, however, in their private divisions, and in the midst of a disorder, otherwise hurtful, of which the force, on many occasions, redounds to the power of the state.

Whatever be the national extent, civil order, and regular government, are advantages of the greatest importance; but it does not follow, that every arrangement made to obtain these ends, and which may, in the making, exercise and cultivate the best qualities of men, is therefore of a nature to produce permanent effects, and to secure the preservation of that national spirit from which it arose.

We have reason to dread the political refinements of ordinary men, when we consider, that repose, or inaction itself, is in a great measure their object; and that they would frequently model their governments, not merely to prevent injustice and error, but to prevent agitation and bustle; and by the barriers they raise against the evil actions of men, would prevent them from acting at all. Every dispute of a free people, in the opinion of such politicians, amounts to disorder, and a breach of the national peace. What heart-burnings? What delay to affairs? What want of secrecy and dispatch? What defect of police? Men of superior genius sometimes seem to imagine, that the vulgar have no title to act, or to think. A great prince is pleased to ridicule the precaution by which judges in a free country are confined to the strict interpretation of law.*

We easily learn to contract our opinions of what men may, in consistence with public order, be safely permitted to do. The agitations of a republic, and the licence of its members, strike the subjects of monarchy with aversion and disgust. The freedom with which the European is left to traverse the streets and the fields, would appear to a Chinese a sure prelude to confusion and anarchy. 'Can men behold their superior and not tremble? Can they converse without a precise and written ceremonial? What hopes of peace, if the streets are not barricaded at an hour? What wild disorder, if men are permitted in any thing to do what they please?'

If the precautions which men thus take against each other be necessary to repress their crimes, and do not arise from a corrupt ambition, or from cruel jealousy in their rulers, the proceeding itself must be applauded, as the best remedy of which the vices of men will admit. The viper must be held at a distance, and the tyger chained. But if a rigorous policy, applied to enslave, not to restrain from crimes, has an actual tendency to corrupt the manners, and to extinguish the spirit of nations; if its severities be applied to terminate the agitations of a free people, not to remedy their corruptions; if forms be often applauded as salutary, because they tend merely to silence the voice of mankind, or be condemned as pernicious, because they allow this voice to be heard; we may expect that many of the boasted improvements of civil society, will be mere devices to lay the political spirit at rest, and will chain up the active virtues more than the restless disorders of men.

If to any people it be the avowed object of policy, in all its internal refinements, to secure the person and the property of the subject, without any regard to his political character, the constitution indeed may be free, but its members may likewise become unworthy of the freedom they possess, and unfit to

* *Memoirs of Brandenburg.*

preserve it. The effects of such a constitution may be to immerse all orders of men in their separate pursuits of pleasure, which they may now enjoy with little disturbance; or of gain, which they may preserve without any attention to the commonwealth.

If this be the end of political struggles, the design, when executed, in securing to the individual his estate, and the means of subsistence, may put an end to the exercise of those very virtues that were required in conducting its execution. A man who, in concert with his fellow-subjects, contends with usurpation in defence of his estate or his person, may find an exertion of great generosity, and of a vigorous spirit; but he who, under political establishments, supposed to be fully confirmed, betakes him, because he is safe, to the mere enjoyment of fortune, has in fact turned to a source of corruption the very advantages which the virtues of the other procured. Individuals, in certain ages, derive their protection chiefly from the strength of the party to which they adhere; but in times of corruption, they flatter themselves, that they may continue to derive from the public that safety which, in former ages, they must have owed to their own vigilance and spirit, to the warm attachment of their friends, and to the exercise of every talent which could render them respected, feared, or beloved. In one period, therefore, mere circumstances serve to excite the spirit, and to preserve the manners of men; in another, great wisdom and zeal for the good of mankind on the part of their leaders, are required for the same purposes.

Rome, it may be thought, did not die of a lethargy, nor perish by the remission of her political ardours at home. Her distemper appeared of a nature more violent and acute. Yet if the virtues of Cato and of Brutus found an exercise in the dying hour of the republic, the neutrality, and the cautious retirement of Atticus, found its security in the same tempestuous season; and the great body of the people lay undisturbed, below the current of a storm, by which the superior ranks of men were destroyed. In the minds of the people, the sense of a public was defaced; and even the animosity of faction had subsided: they only could share in the commotion, who were the soldiers of a legion, or the partisans of a leader. But this state fell not into obscurity for want of eminent men. If at the time of which we speak, we look only for a few names distinguished in the history of mankind, there is no period at which the list was more numerous. But those names became distinguished in the contest for dominion, not in the exercise of equal rights: the people was corrupted; the empire of the known world stood in need of a master.

Republican governments, in general, are in hazard of ruin from the ascendant of particular factions, and from the mutinous spirit of a populace, who being corrupted, are no longer fit to share in the administration of state. But under other establishments, where liberty may be more successfully attained if men are corrupted, the national vigour declines from the abuse of that very security which is procured by the supposed perfection of public order.

A distribution of power and office; an execution of law, by which mutual incroachments and molestations are brought to an end; by which the person and the property are, without friends, without cabal, without obligation, perfectly secured to individuals, does honour to the genius of a nation; and could not have been fully established, without those exertions of understanding and integrity, those trials of a resolute and vigorous spirit, which adorn the annals of a people, and leave to future ages a subject of just admiration and applause. But if we suppose that the end is attained, and that men no longer act, in the enjoyment of liberty, from liberal sentiments, or with a view to the preservation of public manners; if individuals think themselves secure without any attention or effort of their own; this boasted advantage may be found only to give them an opportunity of enjoying, at leisure, the conveniencies and necessaries of life; or, in the language of Cato, teach them to value their houses, their villas, their statues, and their pictures, at a higher rate than they do the republic. They may be found to grow tired in secret of a free constitution, of which they never cease to boast in their conversation, and which they always neglect in their conduct.

The dangers to liberty are not the subject of our present consideration; but they can never be greater from any cause than they are from the supposed remissness of a people, to whose personal vigour every constitution, as it owed its establishment, so must continue to owe its preservation. Nor is this blessing ever less secure than it is in the possession of men who think that they enjoy it in safety, and who therefore consider the public only as it presents to their avarice a number of lucrative employments; for the sake of which they may sacrifice those very rights which render themselves objects of management or consideration.

From the tendency of these reflections, then, it should appear, that a national spirit is frequently transient, not on account of any incurable distemper in the nature of mankind, but on account of their voluntary neglects and corruptions. This spirit subsisted solely, perhaps, in the execution of a few projects, entered into for the acquisition of territory or wealth; it comes, like a useless weapon, to be laid aside after its end is attained.

Ordinary establishments terminate in a relaxation of vigour, and are ineffectual to the preservation of states; because they lead mankind to rely on their arts, instead of their virtues, and to mistake for an improvement of human nature, a mere accession of accommodation, or of riches. Institutions that fortify the mind, inspire courage, and promote national felicity, can never tend to national ruin.

Is it not possible, amidst our admiration of arts, to find some place for these? Let statesmen, who are intrusted with the government of nations, reply for themselves. It is their business to shew, whether they climb into stations of eminence, merely to display a passion for interest, which they had better indulge in obscurity; and whether they have capacity to understand the happiness of a people, the conduct of whose affairs they are so willing to undertake.

SECTION IV.

The same subject continued.

Men frequently, while they study to improve their fortunes, neglect themselves; and while they reason for their country, forget the considerations that most deserve their attention. Numbers, riches, and the other resources of war, are highly important: but nations consist of men; and a nation consisting of degenerate and cowardly men, is weak; a nation consisting of vigorous, public-spirited, and resolute men, is strong. The resources of war, where other advantages are equal, may decide a contest; but the resources of war, in hands that cannot employ them, are of no avail.

Virtue is a necessary constituent of national strength: capacity, and a vigorous understanding, are no less necessary to sustain the fortune of states. Both are improved by discipline, and by the exercises in which men are engaged. We despise, or we pity, the lot of mankind, while they lived under uncertain establishments, and were obliged to sustain in the same person, the character of the senator, the statesman, and the soldier. Polished nations discover, that any one of these characters is sufficient in one person; and that the ends of each, when disjoined, are more easily accomplished. The first, however, were circumstances under which nations advanced and prospered; the second were those in which the spirit relaxed, and the nation went to decay.

We may, with good reason, congratulate our species on their having escaped from a state of barbarous disorder and violence, into a state of domestic peace and regular policy; when they have sheathed the dagger, and disarmed the animosities of civil contention; when the weapons with which they contend are the reasonings of the wise, and the tongue of the eloquent. But we cannot, mean-time, help to regret, that they should ever proceed, in search of perfection, to place every branch of administration behind the counter, and come to employ, instead of the statesman and warrior, the mere clerk and accountant.

By carrying this system to its height, men are educated, who could copy for Caesar his military instructions, or even execute a part of his plans; but none who could act in all the different scenes for which the leader himself must be qualified, in the state and in the field, in times of order or of tumult, in times of division or of unanimity; none who could animate the council when deliberating on ordinary occasions, or when alarmed by attacks from abroad.

The policy of China is the most perfect model of an arrangement, at which the ordinary refinements of government are aimed; and the inhabitants of this empire possess, in the highest degree, those arts on which vulgar minds make the felicity and greatness of nations to depend. The state has acquired, in a measure unequalled in the history of mankind, numbers of men, and the other resources of war. They have done what we are very apt to admire; they have brought national affairs to the level of the meanest capacity; they have broke them into parts, and thrown them into separate departments; they have clothed every proceeding with splendid ceremonies, and majestical forms; and where the reverence of forms cannot repress disorder, a rigorous and severe police, armed with every species of corporal punishment, is applied to the purpose. The whip, and the cudgel, are held up to all orders of men; they are at once employed, and they are dreaded by every magistrate. A mandarine is whipped, for having ordered a pickpocket to receive too few or too many blows.

Every department of state is made the object of a separate profession, and every candidate for office must have passed through a regular education; and, as in the graduations of the university, must have obtained by his proficiency, or his standing, the degree to which he aspires. The tribunals of state, of war, and of the revenue, as well as of literature, are conducted by graduates in their different studies: but while learning is the great road to preferment, it terminates, in being able to read, and to write; and the great object of government consists in raising, and in consuming the fruits of the earth. With all these resources, and this learned preparation, which is made to turn these resources to use, the state is in reality weak; has repeatedly given the example which we seek to explain; and among the doctors of war or of policy, among the millions who are set apart for the military profession, can find none of its members who are fit to stand forth in the dangers of their country, or to form a defence against the repeated inroads of an enemy reputed to be artless and mean.

It is difficult to tell how long the decay of states might be suspended by the cultivation of arts on which their real felicity and strength depend; by cultivating in the higher ranks those talents for the council and the field, which cannot, without great disadvantage, be separated; and in the body of a people, that zeal for their country, and that military character, which enable them to take a share in defending its rights.

Times may come, when every proprietor must defend his own possessions, and every free people maintain their own independence. We may imagine, that against such an extremity, an army of hired troops is a sufficient precaution; but their own troops are the very enemy against which a people is sometimes obliged to fight. We may flatter ourselves, that extremities of this sort, in any particular case, are remote; but we cannot, in reasoning on the general fortunes of mankind, avoid putting the case, and referring to the examples in which it has happened. It has happened in every instance where the polished have fallen a prey to the rude, and where the pacific inhabitant has been reduced to subjection by military force.

If the defence and government of a people be made to depend on a few, who make the conduct of state or of war their profession; whether these be foreigners or natives; whether they be called away of a sudden, like the Roman legion from Britain; whether they turn against their employers, like the army of Carthage, or be overpowered and dispersed by a stroke of fortune, the multitude of a cowardly and undisciplined people must, on such an emergence, receive a foreign or a domestic enemy, as they would a plague or an earthquake, with hopeless amazement and terror, and by their numbers, only swell the triumphs, and enrich the spoil of a conqueror.

Statesmen and leaders of armies, accustomed to the mere observance of forms, are disconcerted by a suspension of customary rules; and on sight grounds despair of their country. They were qualified only to go the rounds of a particular track; and when forced from their stations, are in reality unable to act with men. They only took part in formalities, of which they understood not the tendency; and together with the modes of procedure, even the very state itself, in their apprehension, has ceased to exist. The numbers, possessions, and resources of a great people, only serve, in their view, to constitute a scene of hopeless confusion and terror.

In rude ages, under the appellations of *a community*, *a people*, or *a nation*, was understood a number of men; and the state, while its members remained, was accounted entire. The Scythians, while they fled before Darius, mocked at his childish attempt; Athens survived the devastations of Xerxes; and Rome, in its rude state, those of the Gauls. With polished and mercantile states, the case is sometimes reversed. The nation is a territory, cultivated and improved by its owners; destroy the possession, even while the master remains, the state is undone.

That weakness and effeminacy of which polished nations are sometimes accused, has its place probably in the mind alone. The strength of animals, and that of man in particular, depends on his feeding, and the kind of labour to which he is used. Wholesome food, and hard labour, the portion of many in every polished and commercial nation, secure to the public a number of men endued with bodily strength, and inured to hardship and toil.

Even delicate living, and good accommodation, are not found to enervate the body. The armies of Europe have been obliged to make the experiment; and the children of opulent families, bred in effeminacy, or nursed with tender care, have been made to contend with the savage. By imitating his arts, they have learned, like him, to traverse the forest; and, in every season, to subsist in the desert. They have, perhaps, recovered a lesson, which it has cost civilized nations many ages to unlearn, That the fortune of a man is entire while he remains possessed of himself.

It may be thought, however, that few of the celebrated nations of antiquity, whose fate has given rise to so much reflection on the vicissitudes of human affairs, had made any great progress in those enervating arts we have mentioned; or made those arrangements from which the danger in question could be supposed to arise. The Greeks, in particular, at the time of their fall under the Macedonian yoke, had certainly not carried the commercial arts to so great a height as is common with the most flourishing and prosperous nations of Europe. They had still retained the form of independent republics; the people were generally admitted to a share in the government; and not being able to hire armies, they were obliged, by necessity, to bear a part in the defence of their country. By their frequent wars and domestic commotions, they were accustomed to danger, and were familiar with alarming situations: they were accordingly still accounted the best soldiers and the best statesmen of the known world. The younger Cyrus promised himself the empire of Asia by means of their aid; and after his fall, a body of ten thousand, although bereft of their leaders, baffled, in their retreat, all the military force of the Persian empire. The victor of Asia did not think himself prepared for that conquest, till he had formed an army from the subdued republics of Greece.

It is, however, true, that in the age of Philip, the military and political spirit of those nations appears to have been considerably impaired, and to have suffered, perhaps, from the variety of interests and pursuits, as well as of pleasures, with which their members came to be occupied: they even made a kind of separation between the civil and military character. Phocion, we are told by Plutarch, having observed that the leading men of his time followed different courses, that some applied themselves to civil, others to military affairs, determined rather to follow the examples of Themistocles, Aristides, and Pericles, the leaders of a former age, who were equally prepared for either.

We find in the orations of Demosthenes, a perpetual reference to this state of manners. We find him exhorting the Athenians, not only to declare war, but to arm themselves for the execution of their own military plans. We find that there was an order of military men, who easily passed from the service of one state to that of another; and who, when they were neglected from home, turned away to enterprises on their own account. There were not, perhaps, better warriors in any former age; but those warriors were not attached to any state; and the settled inhabitants of every city thought themselves disqualified for military service. The discipline of armies was perhaps improved; but the vigour of nations was gone to decay. When Philip, or Alexander, defeated the Grecian armies, which were chiefly composed of soldiers of fortune, they found an easy conquest with the other inhabitants: and when the latter, afterwards supported by those soldiers, invaded the Persian empire, he seems to have left little martial spirit behind him; and by removing the military men, to have taken precaution enough, in his absence, to secure his dominion over this mutinous and refractory people.

The subdivision of arts and professions, in certain examples, tends to improve the practice of them, and to promote their ends. By having separated the arts of the clothier and the tanner, we are the better supplied with shoes and with cloth. But to separate the arts which form the citizen and the statesman, the arts of policy and war, is an attempt to dismember the human character, and to destroy those very arts we mean to improve. By this separation, we in effect deprive a free people of what is necessary to their safety; or we prepare a defence against invasions from abroad, which gives a prospect of usurpation, and threatens the establishment of military government at home.

We may be surprised to find the beginning of certain military instructions at Rome, referred to a time no earlier than that of the Cimbric war. It was then, we are told by Valerius Maximus, that Roman soldiers were made to learn from gladiators the use of a sword: and the antagonists of Phyrrhus and of Hannibal were, by the account of this writer, still in need of instruction in the first rudiments of their trade. They had already, by the order and choice of their incampments, impressed the Grecian invader with awe and respect; they had already, not by their victories, but by their national vigour and firmness, under repeated defeats, induced him to sue for peace. But the haughty Roman, perhaps, knew the advantage of order and of union, without having been broke to the inferior arts of the mercenary soldier; and had the courage to face the enemies of his country, without having practised the use of his weapon under the fear of being whipped. He could ill be persuaded, that a time might come, when refined and intelligent nations would make the art of war to consist in a few technical forms; that citizens and soldiers might come to be distinguished as much as women and men; that the citizen would become possessed of a property which he would not be able, or required, to defend; that the soldier would be appointed to keep for another what he would be taught to desire, and what he would be enabled to seize for himself; that, in short, one set of men were to have an interest in the preservation of civil establishments, without the power to defend them; that the other were to have this power, without either the inclination or the interest.

This people, however, by degrees came to put their military force on the very footing to which this description alludes. Marius made a capital change in the manner of levying soldiers at Rome: He filled his legions with the mean and the indigent, who depended on military pay for subsistence; he created a force which rested on mere discipline alone, and the skill of the gladiator; he taught his troops to employ their swords against the constitution of their country, and set the example of a practice which was soon adopted and improved by his successors.

The Romans only meant by their armies to incroach on the freedom of other nations, while they preserved their own. They forgot, that in assembling soldiers of fortune, and in suffering any leader to be master of a disciplined army, they actually resigned their political rights, and suffered a master to arise for the state. This people, in short, whose ruling passion was depredation and conquest, perished by the recoil of an engine which they themselves had erected against mankind.

The boasted refinements, then, of the polished age, are not divested of danger. They open a door, perhaps, to disaster, as wide and accessible as any of those they have shut. If they build walls and ramparts, they enervate the minds of those who are placed to defend them; if they form disciplined armies, they reduce the military spirit of entire nations; and by placing the sword where they have given a distaste to civil establishments, they prepare for mankind the government of force.

It is happy for the nations of Europe, that the disparity between the soldier and the pacific citizen can never be so great as it became among the Greeks and the Romans. In the use of modern arms, the novice is made to learn, and to practise with ease, all that the veteran knows; and if to teach him were a matter of real difficulty, happy are they who are not deterred by such difficulties, and who can discover the arts which tend to fortify and preserve, not to enervate and ruin their country.

SECTION V.

Of National Waste.

The strength of nations consists in the wealth, the numbers, and the character, of their people. The history of their progress from a state of rudeness, is, for the most part, a detail of the struggles they have maintained, and of the arts they have practised, to strengthen, or to secure themselves. Their conquests, their population, and their commerce, their civil and military arrangements, their skill in the construction of weapons, and in the methods of attack and defence; the very distribution of tasks, whether in private business or in public affairs, either tend to bestow, or promise to employ with advantage, the constituents of a national force, and the resources of war.

If we suppose, that together with these advantages, the military character of a people remains, or is improved, it must follow, that what is gained in civilization, is a real increase of strength; and that the ruin of nations could never take its rise from themselves. Where states have stopped short in their progress, or have actually gone to decay, we may suspect, that however disposed to advance, they have found a limit, beyond which they could not proceed; or from a remission of the national spirit, and a weakness of character, were unable to make the most of their resources, and natural advantages. On this supposition, from being stationary, they may begin to relapse, and by a retrograde motion, in a succession of ages, arrive at a state of greater weakness, than that which they quitted in the beginning of their progress; and with the appearance of better arts, and superior conduct, expose themselves to become a prey to barbarians, whom, in the attainment, or the height of their glory, they had easily baffled or despised.

Whatever may be the natural wealth of a people, or whatever may be the limits beyond which they cannot improve on their stock, it is probable, that no nation has ever reached those limits, or has been able to postpone its misfortunes, and the effects of misconduct, until its fund of materials, and the fertility of its soil, were exhausted, or the numbers of its people were greatly reduced. The same errors in policy, and weakness of manners, which prevent the proper use of resources, likewise check their increase, or improvement.

The wealth of the state consists in the fortune of its members. The actual revenue of the state is that share of every private fortune, which the public has been accustomed to demand for national purposes. This revenue cannot be always proportioned to what may be supposed redundant in the private estate, but to what is, in some measure, thought so by the owner; and to what he may be made to spare, without intrenching on his manner of living, and without suspending his projects of expence, or of commerce. It should appear, therefore, that any immoderate increase of private expence is a prelude to national weakness: government, even while each of its subjects consumes a princely estate, may be straitened in point of revenue, and the paradox be explained by example, That the public is poor, while its members are rich.

We are frequently led into error by mistaking money for riches; we think that a people cannot be impoverished by a waste of money which is spent among themselves. The fact is, that men are impoverished, only in two ways; either by having their gains suspended, or by having their substance consumed; and money expended at home, being circulated, and not consumed, cannot, any more than the exchange of a tally, or a counter, among a certain number of hands, tend to diminish the wealth of the company among whom it is handed about. But while money circulates at home, the necessaries of life, which are the real constituents of wealth, may be idly consumed; the industry which might be employed to increase the stock of a people, may be suspended, or turned to abuse.

Great armies, maintained either at home or abroad, without any national object, are so many mouths unnecessarily opened to waste the stores of the public, and so many hands with-held from the arts by which its profits are made. Unsuccessful enterprises are so many ventures thrown away, and losses sustained, proportioned to the capital employed in the service. The Helvetii, in order to invade the Roman province of Gaul, burnt their habitations, dropt their instruments of husbandry, and consumed, in one year, the savings of many. The enterprise failed of success, and the nation was undone.

States have endeavoured, in some instances, by pawning their credit, instead of employing their capital, to disguise the hazards they ran. They have found, in the loans they raised, a casual resource, which encouraged their enterprises. They have seemed, by their manner of erecting transferable funds, to leave the capital for purposes of trade, in the hands of the subject, while it is actually expended by the government. They have, by these means, proceeded to the execution of great national projects, without suspending private industry, and have left future ages to answer, in part, for debts contracted with a view to future emolument. So far the expedient is plausible, and appears to be just. The growing burden too, is thus gradually laid; and if a nation be to sink in some future age, every minister hopes it may still keep afloat in his own. But the measure, for this very reason, is, with all its advantages, extremely dangerous, in the hands of a precipitant and ambitious administration, regarding only the present occasion, and imagining a state to be inexhaustible, while a capital can be borrowed, and the interest be paid.

We are told of a nation, who, during a certain period, rivalled the glories of the ancient world, threw off the dominion of a master armed against them with the powers of a great kingdom, broke the yoke with which they had been oppressed, and almost within the course of a century, raised, by their industry and national vigour, a new and formidable power, which struck the former potentates of Europe with awe and suspense, and turned the badges of poverty with which they set out, into the ensigns of war and dominion. This end was attained by the great efforts of a spirit awaked by oppression, by a successful pursuit of national wealth, and by a rapid anticipation of future revenue. But this illustrious state is supposed, not only in the language of a former section, to have preoccupied the business; they have sequestered the inheritance of many ages to come.

Great national expence, however, does not imply the necessity of any national suffering. While revenue is applied with success, to obtain some valuable end; the profits of every adventure, being more than sufficient to repay its costs, the public should gain, and its resources should continue to multiply. But an expence, whether sustained at home or abroad, whether a waste of the present, or an anticipation of future, revenue, if it bring no proper return, is to be reckoned among the causes of national ruin.

PART SIXTH.

Of Corruption and Political Slavery.

SECTION I.

Of Corruption in general.

If the fortune of nations, and their tendency to aggrandisement, or to ruin, were to be estimated by merely balancing, on the principles of last section, articles of profit and loss, every argument in politics would rest on a comparison of national expence with national gain; on a comparison of the numbers who consume, with those who produce or amass the necessaries of life. The columns of the industrious, and the idle, would include all orders of men; and the state itself, being allowed as many magistrates, politicians, and warriors, as were barely sufficient for its defence and its government, should place, on the side of its loss, every name that is supernumerary on the civil or the military list; all those orders of men, who, by the possession of fortune, subsist on the gains of others, and by the nicety of their choice, require a great expence of time and of labour, to supply their consumption; all those who are idly employed in the train of persons of rank; all those who are engaged in the professions of law, physic, or divinity, together with all the learned, who do not, by their studies, promote or improve the practice of some lucrative trade. The value of every person, in short, should be computed from his labour; and that of labour itself, from its tendency to procure and amass the means of subsistence. The arts employed on mere superfluities should be prohibited, except when their produce could be exchanged with foreign nations, for commodities that might be employed to maintain useful men for the public.

These appear to be the rules by which a miser would examine the state of his own affairs, or those of his country; but schemes of perfect corruption are at least as impracticable as schemes of perfect virtue. Men are not universally misers; they will not be satisfied with the pleasure of hoarding; they must be suffered to enjoy their wealth, in order that they may take the trouble of becoming rich. Property, in the common course of human affairs, is unequally divided: we are therefore obliged to suffer the wealthy to squander, that the poor may subsist; we are obliged to tolerate certain orders of men, who are above the necessity of labour, in order that, in their condition, there may be an object of ambition, and a rank to which the busy aspire. We are not only obliged to admit numbers, who, in strict oeconomy, may be reckoned superfluous, on the civil, the military, and the political list; but because we are men, and prefer the occupation, improvement, and felicity of our nature, to its mere existence, we must even wish, that as many members as possible, of every community, may be admitted to a share of its defence and its government.

Men, in fact, while they pursue in society different objects, or separate views, procure a wide distribution of power, and by a species of chance, arrive at a posture for civil engagements, more favourable to human nature than what human wisdom could ever calmly devise.

If the strength of a nation, in the mean time, consists in the men on whom it may rely, and who are fortunately or wisely combined for its preservation, it follows, that manners are as important as either numbers or wealth; and that corruption is to be accounted a principal cause of national declension and ruin.

Whoever perceives what are the qualities of man in his excellence, may easily, by that standard, distinguish his defects or corruptions. If an intelligent, a courageous, and an affectionate mind, constitutes the perfection of his nature, remarkable failings in any of those particulars, must proportionally sink or debase his character.

We have observed, that it is the happiness of the individual to make a right choice of his conduct; that this choice will lead him to lose in society the sense of a personal interest; and, in the consideration of what is due to the whole, to stifle those anxieties which relate to himself as a part.

The natural disposition of man to humanity, and the warmth of his temper, may raise his character to this fortunate pitch. His elevation, in a great measure, depends on the form of his society; but he can, without incurring the charge of corruption, accommodate himself to great variations in the constitutions of government. The same integrity, and vigorous spirit, which, in democratical states, renders him tenacious of his equality, may, under aristocracy or monarchy, lead him to maintain the subordinations established. He may entertain, towards the different ranks of men with whom he is yoked in the state, maxims of respect and of candour: he may, in the choice of his actions, follow a principle of justice, and of honour, which the considerations of safety, preferment, or profit, cannot efface.

From our complaints of national depravity, it should, notwithstanding, appear, that whole bodies of men are sometimes infected with an epidemical weakness of the head, or corruption of heart, by which they become unfit for the stations they occupy, and threaten the states they compose, however flourishing, with a prospect of decay, and of ruin.

A change of national manners for the worse, may arise from a discontinuance of the scenes in which the talents of men were happily cultivated, and brought into exercise; or from a change in the prevailing opinions relating to the constituents of honours or of happiness. When mere riches, or court-favour, are supposed to constitute rank; the mind is misled from the consideration of qualities on which it ought to rely. Magnanimity, courage, and the love of mankind, are sacrificed to avarice and vanity, or suppressed under a sense of dependence. The individual considers his community so far only as it can be rendered subservient to his personal advancement or profit: he states himself in competition with his fellow-creatures; and, urged by the passions of emulation, of fear and jealousy, of envy and malice, he follows the maxims of an animal destined to preserve his separate existence, and to indulge his caprice or his appetite, at the expence of his species.

On this corrupt foundation, men become either rapacious, deceitful, and violent, ready to trespass on the rights of others; or servile, mercenary, and base, prepared to relinquish their own. Talents, capacity, and force of mind, possessed by a person of the first description, serve to plunge him the deeper in misery, and to sharpen the agony of cruel passions; which lead him to wreak on his fellow-creatures the torments that prey on himself. To a person of the second, imagination, and reason itself, only serve to point out false objects of fear, or desire, and to multiply the subjects of disappointment, and of momentary joy. In either case, and whether we suppose that corrupt men are urged by covetousness, or betrayed by fear, and without specifying the crimes which from either disposition they are prepared to commit, we may safely affirm, with Socrates, 'That every master should pray he may not meet with such a slave; and every such person, being unfit for liberty, should implore that he may meet with a merciful master.'

Man, under this measure of corruption, although he may be bought for a slave by those who know how to turn his faculties and his labour to profit; and although, when kept under proper restraints, his neighbourhood may be convenient or useful; yet is certainly unfit to act on the footing of a liberal combination or concert with his fellow-creatures: his mind is not addicted to friendship or confidence; he is not willing to act for the preservation of others, nor deserves that any other should hazard his own safety for his.

The actual character of mankind, mean-time, in the worst, as well as the best condition, is undoubtedly mixed: and nations of the best description are greatly obliged for their preservation, not only to the good disposition of their members, but likewise to those political institutions, by which the violent are restrained from the commission of crimes, and the cowardly, or the selfish, are made to contribute their part to the public defence or prosperity. By means of such institutions, and the wise precautions of government, nations are enabled to subsist, and even to prosper, under very different degrees of corruption, or of public integrity.

So long as the majority of a people is supposed to act on maxims of probity, the example of the good, and even the caution of the bad, give a general appearance of integrity, and of innocence. Where men are to one another objects of affection and of confidence, where they are generally disposed not to offend, government may be remiss; and every person may be treated as innocent, till he is found to be guilty. As the subject in this case does not hear of the crimes, so he need not be told of the punishments inflicted on persons of a different character. But where the manners of a people are considerably changed for the worse, every subject must stand on his guard, and government itself must act on suitable maxims of fear and distrust. The individual, no longer fit to be indulged in his pretensions to personal consideration, independence, or freedom, each of which he would turn to abuse, must be taught, by external force, and from motives of fear, to counterfeit those effects of innocence, and of duty, to which he is not disposed: he must be referred to the whip, or the gibbet, for arguments in support of a caution, which the state now requires him to assume, on a supposition that he is insensible to the motives which recommend the practice of virtue.

The rules of despotism are made for the government of corrupted men. They were indeed followed on some remarkable occasions, even under the Roman commonwealth; and the bloody axe, to terrify the citizen from his crimes, and to repel the casual and temporary irruptions of vice, was repeatedly committed to the arbitrary will of the dictator. They were finally established on the ruins of the republic itself, when either the people became too corrupted for freedom, or when the magistrate became too corrupted to resign his dictatorial power. This species of government comes naturally in the termination of a continued and growing corruption; but has no doubt, in some instances, come too soon, and has sacrificed remains of virtue, that deserved a better fate, to the jealousy of tyrants, who were in haste to augment their power. This method of government cannot, in such cases, fail to introduce that measure of corruption, against whose external effects it is desired as a remedy. When fear is suggested as the only motive to duty, every heart becomes rapacious or base. And this medicine, if applied to a healthy body, is sure to create the distemper it is destined to cure.

This is the manner of government into which the covetous, and the arrogant, to satiate their unhappy desires, would hurry their fellow-creatures: it is a manner of government to which the timorous and the servile submit at discretion; and when these characters of the rapacious and the timid divide mankind, even the virtues of Antoninus or Trajan, can do no more than apply, with candour and with vigour, the whip and the sword; and endeavour, by the hopes of reward, or the fear of punishment, to find a speedy and a temporary cure for the crimes, or the imbecilities of men.

Other states may be more or less corrupted: this has corruption for its basis. Here justice may sometimes direct the arm of the despotical sovereign; but the name of justice is most commonly employed to signify the interest, or the caprice, of a reigning power. Human society, susceptible of such a variety of forms, here finds the simplest of all. The toils and possessions of many are destined to asswage the passions of one or a few; and the only parties that remain among mankind, are the oppressor who demands, and the oppressed who dare not refuse.

Nations, while they were intitled to a milder fate, as in the case of the Greeks, repeatedly conquered, have been reduced to this condition by military force. They have reached it too in the maturity of their own depravations; when, like the Romans, returned from the conquest, and loaded with the spoils, of the world, they gave loose to faction, and to crimes too bold and too frequent for the correction of ordinary government; and when the sword of justice, dropping with blood, and perpetually required to suppress accumulating disorders on every side, could no longer await the delays and precautions of an administration fettered by laws.

It is, however, well known from the history of mankind, that corruption of this, or of any other degree, is not peculiar to nations in their decline, or in the result of signal prosperity, and great advances in the arts of commerce. The bands of society, indeed, in small and infant establishments, are generally strong; and their subjects, either by an ardent devotion to their own tribe, or a vehement animosity against enemies, and by a vigorous courage founded on both, are well qualified to urge, or to sustain, the fortune of a growing community. But the savage, and the barbarian, have given, notwithstanding, in the case of entire nations, some examples of a weak and timorous character.* They have, in more instances, fallen into that species of corruption which we have already described in treating of barbarous nations; they have made rapine their trade, not merely as a species of warfare, or with a view to enrich their community, but to possess, in property, what they learned to prefer even to the ties of affection or of blood.

In the lowest state of commercial arts, the passions for wealth, and for dominion, have exhibited scenes of oppression, or servility, which the most finished corruption of the arrogant, the cowardly, and the mercenary, founded on the desire of procuring, or the fear of losing, a fortune, could not exceed. In such cases, the vices of men, unrestrained by forms, and unawed by police, are suffered to riot at large, and to produce their entire effects. Parties accordingly unite, or separate, on the maxims of a gang of robbers; they sacrifice to interest the tenderest affections of human nature. The parent supplies the market for slaves, even by the sale of his own children; the cottage ceases to be a sanctuary for the weak and the defenceless stranger; and rites of hospitality, often so sacred among nations in their primitive state, come to be violated, like every other tie of humanity, without fear or remorse.†

Nations, which in later periods of their history became eminent for civil wisdom and justice, had, perhaps, in a former age, paroxysms of lawless disorder, to which this description might in part be applied. The very policy by which they arrived at their degree of national felicity, was devised as a remedy for outrageous abuse. The establishment of order was dated from the commis-

---

* The barbarous nations of Siberia, in general, are servile and timid.

† Chardin's travels through Mingrelia into Persia.

sion of rapes and murders; indignation, and private revenge, were the principles on which nations proceeded to the expulsion of tyrants, to the emancipation of mankind, and the full explanation of their political rights.

Defects of government, and of law, may be in some cases considered as a symptom of innocence and of virtue. But where power is already established, where the strong are unwilling to suffer restraint, or the weak unable to find a protection, the defects of law are marks of the most perfect corruption.

Among rude nations, government is often defective; both because men are not yet acquainted with all the evils for which polished nations have endeavoured to find a redress; and because, even where evils of the most flagrant nature have long afflicted the peace of society, they have not yet been able to apply the cure. In the progress of civilization, new distempers break forth, and new remedies are applied: but the remedy is not always applied the moment the distemper appears; and laws, though suggested by the commission of crimes, are not the symptom of a recent corruption, but of a desire to find a remedy that may cure, perhaps, some inveterate evil which has long afflicted the state.

There are corruptions, however, under which men still possess the vigour and the resolution to correct themselves. Such are the violence and the outrage which accompany the collision of fierce and daring spirits, occupied in the struggles which sometimes precede the dawn of civil and commercial improvements. In such cases, men have frequently discovered a remedy for evils, of which their own misguided impetuosity, and superior force of mind, were the principal causes. But if to a depraved disposition, we suppose to be joined a weakness of spirit; if to an admiration, and desire of riches, be joined an aversion to danger or business; if those orders of men whose valour is required by the public, cease to be brave; if the members of society, in general, have not those personal qualities which are required to fill the stations of equality, or of honour, to which they are invited by the forms of the state; they must sink to a depth from which their imbecility, even more than their depraved inclinations, may prevent their rise.

SECTION II.

Of Luxury.

We are far from being agreed on the application of the term *luxury*, or on that degree of its meaning which is consistent with national prosperity, or with the moral rectitude of our nature. It is sometimes employed to signify a manner of life which we think necessary to civilization, and even to happiness. It is, in our panegyric of polished ages, the parent of arts, the support of commerce, and the minister of national greatness, and of opulence. It is, in our censure of degenerate manners, the source of corruption, and the presage of national declension and ruin. It is admired, and it is blamed; it is treated as ornamental and useful; and it is proscribed as a vice.

With all this diversity in our judgements, we are generally uniform in employing the term to signify that complicated apparatus which mankind devise for the ease and convenience of life. Their buildings, furniture, equipage, cloathing, train of domestics, refinement of the table, and, in general, all that assemblage which is rather intended to please the fancy, than to obviate real wants, and which is rather ornamental than useful.

When we are disposed, therefore, under the appellation of *luxury*, to rank the enjoyment of these things among the vices, we either tacitly refer to the habits of sensuality, debauchery, prodigality, vanity, and arrogance, with which the possession of high fortune is sometimes attended; or we apprehend a certain measure of what is necessary to human life, beyond which all enjoyments are supposed to be excessive and vicious. When, on the contrary, luxury is made an article of national lustre and felicity, we only think of it as an innocent consequence of the unequal distribution of wealth, and as a method by which different ranks are rendered mutually dependent, and mutually useful. The poor are made to practise arts, and the rich to reward them. The public itself is made a gainer by what seems to waste its stock, and it receives a perpetual increase of wealth, from the influence of those growing appetites, and delicate tastes, which seem to menace consumption and ruin.

It is certain, that we must either, together with the commercial arts, suffer their fruits to be enjoyed, and even, in some measure, admired; or, like the Spartans, prohibit the art itself, while we are afraid of its consequences, or while we think that the conveniencies it brings exceed what nature requires.

We may propose to stop the advancement of arts at any stage of their progress, and still incur the censure of luxury from those who have not advanced so far. The house-builder and the carpenter at Sparta were limited to the use of the axe and the saw; but a Spartan cottage might have passed for a palace in Thrace: and if the dispute were to turn on the knowledge of what is physically necessary to the preservation of human life, as the standard of what is morally lawful, the faculties of physic, as well as of morality, would probably divide on the subject, and leave every individual, as at present, to find some rule for himself. The casuist, for the most part, considers the practice of his own age and condition, as a standard for mankind. If in one age or condition, he condemn the use of a coach, in another he would have no less censured the wearing of shoes; and the very person who exclaims against the first, would probably not have spared the second, if it had not been already familiar in ages before his own. A censor born in a cottage, and accustomed to sleep upon straw, does not propose that men should return to the woods and the caves for shelter; he admits the reasonableness and the utility of what is already familiar; and apprehends an excess and corruption, only in the newest refinement of the rising generation.

The clergy of Europe have preached successively against every new fashion, and every innovation in dress. The modes of youth are the subject of censure to the old; and modes of the last age, in their turn, are matter of ridicule to the flippant, and the young. Of this there is not always a better account to be given, than that the old are disposed to be severe, and the young to be merry.

The argument against many of the conveniences of life,

drawn from the mere consideration of their not being necessary, was equally proper in the mouth of the savage, who dissuaded from the first applications of industry, as it is in that of the moralist, who insists on the vanity of the last. 'Our ancestors,' he might say, 'found their dwelling under this rock; they gathered their food in the forest; they allayed their thirst from the fountain; and they were clothed in the spoils of the beast they had slain. Why should we indulge a false delicacy, or require from the earth fruits which she is not accustomed to yield? The bow of our fathers is already too strong for our arms; and the wild beast begins to lord it in the woods.'

Thus the moralist may have found, in the proceedings of every age, those topics of blame, from which he is so much disposed to arraign the manners of his own; and our imbarrassment on the subject, is, perhaps, but a part of that general perplexity which we undergo, in trying to define moral characters by external circumstances, which may, or may not, be attended with faults in the mind and the heart. One man finds a vice in the wearing of linen; another does not, unless the fabric be fine: and if, mean-time, it be true, that a person may be dressed in manufacture, either coarse or fine; that he may sleep in the fields, or lodge in a palace; tread upon carpet, or plant his foot on the ground; while the mind either retains, or has lost, its penetration, and its vigour, and the heart its affection to mankind, it is vain, under any such circumstance, to seek for the distinctions of virtue and vice, or to tax the polished citizen with weakness for any part of his equipage, or for his wearing a fur, perhaps, in which some savage was dressed before him. Vanity is not distinguished by any peculiar species of dress. It is betrayed by the Indian in the phantastic assortments of his plumes, his shells, his party-coloured furs, and in the time he bestows at the glass and the toilet. Its projects in the woods and in the town are the same: in the one, it seeks, with the visage bedaubed, and with teeth artificially stained, for that admiration, which it courts in the other with a gilded equipage, and liveries of state.

Polished nations, in their progress, often come to surpass the rude in moderation, and severity of manners. 'The Greeks,' says Thucydides, 'not long ago, like barbarians, wore golden spangles in the hair, and went armed in times of peace.' Simplicity of dress in this people, became a mark of politeness: and the mere materials with which the body is nourished or clothed, are probably of little consequence to any people. We must look for the characters of men in the qualities of the mind, not in the species of their food, or in the mode of their apparel. What are now the ornaments of the grave, and severe; what is owned to be a real conveniency, were once the fopperies of youth, or were devised to please the effeminate. The new fashion, indeed, is often the mark of the coxcomb; but we frequently change our fashions, without increasing the measures of our vanity or folly.

Are the apprehensions of the severe, therefore, in every age, equally groundless and unreasonable? Are we never to dread any error in the article of a refinement bestowed on the means of subsistence, or the conveniencies of life? The fact is, that men are perpetually exposed to the commission of error in this article, not merely where they are accustomed to high measures of accommodation, or to any particular species of food, but where-ever these objects, in general, may come to be preferred to friends, to a country, or to mankind; they actually commit such error, where-ever they admire paultry distinctions or frivolous advantages; where-ever they shrink from small inconveniencies, and are incapable of discharging their duty with vigour. The use of morality on this subject, is not to limit men to any particular species of lodging, diet, or cloaths; but to prevent their considering these conveniencies as the principal objects of human life. And if we are asked, Where the pursuit of trifling accommodations should stop, in order that a man may devote himself entirely to the higher engagements of life? we may answer, That it should stop where it is. This was the rule followed at Sparta: The object of the rule was, to preserve the heart entire for the public, and to occupy men in cultivating their own nature, not in accumulating wealth, and external conveniencies. It was not expected otherwise, that the axe or the saw should be attended with greater political advantage, than the plane and the chisel. When Cato walked the streets of Rome without his robe, and without shoes, he did so, most probably, in contempt of what his countrymen were so prone to admire; not in hopes of finding a virtue in one species of dress, or a vice in another.

Luxury, therefore, considered as a predilection in favour of the objects of vanity, and the costly materials of pleasure, is ruinous to the human character; considered as the mere use of accommodations and conveniencies which the age has procured, rather depends on the progress which the mechanical arts have made, and on the degree in which the fortunes of men are unequally parcelled, than on the dispositions of particular men either to vice or to virtue.

Different measures of luxury are, however, variously suited to different constitutions of government. The advancement of arts supposes an unequal distribution of fortune; and the means of distinction they bring, serve to render the separation of ranks more sensible. Luxury is, upon this account, apart from all its moral effects, adverse to the form of democratical government; and in any state of society, can be safely admitted in that degree only in which the members of the community are supposed of unequal rank, and constitute public order by means of a regular subordination. High degrees of it appear salutary, and even necessary, in monarchical and mixed governments; where, besides the encouragement to arts and commerce, it serves to give lustre to those hereditary or constitutional dignities which have a place of importance in the political system. Whether even here luxury leads to abuse peculiar to ages of high refinement and opulence, we shall proceed to consider in the following sections.

SECTION III.

Of the Corruption incident to Polished Nations.

Luxury and corruption are frequently coupled together, and even pass for synonymous terms. But in order to avoid any dispute about words, by the first we may understand that accumulation of wealth, and that refinement on the ways of enjoying it, which are the objects of industry, or the fruits of mechanic and commercial arts: And by the second a real weakness, or depravity of the human character, which may accompany any state of those arts, and be found under any external circumstances or condition whatsoever. It remains to inquire, What are the corruptions incident to polished nations, arrived at certain measures of luxury, and possessed of certain advantages, in which they are generally supposed to excel?

We need not have recourse to a parallel between the manners of entire nations, in the extremes of civilization and rudeness, in order to be satisfied, that the vices of men are not proportioned to their fortunes; or that the habits of avarice, or of sensuality, are not founded on any certain measures of wealth, or determinate kind of enjoyment. Where the situations of particular men are varied as much by their personal stations, as they can be by the state of national refinements, the same passions for interest, or pleasure, prevail in every condition. They arise from temperament, or an acquired admiration of property; not from any particular manner of life in which the parties are engaged, nor from any particular species of property, which may have occupied their cares and their wishes.

Temperance and moderation are, at least, as frequent among those whom we call the superior, as they are among the lower classes of men; and however we may affix the character of sobriety to mere cheapness of diet, and other accommodations with which any particular age, or rank of men, appear to be contented, it is well known, that costly materials are not necessary to constitute a debauch, nor profligacy less frequent under the thatched roof, than under the lofty ceiling. Men grow equally familiar with different conditions, receive equal pleasure, and are equally allured to sensuality, in the palace, and in the cave. Their acquiring in either habits of intemperance or sloth, depends on the remission of other pursuits, and on the distaste of the mind to other engagements. If the affections of the heart be awake, and the passions of love, admiration, or anger, be kindled, the costly furniture of the palace, as well as the homely accommodations of the cottage, are neglected: and men, when roused, reject their repose; or, when wearied, embrace it alike on the silken bed, or on the couch of straw.

We are not, however, from hence to conclude, that luxury, with all its concomitant circumstances, which either serve to favour its increase, or which, in the arrangements of civil society, follow it as consequences, can have no effect to the disadvantage of national manners. If that respite from public dangers and troubles which gives a leisure for the practice of commercial arts, be continued, or increased, into a disuse of national efforts; if the individual, not called to unite with his country, be left to pursue his private advantage; we may find him become effeminate, mercenary, and sensual; not because pleasures and profits are become more alluring, but because he has fewer calls to attend to other objects; and because he has more encouragement to study his personal advantages, and pursue his separate interests.

If the disparities of rank and fortune which are necessary to the pursuit or enjoyment of luxury, introduce false grounds of precedency and estimation; if, on the mere considerations of being rich or poor, one order of men are, in their own apprehension, elevated, another debased; if one be criminally proud, another meanly dejected; and every rank in its place, like the tyrant, who thinks that nations are made for himself, be disposed to assume on the rights of mankind: although, upon the comparison, the higher order may be least corrupted; or from education, and a sense of personal dignity, have most good qualities remaining; yet the one becoming mercenary and servile; the other imperious and arrogant; both regardless of justice, and of merit; the whole mass is corrupted, and the manners of a society changed for the worse, in proportion as its members cease to act on principles of equality, independence, or freedom.

Upon this view, and considering the merits of men in the abstract, a mere change from the habits of a republic to those of a monarchy; from the love of equality, to the sense of a subordination founded on birth, titles, and fortune, is a species of corruption to mankind. But this degree of corruption is still consistent with the safety and prosperity of some nations; it admits of a vigorous courage, by which the rights of individuals, and of kingdoms, may be long preserved.

Under the form of monarchy, while yet in its vigour, superior fortune is, indeed, one mark by which the different orders of men are distinguished; but there are some other ingredients, without which wealth is not admitted as a foundation of precedency, and in favour of which it is often despised, and lavished away. Such are birth and titles, the reputation of courage, courtly manners, and a certain elevation of mind. If we suppose, that these distinctions are forgotten, and nobility itself only to be known by the sumptuous retinue which money alone may procure; and by a lavish expence, which the more recent fortunes can generally best sustain; luxury must then be allowed to corrupt the monarchical as much as the republican state, and to introduce a fatal dissolution of manners, under which men of every condition, although they are eager to acquire, or to display their wealth, have no remains of real ambition. They have neither the elevation of nobles, nor the fidelity of subjects; they have changed into effeminate vanity, that sense of honour which gave rules to the personal courage; and into a servile baseness, that loyalty, which bound each in his place, to his immediate superior, and the whole to the throne.

Nations are most exposed to corruption from this quarter, when the mechanical arts, being greatly advanced, furnish numberless articles, to be applied in ornament to the person, in furniture, entertainment, or equipage; when such articles as the rich alone can procure are admired; and when consideration, precedence, and rank, are accordingly made to depend on fortune.

In a more rude state of the arts, although wealth be unequally divided, the opulent can amass only the simple means of subsistence: They can only fill the granary, and furnish the stall; reap from more extended fields, and drive their herds over a larger pasture. To enjoy their magnificence, they must live in a croud; and to secure their possessions, they must be surrounded with friends that espouse their quarrels. Their honours, as well as their safety, consist in the numbers who attend them; and their personal distinctions are taken from their liberality, and supposed elevation of mind. In this manner, the possession of riches serves only to make the owner assume a character of magnanimity, to become the guardian of numbers, or the public object of respect and affection. But when the bulky constituents of wealth, and of rustic magnificence, can be exchanged for refinements; and when the produce of the soil may be turned into equipage, and mere decoration; when the combination of many is no longer required for personal safety; the master may become the sole consumer of his own estate: he may refer the use of every subject to himself; he may employ the materials of generosity to feed a personal vanity, or to indulge a sickly and effeminate fancy, which has learned to enumerate the trappings of weakness or folly among the necessaries of life.

The Persian satrape, we are told, when he saw the King of Sparta at the place of their conference, stretched on the grass with his soldiers, blushed at the provision he had made for the accommodation of his own person: he ordered the furs and the carpets to be withdrawn; he felt his own inferiority; and recollected, that he was to treat with a man, not to vie with a pageant in costly attire and magnificence.

When, amidst circumstances that make no trial of the virtues or talents of men, we have been accustomed to the air of superiority, which people of fortune derive from their retinue, we are apt to lose every sense of distinction arising from merit, or even from abilities. We rate our fellow-citizens by the *figure* they are able to make; by their buildings, their dress, their equipage, and the train of their followers. All these circumstances make a part in our estimate of what is excellent; and if the master himself is known to be a pageant in the midst of his fortune, we nevertheless pay our court to his station, and look up with an envious, servile, or dejected mind, to what is, in itself, scarcely fit to amuse children; though, when it is worn as a badge of distinction, it inflames the ambition of those we call the great, and strikes the multitude with awe and respect.

We judge of entire nations by the productions of a few mechanical arts, and think we are talking of men, while we are boasting of their estates, their dress, and their palaces. The sense in which we apply the terms, *great*, and *noble*, *high rank*, and *high life*, shew, that we have, on such occasions, transferred the idea of perfection from the character to the equipage; and that excellence itself is, in our esteem, a mere pageant, adorned at a great expence, by the labours of many workmen.

To those who overlook the subtile transitions of the imagination, it might appear, since wealth can do no more than furnish the means of subsistence, and purchase animal pleasures, that covetousness, and venality itself, should keep pace with our fears of want, or with our appetite for sensual enjoyments; and that where the appetite is satiated, and the fear of want is removed, the mind should be at ease on the subject of fortune. But they are not the mere pleasures that riches procure, nor the choice of viands which cover the board of the wealthy, that inflame the passions of the covetous and the mercenary. Nature is easily satisfied in all her enjoyments. It is an opinion of eminence, connected with fortune; it is a sense of debasement attending on poverty, which renders us blind to every advantage, but that of the rich; and insensible to every disgrace, but that of the poor. It is this unhappy apprehension, that occasionally prepares us for the desertion of every duty, for a submission to every indignity, and for the commission of every crime that can be accomplished in safety.

Aurengzebe was not more renowned for sobriety in his private station, and in the conduct of a supposed dissimulation, by which he aspired to sovereign power, than he continued to be, even on the throne of Indostan. Simple, abstinent, and severe in his diet, and other pleasures, he still led the life of a hermit, and occupied his time with a seemingly painful application to the affairs of a great empire.* He quitted a station in which, if pleasure had been his object, he might have indulged his sensuality without reserve; he made his way to a scene of disquietude and care; he aimed at the summit of human greatness, in the possession of imperial fortune, not at the gratifications of animal appetite, or the enjoyment of ease. Superior to sensual pleasure, as well as to the feelings of nature, he dethroned his father, and he murdered his

* Gemelli Carceri.

brothers, that he might roll on a carriage incrusted with diamond and pearl; that his elephants, his camels, and his horses, on the march, might form a line extending many leagues; might present a glittering harness to the sun; and loaded with treasure, usher to the view of an abject and admiring croud, that awful majesty, in whose presence they were to strike the forehead on the ground, and be overwhelmed with the sense of his greatness, and with that of their own debasement.

As these are the objects which prompt the desire of dominion, and excite the ambitious to aim at the mastery of their fellow-creatures; so they inspire the ordinary race of men with a sense of infirmity and meanness, that prepares them to suffer indignities, and to become the property of persons, whom they consider as of a rank and a nature so much superior to their own.

The chains of perpetual slavery, accordingly, appear to be rivetted in the East, no less by the pageantry which is made to accompany the possession of power, than they are by the fears of the sword, and the terrors of a military execution. In the West, as well as the East, we are willing to bow to the splendid equipage, and stand at an awful distance from the pomp of a princely estate. We too, may be terrified by the frowns, or won by the smiles, of those whose favour is riches and honour, and whose displeasure is poverty and neglect. We too may overlook the honours of the human soul, from an admiration of the pageantries that accompany fortune. The procession of elephants harnessed with gold might dazzle into slaves, the people who derive corruption and weakness from the effect of their own arts and contrivances, as well as those who inherit servility from their ancestors, and are enfeebled by their natural temperament, and the enervating charms of their soil, and their climate.

It appears, therefore, that although the mere use of materials which constitute luxury, may be distinguished from actual vice; yet nations under a high state of the commercial arts, are exposed to corruption, by their admitting wealth, unsupported by personal elevation and virtue, as the great foundation of distinction, and by having their attention turned on the side of interest, as the road to consideration and honour.

With this effect, luxury may serve to corrupt democratical states, by introducing a species of monarchical subordination, without that sense of high birth and hereditary honours which render the boundaries of rank fixed and determinate, and which teach men to act in their stations with force and propriety. It may prove the occasion of political corruption, even in monarchical governments, by drawing respect towards mere wealth; by casting a shade on the lustre of personal qualities, or family-distinctions; and by infecting all orders of men, with equal venality, servility, and cowardice.

SECTION IV.

The same subject continued.

The increasing regard with which men appear, in the progress of commercial arts, to study their profit, or the delicacy with which they refine on their pleasures; even industry itself, or the habit of application to a tedious employment, in which no honours are won, may, perhaps, be considered as indications of a growing attention to interest, or of effeminacy, contracted in the enjoyment of ease and conveniency. Every successive art, by which the individual is taught to improve on his fortune, is, in reality, an addition to his private engagements, and a new avocation of his mind from the public.

Corruption, however, does not arise from the abuse of commercial arts alone; it requires the aid of political situation; and is not produced by the objects that occupy a sordid and a mercenary spirit, without the aid of circumstances that enable men to indulge in safety any mean disposition they have acquired.

Providence has fitted mankind for the higher engagements which they are sometimes obliged to fulfil; and it is in the midst of such engagements that they are most likely to acquire or to preserve their virtues. The habits of a vigorous mind are formed in contending with difficulties, not in enjoying the repose of a pacific station; penetration and wisdom are the fruits of experience, not the lessons of retirement and leisure; ardour and generosity are the qualities of a mind roused and animated in the conduct of scenes that engage the heart, not the gifts of reflection or knowledge. The mere intermission of national and political efforts is, notwithstanding, sometimes mistaken for public good; and there is no mistake more likely to foster the vices, or to flatter the weakness, of feeble and interested men.

If the ordinary arts of policy, or rather, if a growing indifference to objects of a public nature, should prevail, and, under any free constitution, put an end to those disputes of party, and silence that noise of dissension, which generally accompany the exercise of freedom, we may venture to prognosticate corruption to the national manners, as well as remissness to the national spirit. The period is come, when, no engagement remaining on the part of the public, private interest, and animal pleasure, become the sovereign objects of care. When men, being relieved from the pressure of great occasions, bestow their attention on trifles; and having carried what they are pleased to call *sensibility* and *delicacy*, on the subject of ease or molestation, as far as real weakness or folly can go, have recourse to affectation, in order to enhance the pretended demands, and accumulate the anxieties, of a sickly fancy, and enfeebled mind.

In this condition, mankind generally flatter their own imbecility under the name of *politeness*. They are persuaded, that the celebrated ardour, generosity, and fortitude, of former ages, bordered on frenzy, or were the mere effects of necessity, on men who had not the means of enjoying their ease, or their pleasure. They congratulate themselves on having escaped the storm which required the exercise of such arduous virtues; and with that vanity which accompanies the human race in their meanest condition, they boast of a scene of affectation, of languor, or of folly, as the standard of human felicity, and as furnishing the properest exercise of a rational nature.

It is none of the least menacing symptoms of an age prone to degeneracy, that the minds of men become perplexed in the discernment of merit, as much as the spirit becomes enfeebled in conduct, and the heart misled in the choice of its objects. The care of mere fortune is supposed to constitute wisdom; retirement from public affairs, and real indifference to mankind, receive the applauses of moderation and virtue.

Great fortitude, and elevation of mind, have not always, indeed, been employed in the attainment of valuable ends; but they are always respectable, and they are always necessary when we would act for the good of mankind, in any of the more arduous stations of life. While, therefore, we blame their misapplication, we should beware of depreciating their value. Men of a severe and sententious morality have not always sufficiently observed this caution; nor have they been duly aware of the corruptions they flattered, by the satire they employed against what is aspiring and prominent in the character of the human soul.

It might have been expected, that in an age of hopeless debasement,* the talents of Demosthenes and Tully, even the ill-governed magnanimity of a Macedonian, or the daring enterprise of a Carthaginian leader, might have escaped the acrimony of a satirist, who had so many objects of correction in his view, and who possessed the arts of declamation in so high a degree:

> *I, demens, et saevos per Alpes,*
> *Ut pueris placeas, et declamatio fias,*

is part of the illiberal censure which is thrown by this poet on the person and action of a leader, who, by his courage and conduct, in the very service to which the satire referred, had well nigh saved his country from the ruin with which it was at last overwhelmed.

> Heroes are much the same, the point's agreed,
> From Macedonia's madman to the Swede,

is a distich, in which another poet of beautiful talents, has attempted to depreciate a name, to which, probably, few of his readers are found to aspire.

If men must go wrong, there is a choice of their very errors, as well as of their virtues. Ambition, the love of personal eminence, and the desire of fame, although they sometimes lead to the com-

* Juvenal's 10th satire.

mission of crimes, yet always engage men in pursuits that require to be supported by some of the greatest qualities of the human soul; and if eminence is the principal object of pursuit, there is, at least, a probability, that those qualities may be studied on which a real elevation of mind is raised. But when public alarms have ceased, and contempt of glory is recommended as an article of wisdom, the sordid habits, and mercenary dispositions, to which, under a general indifference to national objects, the members of a polished or commercial state are exposed, must prove at once the most effectual suppression of every liberal sentiment, and the most fatal reverse of all those principles from which communities derive their hopes of preservation, and their strength.

It is noble to possess happiness and independence, either in retirement, or in public life. The characteristic of the happy, is to acquit themselves well in every condition; in the court, or in the village; in the senate, or in the private retreat. But if they affect any particular station, it is surely that in which their actions may be rendered most extensively useful. Our considering mere retirement, therefore, as a symptom of moderation, and of virtue, is either a remnant of that system, under which monks and anchorets, in former ages, have been canonized; or proceeds from a habit of thinking, which appears equally fraught with moral corruption, from our considering public life as a scene for the gratification of mere vanity, avarice, and ambition; never as furnishing the best opportunity for a just and a happy engagement of the mind and the heart.

Emulation, and the desire of power, are but sorry motives to public conduct; but if they have been, in any case, the principal inducements from which men have taken part in the service of their country, any diminution of their prevalence or force is a real corruption of national manners; and the pretended moderation assumed by the higher orders of men, has a fatal effect in the state. The disinterested love of the public, is a principle without which some constitutions of government cannot subsist: but when we consider how seldom this has appeared a reigning passion, we have little reason to impute the prosperity of preservation of nations, in every case, to its influence.

It is sufficient, perhaps, under one form of government, that men should be fond of their independence; that they should be ready to oppose usurpation, and to repel personal indignities: under another, it is sufficient, that they should be tenacious of their rank, and of their honours; and instead of a zeal for the public, entertain a vigilant jealousy of the rights which pertain to themselves. When numbers of men retain a certain degree of elevation and fortitude, they are qualified to give a mutual check to their several errors, and are able to act in that variety of situations which the different constitutions of government have prepared for their members: but, under the disadvantages of a feeble spirit, however directed, and however informed, no national constitution is safe; nor can any degree of enlargement to which a state has arrived, secure its political welfare.

In states where property, distinction, and pleasure, are thrown out as baits to the imagination, and incentives to passion, the public seems to rely for the preservation of its political life, on the degree of emulation and jealousy with which parties mutually oppose and restrain each other. The desires of preferment and profit in the breast of the citizen, are the motives from which he is excited to enter on public affairs, and are the considerations which direct his political conduct. The suppression, therefore, of ambition, of party-animosity, and of public envy, is probably, in every such case, not a reformation, but a symptom of weakness, and a prelude to more sordid pursuits, and ruinous amusements.

On the eve of such a revolution in manners, the higher ranks, in every mixed or monarchical government, have need to take care of themselves. Men of business, and of industry, in the inferior stations of life, retain their occupations, and are secured, by a kind of necessity, in the possession of those habits on which they rely for their quiet, and for the moderate enjoyments of life. But the higher orders of men, if they relinquish the state, if they cease to possess that courage and elevation of mind, and to exercise those talents which are employed in its defence, and its government, are, in reality, by the seeming advantages of their station, become the refuse of that society of which they once were the ornament; and from being the most respectable, and the most happy, of its members, are become the most wretched and corrupt. In their approach to this condition, and in the absence of every manly occupation, they feel a dissatisfaction and languor which they cannot explain: They pine in the midst of apparent enjoyments; or, by the variety and caprice of their different pursuits and amusements, exhibit a state of agitation, which, like the disquiet of sickness, is not a proof of enjoyment or pleasure, but of suffering and pain. The care of his buildings, his equipage, or his table, is chosen by one; literary amusement, or some frivolous study, by another. The sports of the country, and the diversions of the town; the gaming-table,* dogs, horses, and wine, are employed to fill up the blank of a listless and unprofitable life. They speak of human pursuits, as if the whole difficulty were to find something to do: They fix on some frivolous occupation, as if there was nothing that deserved to be done: They consider what tends to the good of their fellow-creatures, as a disadvantage to themselves: They fly from every scene, in which any efforts of vigour are required, or in which they might be allured to perform any service to their country. We misapply our compassion in pitying the poor; it were much more justly applied to the rich, who become the first victims of that wretched insignificance, into which the members of every corrupted state, by the tendency of their weaknesses, and their vices, are in haste to plunge themselves.

It is in this condition, that the sensual invent all those refinements on pleasure, and devise those incentives to a satiated appetite, which tend to foster the corruptions of a dissolute age. The effects of brutal appetite, and the mere debauch, are more flagrant, and more violent, perhaps, in rude ages, than they are in the later periods of commerce and luxury: but that perpetual habit of searching for animal pleasure where it is not to be found, in the gratifications of an appetite that is cloyed, and among the

* These different occupations differ from each other, in respect to their dignity, and their innocence; but none of them are the schools from which men are brought to sustain the tottering fortune of nations; they are equally avocations from what ought to be the principal pursuit of man, the good of mankind.

ruins of an animal constitution, is not more fatal to the virtues of the soul, than it is even to the enjoyment of sloth, or of pleasure; it is not a more certain avocation from public affairs, or a surer prelude to national decay, than it is a disappointment to our hopes of private felicity.

In these reflections, it has been the object, not to ascertain a precise measure to which corruption has risen in any of the nations that have attained to eminence, or that have gone to decay; but to describe that remissness of spirit, that weakness of soul, that state of national debility, which is likely to end in political slavery; an evil which remains to be considered as the last object of caution, and beyond which there is no subject of disquisition in the perishing fortunes of nations.

SECTION V.

Of Corruption, as it tends to Political Slavery.

Liberty, in one sense, appears to be the portion of polished nations alone. The savage is personally free, because he lives unrestrained, and acts with the members of his tribe on terms of equality. The barbarian is frequently independent from a continuance of the same circumstances, or because he has courage and a sword. But good policy alone can provide for the regular administration of justice, or constitute a force in the state, which is ready on every occasion to defend the rights of its members.

It has been found, that, except in a few singular cases, the commercial and political arts have advanced together. These arts have been in modern Europe so interwoven, that we cannot determine which were prior in the order of time, or derived most advantage from the mutual influences with which they act and re-act upon one another. It has been observed, that in some nations the spirit of commerce, intent on securing its profits, has led the way to political wisdom. A people, possessed of wealth, and become jealous of their properties, have formed the project of emancipation, and have proceeded, under favour of an importance recently gained, still farther to enlarge their pretensions, and to dispute the prerogatives which their sovereign had been in use to employ. But it is in vain that we expect in one age, from the possession of wealth, the fruit which it is said to have borne in a former. Great accessions of fortune, when recent, when accompanied with frugality, and a sense of independence, may render the owner confident in his strength, and ready to spurn at oppression. The purse which is open, not to personal expence, or to the indulgence of vanity, but to support the interests of a faction, to gratify the higher passions of party, render the wealthy citizen formidable to those who pretend to dominion; but it does not follow, that in a time of corruption, equal, or greater, measures of wealth should operate to the same effect.

On the contrary, when wealth is accumulated only in the hands of the miser, and runs to waste from those of the prodigal; when heirs of family find themselves straitened and poor, in the midst of affluence; when the cravings of luxury silence even the voice of party and faction; when the hopes of meriting the rewards of compliance, or the fear of losing what is held at discretion, keep men in a state of suspense and anxiety; when fortune, in short, instead of being considered as the instrument of a vigorous spirit, becomes the idol of a covetous or a profuse, of a rapacious or a timorous mind; the foundation on which freedom was built, may serve to support a tyranny; and what, in one age, raised the pretensions, and fostered the confidence of the subject, may, in another, incline him to servility, and furnish the price to be paid for his prostitutions. Even those, who, in a vigorous age, gave the example of wealth, in the hands of the people, becoming an occasion of freedom, may, in times of degeneracy, verify likewise the maxim of Tacitus, That the admiration of riches leads to despotical government.*

Men who have tasted of freedom, and who have felt their personal rights, are not easily taught to bear with incroachments on either, and cannot, without some preparation, come to submit to oppression. They may receive this unhappy preparation, under

---

* Est apud illos et opibus honos; eoque unus imperitat, &c. Tacitus *De mor. Ger. c.* 44.

different forms of government, from different hands, and arrive at the same end by different ways. They follow one direction in republics, another in monarchies, and in mixed governments. But where-ever the state has, by means that do not preserve the virtue of the subject, effectually guarded his safety; remissness, and neglect of the public, are likely to follow; and polished nations of every description, appear to encounter a danger, on this quarter, proportioned to the degree in which they have, during any continuance, enjoyed the uninterrupted possession of peace and prosperity.

Liberty results, we say, from the government of laws; and we are apt to consider statutes, not merely as the resolutions and maxims of a people determined to be free, not as the writings by which their rights are kept on record; but as a power erected to guard them, and as a barrier which the caprice of man cannot transgress.

When a basha, in Asia, pretends to decide every controversy by the rules of natural equity, we allow that he is possessed of discretionary powers. When a judge in Europe is left to decide, according to his own interpretation of written laws, is he in any sense more restrained than the former? Have the multiplied words of a statute an influence over the conscience, and the heart, more powerful than that of reason and nature? Does the party, in any judicial proceeding, enjoy a less degree of safety, when his rights are discussed, on the foundation of a rule that is open to the understandings of mankind, than when they are referred to an intricate system, which it has become the object of a separate profession to study and to explain?

If forms of proceeding, written statutes, or other constituents of law, cease to be enforced by the very spirit from which they arose; they serve only to cover, not to restrain, the iniquities of power: they are possibly respected even by the corrupt magistrate, when they favour his purpose; but they are contemned or evaded, when they stand in his way: And the influence of laws, where they have any real effect in the preservation of liberty, is not any magic power descending from shelves that are loaded with books, but is, in reality, the influence of men resolved to be free; of men, who, having adjusted in writing the terms on which they are to live with the state, and with their fellow-subjects, are determined, by their vigilance and spirit, to make these terms be observed.

We are taught, under every form of government, to apprehend usurpations, from the abuse, or from the extension of the executive power. In pure monarchies, this power is commonly hereditary, and made to descend in a determinate line. In elective monarchies, it is held for life. In republics, it is exercised during a limited time. Where men, or families, are called by election to the possession of temporary dignities, it is more the object of ambition to perpetuate, than to extend their powers. In hereditary monarchies, the sovereignty is already perpetual; and the aim of every ambitious prince, is to enlarge his prerogative. Republics, and, in times of commotion, communities of every form, are exposed to hazard, not from those only who are formally raised to places of trust, but from every person whatever, who is incited by ambition, and who is supported by faction.

It is no advantage to a prince, or other magistrate, to enjoy more power than is consistent with the good of mankind; nor is it of any benefit to a man to be unjust: but these maxims are a feeble security against the passions and follies of men. Those who are intrusted with any measures of influence, are disposed, from a mere aversion to constraint, to remove opposition. Not only the monarch who wears a hereditary crown, but the magistrate who holds his office for a limited time, grows fond of his dignity. The very minister, who depends for his place on the momentary will of his prince, and whose personal interests are, in every respect, those of a subject, still has the weakness to take an interest in the growth of prerogative, and to reckon as gain to himself the incroachments he has made on the rights of a people, with whom he himself and his family are soon to be numbered.

Even with the best intentions towards mankind, we are inclined to think, that their welfare depends, not on the felicity of their own inclinations, or the happy employment of their own talents, but on their ready compliance with what we have devised for their good. Accordingly, the greatest virtue of which any sovereign has hitherto shown an example, is not a desire of cherishing in his people the spirit of freedom and independence; but what is in itself sufficiently rare, and highly meritorious, a steady regard to the distribution of justice in matters of property, a disposition to protect and to oblige, to redress the grievances, and to promote the interest of his subjects. It was from a reference to these objects, that Titus computed the value of his time, and judged of its application. But the sword, which in this beneficent hand was drawn to protect the subject, and to procure a speedy and effectual distribution of justice, was likewise sufficient in the hands of a tyrant, to shed the blood of the innocent, and to cancel the rights of men. The temporary proceedings of humanity, though they suspended the exercise of oppression, did not break the national chains: the prince was even the better enabled to procure that species of good which he studied; because there was no freedom remaining, and because there was no where a force to dispute his decrees, or to interrupt their execution.

Was it in vain, that Antoninus became acquainted with the characters of Thrasea, Helvidius, Cato, Dion, and Brutus? Was it in vain, that he learned to understand the form of a free community, raised on the basis of equality and justice; or of a monarchy, under which the liberties of the subject were held the most sacred object of administration?* Did he mistake the means of procuring to mankind what he points out as a blessing? Or did the absolute power with which he was furnished, in a mighty empire, only disable him from executing what his mind had perceived as a national good? In such a case, it were vain to flatter the monarch or his people. The first cannot bestow liberty, without raising a spirit, which may, on occasion, stand in opposition to his own designs; nor the latter receive this blessing, while they own that it is in the right of a master to give or to with-hold it. The claim of justice is firm and peremptory. We receive favours with a sense of obligation and kindness; but we would inforce our rights, and the spirit of freedom in this exertion cannot take the tone of supplication, or of thankfulness, without

---

* M. Antoninus, lib. I.

betraying itself. 'You have intreated Octavius,' says Brutus to Cicero, 'that he would spare those who stand foremost among the citizens of Rome. What if he will not? Must we perish? Yes; rather than owe our safety to him.'

Liberty is a right which every individual must be ready to vindicate for himself, and which he who pretends to bestow as a favour, has by that very act in reality denied. Even political establishments, though they appear to be independent of the will and arbitration of men, cannot be relied on for the preservation of freedom; they may nourish, but should not supersede that firm and resolute spirit, with which the liberal mind is always prepared to resist indignities, and to refer its safety to itself.

Were a nation, therefore, given to be moulded by a sovereign, as the clay is put into the hands of the potter, this project of bestowing liberty on a people who are actually servile, is, perhaps, of all others, the most difficult, and requires most to be executed in silence, and with the deepest reserve. Men are qualified to receive this blessing, only in proportion as they are made to apprehend their own rights; and are made to respect the just pretensions of mankind; in proportion as they are willing to sustain, in their own persons, the burden of government, and of national defence; and are willing to prefer the engagements of a liberal mind, to the enjoyments of sloth, or the delusive hopes of a safety purchased by submission and fear.

I speak with respect, and, if I may be allowed the expression, even with indulgence, to those who are intrusted with high prerogatives in the political system of nations. It is, indeed, seldom their fault that states are inslaved. What should be expected from them, but that being actuated by human desires, they should be averse to disappointment, or even to delay; and in the ardour with which they pursue their object, that they should break through the barriers that would stop their career? If millions recede before single men, and senates are passive, as if composed of members who had no opinion or sense of their own; on whose side have the defences of freedom given way, or to whom shall we impute their fall? to the subject, who has deserted his station; or to the sovereign, who has only remained in his own; and who, if the collateral or subordinate members of government shall cease to question his power, must continue to govern without any restraint?

It is well known, that constitutions framed for the preservation of liberty, must consist of many parts; and that senates, popular assemblies, courts of justice, magistrates of different orders, must combine to balance each other, while they exercise, sustain, or check the executive power. If any part is struck out, the fabric must totter, or fall; if any member is remiss, the others must incroach. In assemblies constituted by men of different talents, habits, and apprehensions, it were something more than human that could make them agree in every point of importance; having different opinions and views, it were want of integrity to abstain from disputes: our very praise of unanimity, therefore, is to be considered as a danger to liberty. We wish for it, at the hazard of taking in its place, the remissness of men grown indifferent to the public; the venality of those who have sold the rights of their country; or the servility of others, who give implicit obedience to a leader by whom their minds are subdued. The love of the public, and respect to its laws, are the points in which mankind are bound to agree; but if, in matters of controversy, the sense of any individual or party is invariably pursued, the cause of freedom is already betrayed.

He whose office it is to govern a supine or an abject people, cannot, for a moment, cease to extend his powers. Every execution of law, every movement of the state, every civil and military operation, in which his power is exerted, must serve to confirm his authority, and present him to the view of the public, as the sole object of consideration, fear, and respect. Those very establishments which were devised, in one age, to limit, or to direct the exercise of an executive power, will serve, in another, to settle its foundations, and to give it stability; they will point out the channels in which it may run, without giving offence, or without exciting alarms, and the very councils which were instituted to check its incroachments, will, in a time of corruption, furnish an aid to its usurpations.

The passion for independence, and the love of dominion,

frequently arise from a common source: There is, in both, an aversion to controul; and he, who, in one situation, cannot bruik a superior, must, in another, dislike to be joined with an equal.

What the prince, under a pure or limited monarchy, is, by the constitution of his country, the leader of a faction would willingly become in republican governments. If he attains to this envied condition, his own inclination, or the tendency of human affairs, seem to open before him the career of a royal ambition: but the circumstances in which he is destined to act, are very different from those of a king. He encounters with men who are unused to disparity; he is obliged, for his own security, to hold the dagger continually unsheathed. When he hopes to be safe, he possibly means to be just; but is hurried, from the first moment of his usurpation, into every exercise of despotical power. The heir of a crown has no such quarrel to maintain with his subjects: his situation is flattering; and the heart must be uncommonly bad, that does not glow with affection to a people, who are, at once, his admirers, his support, and the ornaments of his reign. In him, perhaps, there is no explicit design of trespassing on the rights of his subjects; but the forms intended to preserve their freedom, are not, on this account, always safe in his hands.

Slavery has been imposed upon mankind in the wantonness of a depraved ambition, and tyrannical cruelties have been committed in the gloomy hours of jealousy and terror: yet these demons are not necessary to the creation, or to the support of an arbitrary power. Although no policy was ever more successful than that of the Roman republic in maintaining a national fortune; yet subjects, as well as their princes, frequently imagine that freedom is a clog on the proceedings of government: they imagine, that despotical power is best fitted to procure dispatch and secrecy in the execution of public councils; to maintain what they are pleased to call *political order*,* and to give a speedy re-

---

* Our notion of order in civil society is frequently false: it is taken from the analogy of subjects inanimate and dead; we consider commotion and action as contrary to its nature; we think it consistent only with obedience, secrecy, and the silent passing of affairs through the hands of a few. The good order of stones in a wall, is their being properly fixed in the places for which they are hewn; were they to stir the building must fall: but the order of men in society,

dress of complaints. They even sometimes acknowledge, that if a succession of good princes could be found, despotical government is best calculated for the happiness of mankind. While they reason thus, they cannot blame a sovereign who, in the confidence that he is to employ his power for good purposes, endeavours to extend its limits; and, in his own apprehension, strives only to shake off the restraints which stand in the way of reason, and which prevent the effect of his friendly intentions.

Thus prepared for usurpation, let him, at the head of a free state, employ the force with which he is armed, to crush the seeds of apparent disorder in every corner of his dominions; let him effectually curb the spirit of dissension and variance among his people; let him remove the interruptions to government, arising from the refractory humours and the private interests of his subjects; let him collect the force of the state against its enemies, by availing himself of all it can furnish in the way of taxation and personal service: it is extremely probable, that, even under the direction of wishes for the good of mankind, he may break through every barrier of liberty, and establish a despotism, while he flatters himself, that he only follows the dictates of sense and propriety.

When we suppose government to have bestowed a degree of tranquillity, which we sometimes hope to reap from it, as the best of its fruits, and public affairs to proceed, in the several departments of legislation and execution, with the least possible interruption to commerce and lucrative arts; such a state, like that of China, by throwing affairs into separate offices, where conduct consists in detail, and in the observance of forms, by superseding all the exertions of a great or a liberal mind, is more akin to despotism than we are apt to imagine.

Whether oppression, injustice, and cruelty, are the only evils which attend on despotical government, may be considered apart. In the mean time it is sufficient to observe, that liberty is never

---

is their being placed where they are properly qualified to act. The first is a fabric made of dead and inanimate parts, the second is made of living and active members. When we seek in society for the order of mere inaction and tranquillity, we forget the nature of our subject, and find the order of slaves, not that of free men.

in greater danger than it is when we measure national felicity by the blessings which a prince may bestow, or by the mere tranquillity which may attend on equitable administration. The sovereign may dazzle with his heroic qualities; he may protect his subjects in the enjoyment of every animal advantage or pleasure: but the benefits arising from liberty are of a different sort; they are not the fruits of a virtue, and of a goodness, which operate in the breast of one man, but the communication of virtue itself to many; and such a distribution of functions in civil society, as gives to numbers the exercises and occupations which pertain to their nature.

The best constitutions of government are attended with inconvenience; and the exercise of liberty may, on many occasions, give rise to complaints. When we are intent on reforming abuses, the abuses of freedom may lead us to incroach on the subject from which they are supposed to arise. Despotism itself has certain advantages, or at least, in time of civility and moderation, may proceed with so little offence, as to give no public alarm. These circumstances may lead mankind, in the very spirit of reformation, or by mere inattention, to apply or to admit of dangerous innovations in the state of their policy.

Slavery, however, is not always introduced by mere mistake; it is sometimes imposed in the spirit of violence and rapine. Princes become corrupt as well as their people; and whatever may have been the origin of despotical government, its pretensions, when fully explained, give rise to a contest between the sovereign and his subjects, which force alone can decide. These pretensions have a dangerous aspect to the person, the property, or the life of every subject; they alarm every passion in the human breast; they disturb the supine; they deprive the venal of his hire; they declare war on the corrupt as well as the virtuous; they are tamely admitted only by the coward; but even to him must be supported by a force that can work on his fears. This force the conqueror brings from abroad; and the domestic usurper endeavours to find in his faction at home.

When a people is accustomed to arms, it is difficult for a part to subdue the whole; or before the establishment of disciplined armies, it is difficult for any usurper to govern the many by the help of a few. These difficulties, however, the policy of civilized and commercial nations has sometimes removed; and by forming a distinction between civil and military professions, by committing the keeping and the enjoyment of liberty to different hands, has prepared the way for the dangerous alliance of faction with military power, in opposition to mere political forms, and the rights of mankind.

A people who are disarmed in compliance with this fatal refinement, have rested their safety on the pleadings of reason and justice at the tribunal of ambition and of force. In such an extremity, laws are quoted, and senates are assembled, in vain. They who compose a legislature, or who occupy the civil departments of state, may deliberate on the messages they receive from the camp or the court; but if the bearer, like the centurion who brought the petition of Octavius to the Roman senate, shew the hilt of his sword,* they find that petitions are become commands, and that they themselves are become the pageants, not the repositories of sovereign power.

The reflections of this section may be unequally applied to nations of unequal extent. Small communities, however corrupted, are not prepared for despotical government: their members, crouded together, and contiguous to the seats of power, never forget their relation to the public; they pry, with habits of familiarity and freedom, into the pretensions of those who would rule; and where the love of equality, and the sense of justice, have failed, they act on motives of faction, emulation, and envy. The exiled Tarquin had his adherents at Rome; but if by their means he had recovered his station, it is probable, that in the exercise of his royalty, he must have entered on a new scene of contention with the very party that restored him to power.

In proportion as territory is extended, its parts lose their relative importance to the whole. Its inhabitants cease to perceive their connection with the state, and are seldom united in the execution of any national, or even of any factious, designs. Distance from the feats of administration, and indifference to the persons

* Sueton.

who contend for preferment, teach the majority to consider themselves as the subjects of a sovereignty, not as the members of a political body. It is even remarkable, that enlargement of territory, by rendering the individual of less consequence to the public, and less able to intrude with his counsel, actually tends to reduce national affairs within a narrower compass, as well as to diminish the numbers who are consulted in legislation, or in other matters of government.

The disorders to which a great empire is exposed, require speedy prevention, vigilance, and quick execution. Distant provinces must be kept in subjection by military force; and the dictatorial powers, which, in free states, are sometimes raised to quell insurrections, or to oppose other occasional evils, appear, under a certain extent of dominion, at all times equally necessary to suspend the dissolution of a body, whose parts were assembled, and must be cemented, by measures forcible, decisive, and secret. Among the circumstances, therefore, which in the event of national prosperity, and in the result of commercial arts, lead to the establishment of despotism, there is none, perhaps, that arrives at this termination, with so sure an aim, as the perpetual enlargement of territory. In every state, the freedom of its members depends on the balance and adjustment of its interior parts; and the existence of any such freedom among mankind, depends on the balance of nations. In the progress of conquest, those who are subdued are said to have lost their liberties; but from the history of mankind, to conquer, or to be conquered, has appeared, in effect, the same.

SECTION VI.

Of the Progress and Termination of Despotism.

Mankind, when they degenerate, and tend to their ruin, as well as when they improve, and gain real advantages, frequently proceed by slow, and almost insensible, steps. If, during ages of activity and vigour, they fill up the measure of national greatness to a height which no human wisdom could at a distance foresee; they actually incur, in ages of relaxation and weakness, many evils which their fears did not suggest, and which, perhaps, they had thought far removed by the tide of success and prosperity.

We have already observed, that where men are remiss or corrupted, the virtue of their leaders, or the good intention of their magistrates, will not always secure them in the possession of political freedom. Implicit submission to any leader, or the uncontrouled exercise of any power, even when it is intended to operate for the good of mankind, may frequently end in the subversion of legal establishments. This fatal revolution, by whatever means it is accomplished, terminates in military government; and this, though the simplest of all governments, is rendered complete by degrees. In the first period of its exercise over men who have acted as members of a free community, it can have only laid the foundation, not completed the fabric, of a despotical policy. The usurper, who has possessed, with an army, the centre of a great empire, sees around him, perhaps, the shattered remains of a former constitution; he may hear the murmurs of a reluctant and unwilling submission; he may even see danger in the aspect of many, from whose hands he may have wrested the sword, but whose minds he has not subdued, nor reconciled to his power.

The sense of personal rights, or the pretension to privilege and honours, which remain among certain orders of men, are so many bars in the way of a recent usurpation. If they are not suffered to decay with age, and to wear away in the progress of a growing corruption, they must be broken with violence, and the entrance to every new accession of power must be stained with blood. The effect, even in this case, is frequently tardy. The Roman spirit, we know, was not entirely extinguished under a succession of masters, and under a repeated application of bloodshed and poison. The noble and respectable family still aspired to its original honours: The history of the republic, the writings of former times, the monuments of illustrious men, and the lessons of a philosophy fraught with heroic conceptions, continued to nourish the soul in retirement, and formed those eminent characters, whose elevation, and whose fate, are, perhaps, the most affecting subjects of human story. Though unable to oppose the general bent to servility, they became, on account of their supposed inclinations, objects of distrust and aversion; and were made to pay with their blood, the price of a sentiment which they fostered in silence, and which glowed only in the heart.

While despotism proceeds in its progress, by what principle is the sovereign conducted in the choice of measures that tend to establish his government? By a mistaken apprehension of his own good, sometimes even of that of his people, and by the desire which he feels on every particular occasion, to remove the obstructions which impede the execution of his will. When he has fixed a resolution, whoever reasons or remonstrates against it is an enemy; when his mind is elated, whoever pretends to eminence, and is disposed to act for himself, is a rival. He would leave no dignity in the state, but what is dependent on himself; no active power, but what carries the expression of his momentary pleasure. Guided by a perception as unerring as that of instinct, he never fails to select the proper objects of his antipathy or of his favour. The aspect of independence repels him; that of servility attracts. The tendency of his administration is to quiet every restless spirit, and to assume every function of government to himself.* When the power is adequate to the end, it operates as much in the hands of those who do not perceive the termination, as it does in the hands of others by whom it is best understood: the mandates of either, when just, should not be disputed; when erroneous or wrong, they are supported by force.

You must die, was the answer of Octavius to every suit, from a people that implored his mercy. It was the sentence which some of his successors pronounced against every citizen that was eminent for his birth or his virtues. But are the evils of despotism confined to the cruel and sanguinary methods, by which a recent

---

* It is ridiculous to hear men of a restless ambition, who would be the only actors in every scene, sometimes complain of a refractory spirit in mankind; as if the same disposition from which they desire to usurp every office, did not incline every other person to reason and to act at least for himself.

dominion over a refractory and a turbulent people is established or maintained? And is death the greatest calamity which can afflict mankind under an establishment by which they are divested of all their rights? They are, indeed, frequently suffered to live; but distrust, and jealousy, the sense of personal meanness, and the anxieties which arise from the care of a wretched interest, are made to possess the soul; every citizen is reduced to a slave; and every charm by which the community engaged its members, has ceased to exist. Obedience is the only duty that remains, and this is exacted by force. If under such an establishment, it be necessary to witness scenes of debasement and horror, at the hazard of catching the infection, death becomes a relief; and the libation which Thrasea was made to pour from his arteries, is to be considered as a proper sacrifice of gratitude to Jove the Deliverer.*

Oppression and cruelty are not always necessary to despotical government; and even when present, are but a part of its evils. It is founded on corruption, and on the suppression of all the civil and the political virtues; it requires its subjects to act from motives of fear; it would asswage the passions of a few men at the expence of mankind; and would erect the peace of society itself on the ruins of that freedom and confidence from which alone the enjoyment, the force, and the elevation of the human mind, are found to arise.

During the existence of any free constitution, and whilst every individual possessed his rank and his privilege, or had his apprehension of personal rights, the members of every community were to one another objects of consideration and of respect; every point to be carried in civil society, required the exercise of talents, of wisdom, persuasion, and vigour, as well as of power. But it is the highest refinement of a despotical government, to rule by simple commands, and to exclude every art but that of compulsion. Under the influence of this policy, therefore, the

---

* Porrectisque utriuque brachii venis, postquam cruorem effudit, humum super spargens, proprius vocato Quaestore, *Libemus*, inquit, *Jovi Liberatori.* Specta juvenis; et omen quidem Dii prohibeant; ceterum in ea tempora natus es, quibus, firmare animum deceat constantibus exemplis. Tacit. *Ann. lib.* 16.

occasions which employed and cultivated the understandings of men, which awakened their sentiments, and kindled their imaginations, are gradually removed; and the progress by which mankind attained to the honours of their nature, in being engaged to act in society upon a liberal footing, was not more uniform, or less interrupted, than that by which they degenerate in this unhappy condition.

When we hear of the silence which reigns in the seraglio, we are made to believe, that speech itself is become unnecessary; and that the signs of the mute are sufficient to carry the most important mandates of government. No arts, indeed, are require l to maintain an ascendant where terror alone is opposed to force, where the powers of the sovereign are delegated entire to every subordinate officer: nor can any station bestow a liberality of mind in a scene of silence and dejection, where every breast is possessed with jealousy and caution, and where no object, but animal pleasure, remains to balance the sufferings of the sovereign himself, or those of his subjects.

In other states, the talents of men are sometimes improved by the exercises which belong to an eminent station: but here the master himself is probably the rudest and least cultivated animal of the herd; he is inferior to the slave whom he raises from a servile office to the first places of trust or of dignity in his court. The primitive simplicity which formed ties of familiarity and affection betwixt the sovereign and the keeper of his herds,* appears, in the absence of all affections, to be restored, or to be counterfeited amidst the ignorance and brutality which equally characterise all orders of men, or rather which level the ranks, and destroy the distinction of persons in a despotical court.

Caprice and passion are the rules of government with the prince. Every delegate of power is left to act by the same direction; to strike when he is provoked; to favour when he is pleased. In what relates to revenue, jurisdiction, or police, every governor of a province acts like a leader in an enemy's country; comes armed with the terrors of fire and sword; and instead of a tax,

* See *Odyssey*.

levies a contribution by force: he ruins or spares as either may serve his purpose. When the clamours of the oppressed, or the reputation of a treasure amassed at the expence of a province, have reached the ears of the sovereign, the extortioner is indeed made to purchase impunity by imparting a share, or by forfeiting the whole of his spoil; but no reparation is made to the injured; nay, the crimes of the minister are first employed to plunder the people, and afterwards punished to fill the coffers of the sovereign.

In this total discontinuance of every art that relates to just government and national policy, it is remarkable, that even the trade of the soldier is itself greatly neglected. Distrust and jealousy on the part of the prince, come in aid of his ignorance and incapacity; and these causes operating together, serve to destroy the very foundation on which his power is established. Any undisciplined rout of armed men passes for an army, whilst a weak, dispersed, and unarmed people, are sacrificed to military disorder, or exposed to depredation on the frontier from an enemy, whom the desire of spoil, or the hopes of conquest, may have drawn to their neighbourhood.

The Romans extended their empire till they left no polished nation to be subdued, and found a frontier which was every where surrounded by fierce and barbarous tribes; they even pierced through uncultivated deserts, in order to remove to a greater distance the molestation of such troublesome neighbours, and in order to possess the avenues through which they feared their attacks. But this policy put the finishing hand to the internal corruption of the state. A few years of tranquillity were sufficient to make even the government forget its danger; and in the cultivated province, prepared for the enemy, a tempting prize and an easy victory.

When by the conquest and annexation of every rich and cultivated province, the measure of empire is full, two parties are sufficient to comprehend mankind; that of the pacific and the wealthy, who dwell within the pale of empire; and that of the poor, the rapacious, and the fierce, who are inured to depredation and war. The last bear to the first nearly the same relation which the wolf and the lion bear to the fold; and they are naturally engaged in a state of hostility.

Were despotic empire, mean-time, to continue for ever unmolested from abroad, while it retains that corruption on which it was founded, it appears to have in itself no principle of new life, and presents no hope of restoration to freedom and political vigour. That which the despotical *master has sown, cannot quicken unless it die*; it must languish and expire by the effect of its own abuse, before the human spirit can spring up anew, or bear those fruits which constitute the honour and the felicity of human nature. In time of the greatest debasement, indeed, commotions are felt; but very unlike the agitations of a free people: they are either the agonies of nature, under the sufferings to which men are exposed; or mere tumults, confined to a few who stand in arms about the prince, and who, by their conspiracies, assassinations, and murders, serve only to plunge the pacific inhabitant still deeper in the horrors of fear or despair. Scattered in the provinces, unarmed, unacquainted with the sentiments of union and confederacy, restricted by habit to a wretched oeconomy, and dragging a precarious life on those possessions which the extortions of government have left; the people can no where, under these circumstances, assume the spirit of a community, nor form any liberal combination for their own defence. The injured may complain; and while he cannot obtain the mercy of government, he may implore the commiseration of his fellow-subject. But that fellow-subject is comforted, that the hand of oppression has not seized on himself: he studies his interest, or snatches his pleasure, under that degree of safety which obscurity and concealment bestow.

The commercial arts, which seem to require no foundation in the minds of men, but the regard to interest; no encouragement, but the hopes of gain, and the secure possession of property, must perish under the precarious tenure of slavery, and under the apprehension of danger arising from the reputation of wealth. National poverty, however, and the suppression of commerce, are the means by which despotism comes to accomplish its own destruction. Where there are no longer any profits to corrupt, or fears to deter, the charm of dominion is broken, and the naked slave, as awake from a dream, is astonished to find he is free. When the fence is destroyed, the wilds are open, and the herd breaks loose. The pasture of the cultivated field is no longer preferred to that of the desert. The sufferer willingly flies where the extortions of government cannot overtake him; where even the timid and the servile may recollect they are men; where the tyrant may threaten, but where he is known to be no more than a fellow-creature; where he can take nothing but life, and even this at the hazard of his own.

Agreeably to this description, the vexations of tyranny have overcome, in many parts of the East, the desire of settlement. The inhabitants of a village quit their habitations, and infest the public ways; those of the valleys fly to the mountains, and, equipt for flight, or possessed of a strong hold, subsist by depredation, and by the war they make on their former masters.

These disorders conspire with the impositions of government to render the remaining settlements still less secure: but while devastation and ruin appear on every side, mankind are forced anew upon those confederacies, acquire again that personal confidence and vigour, that social attachment, that use of arms, which, in former times, rendered a small tribe the seed of a great nation; and which may again enable the emancipated slave to begin the career of civil and commercial arts. When human nature appears in the utmost state of corruption, it has actually begun to reform.

In this manner, the scenes of human life have been frequently shifted. Security and presumption forfeit the advantages of prosperity; resolution and conduct retrieve the ills of adversity; and mankind, while they have nothing on which to rely but their virtue, are prepared to gain every advantage; and when they confide most in their fortune, are most exposed to feel its reverse. We are apt to draw these observations into rule; and when we are no longer willing to act for our country, we plead in excuse of our own weakness or folly, a supposed fatality in human affairs.

The institutions of men are, indeed, likely to have their end as well as their beginning: but their duration is not fixed to any limited period; and no nation ever suffered internal decay but from the vice of its members. We are sometimes willing to acknowledge this vice in our countrymen; but who was ever willing to acknowledge it in himself? It may be suspected, however, that we do more than acknowledge it, when we cease to oppose its effects, and when we plead a fatality, which, at least, in the breast of every individual, is dependent on himself. Men of real fortitude, integrity, and ability, are well placed in every scene; they reap, in every condition, the principal enjoyments of their nature; they are the happy instruments of providence employed for the good of mankind; or, if we must change this language, they show, that while they are destined to live, the states they compose are likewise doomed by the fates to survive, and to prosper.

THE END.

VARIANTS

This list of variants does not include small changes in punctuation, syntax or spelling. The left-hand column gives the folio references to this reprint of the 1767 edition; the right, the corresponding folio reference in the edition of 1814; the figures 43^{10} indicate that the start of the entry is on page 43 line 10.

1767		1814
page		*page*
1^2 grow	are raised	1^2
1^3 destined to act	active	1^4
1^3 extend their operations as their powers increase	extend together their operations and their powers	1^4
1^4 exhibit a progress	have a progress	1^5
1^6 man	Man	1^7
1^{21} nature	Nature	2^{20}
3^{10} great purposes of human life	purposes of human life	4^{23}
3^{25} are made to occupy a place	have a place	5^{12}
4^8 pertain to society	arise in society	6^8
4^{34}-5 Yet one property by which man is distinguished, has been sometimes overlooked in the account of his nature, or has only served to mislead our attention. In other classes of animals, the individual advances from infancy to age or maturity; and he attains, in the compass of a single life, to all the perfection his nature can reach: but, in the human kind, the species has a progress as well as the individual; they build	The attainments of the parent do not descend in the blood of his children, nor is the progress of man to be considered as a physical mutation of the species. The individual, in every age, has the same race to run from infancy to manhood, and every infant, or ignorant person, now, is a model of what man was in his original state. He enters on his career with advantages peculiar to his age; but his natural talent is probably the same. The use and application of this talent is	

1767	1814
page	*page*
4-5 contd.	contd.

in every subsequent age on foundations formerly laid; and, in a succession of years, tend to a perfection in the application of their faculties, to which the aid of long experience is required and to which many generations must have combined their endeavours.

changing, and men continue their works in progression through many ages together: They build on foundations laid by their ancestors; and in a succession of years, tend to a perfection in the application of their faculties, to which the aid of long experience is required, and to which many generations must have combined their endeavours. 7^{10}

6^{27} come to perceive — perceive 10^{11}

10^{22} men are themselves — this nature itself 17^{3}

10^{24} So far as we are able to account for this diversity on principles either moral or physical, we perform a task of great curiosity or signal utility.

The varieties merit our attention, and the course of every stream into which this mighty current divides, deserves to be followed to its source. 17^{5}

11^{3} many functions of nature — many functions which terminate in himself, or have a relation to his fellow-creatures. 17^{18}

11^{11} refer to — tend to 18^{29}

12^{36} beyond itself, and has a quality, which we call *tenderness*, that never can accompany the considerations of interest. This affection being a complacency

beyond itself, and is the sense of a relation to some fellow-creature as to its object. Being a complacency 20^{22}

13^{3} unknown to those who act without any regard to their fellow creatures — unknown to those who are guided by mere considerations of interest 20^{27}

13^{27} restore his relish for food — renew his enjoyment 21^{29}

1767	1814
page	*page*

14^{20} *selfishness*, by which they express their desire of the welfare of others, or the care of their own

selfishness, by the first of which they express their friendly affections, and by the second their interest. 23^{6}

14^{26} they will disturb the order of vulgar apprehension

they will attempt to change the application of words. 23^{13}

15^{2} the reasonings of men

our reasonings 23^{30}

15^{19} regard to property

property 24^{21}

21^{12} brought us to the knowledge

brought to our knowledge 34^{1}

24^{18} a path that leads to

a way to 39^{3}

27^{26} pertains to

requisite to 44^{29}

28^{20} That they understand well the subjects to which they apply, is all that can be said, in commending

No more can be said, in commending 46^{8}

32^{26} peculiar attention

peculiar emotion 53^{18}

33^{27} and with acrimony

or with acrimony 55^{4}

34^{12} general rules

general rule 56^{3}

34^{36} converse with one another, without feeling that the part they maintain

associate together, without feeling that the treatment they give or receive 57^{4}

36^{15} *Addition after*: . . . his applauses refer.

Applause, however, is the expression of a peculiar sentiment; an expression of esteem the reverse of contempt. Its object is perfection, the reverse of defect. This sentiment is not the love of mankind; it is that by which we estimate the qualities of men, and the objects of our pursuit; that which doubles the force of every desire or aversion, when we consider its object as tending to raise or to sink our nature. 59^{20}

1767	1814
page	*page*
36²⁰ love and compassion are the most	love and compassion are, next to the desire of elevation, the most 60^3
39³ it is, perhaps, of consequence	And it is of consequence 64^2
39¹⁰ To love, and even to hate, on the apprehension of moral qualities, to espouse	To distinguish men by the difference of their moral qualities, to espouse 64^{10}
43¹⁰ *Addition after* . . . melancholy spectacle.	The difficulties and hardships of human life are supposed to detract from the goodness of God; yet many of the pastimes men devise for themselves are fraught with difficulty and danger. The great inventor of the game of human life, knew well how to accommodate the players. The chances are matter of complaint: But if these were removed, the game itself would no longer amuse the parties. 71^{12}
43³⁴ bond of society	band of society 72^{21}
44¹ human felicity	happiness 72^{27}
54-55 order changed	In 1814 edition 'We commonly apprehend . . . happy character.' comes immediately after the quotation from Pope, followed by 'If this be the good . . . in the world.' and then the Epictetus quotation. 90
64¹⁶ *Addition after* . . . defect of power.	Whoever, therefore, has power, may employ it to this extent; and no previous convention is required to justify his conduct. 106^9

1767	1814
page	*page*
69^{28} to aid them in procuring what must weaken a force, with which	to aid them in reducing pretensions, with which he himself is, on many occasions, obliged to contend. 115^2
72^{21} to which constitutions of government are sometimes carried.	at which constitutions of government furthest recede from each other. 119^{16}
81^{29} suffer themselves to be classed according to their measures of wealth.	and by the measures of fortune determine their station. 136^7
$83n^*$ *Addition after*: Charlevoix.	Charlevoix. This account of Rude Nations, in most points of importance, so far it relates to the original North Americans, is not founded so much on the testimony of this or of the other writers cited, as it is on the concurring representations of living witnesses, who, in the course of trade, of war, and of treaties, have had ample occasion to observe the manners of that people. It is necessary, however, for the sake of those who may not have conversed with the living witnesses, to refer to printed authorities. 137-$8n$
84^{18} motives	motive 140^{15}
88^{35} air of	sentiment of 147^{25}
90^{32} superstitious observances	charms 150^{26}
$92n\dagger$ who would shake it off first	who could endure it longest $153n$
94^{15} the subject	the materials 156^{22}
94^{16} cultivation	this improvement 156^{23}

1767	1814
page	*page*
94^{22} to operate on the materials we have described	to find a plan of government for the people 157^{1}
96^{7} and be seized with the folly of breeding and attending his cattle	have the folly of troubling himself with the charge of cattle 160^{4}
96^{14} retards their progress in extending the notion of property	retards the progress of industry and impropriation 160^{12}
96^{17} that this notion is already applied to different subjects; as the fur	that property is apprehended in different subjects; that the fur 160^{16}
96^{18} pertain to	belong to 160^{18}
97^{9} they are taught to abstain from unlawful profits	they are restrained from rapine 161^{24}
97^{23} In the east and the north of Asia	In the north and middle regions of Asia 162^{12}
98^{20} any community	every community 163^{28}
98^{21} unequal shares in the distribution of property	unequal possessions 164^{1}
99^{35} eloquence	persuasion 166^{7}
100^{6} is admitted	was admitted 166^{16}
100^{8} matter of choice, must arrive at	requisite, they must have arrived at 166^{19}
108^{14} polar circle	polar system 182^{5}
110^{1} national pursuit	national change 184^{6}
120^{3} to its members	of its members 200^{18}
120^{7} barbarity	ignorance 200^{22}
121 SECT. II *The History of Subordination*	SECT. II *The History of Political Establishments* 203
121^{30} national union	natural union 204^{6}
125^{6} conduct, these motives are balanced or restrained by other habits and other pursuits	conduct, are guided or restrained by different motives 209^{14}

1767

page

125^9 These circumstances

125^{12} slavery and rapine

126^{18} its abuses

132^{27} in that grave which

133^4 like the materials

138^{32} arise from a disregard to
numbers on the part of states

145^2 ablest writers who have
left nothing so important to
be offered on the subject, as
the general caution, not to
consider these articles as
making the sum of national
felicity, or the principal object of any state.

145^{21} of nothing but the increase of their stock; assemble
to deliberate on profit and
loss; and

1814

page

These motives or habits 209^{18}

slavery and rapine, in the case of
every community 209^{22}

the abuses of power 211^{19}

in a grave like that which 221^{26}

like the wrought materials 222^{15}

arise from the negligence of
those who ought to repair it
                        231^{27}

ablest writers; and the public
will probably soon be furnished
with a theory of national econ-
omy, equal to what has ever
appeared on any subject of
science whatever.* But in the
view which I have taken of
human affairs, nothing seems
more important than the general
caution which the authors to
whom I refer so well understand, not to consider these
articles as making the sum of
national felicity, or the principal
object of any state. In science
we consider our objects apart;
in practice it were an error not
to have them all in our view at
once. (* By Mr Smith, author of
the Theory of Moral Sentiment.) 241^{29}

nothing but monopolies and the
profit of trade, and 243^5

1767	1814
page	*page*
157[1] every people is apt to imagine, that its signification is to be found only among themselves	every free nation is apt to suppose, that freedom is to be found only among themselves; they measure it by their own peculiar habits and system of manners. 262[14]
157[4] foundation of freedom	foundation of public justice 262[20]
163[27] assembled in their tribes	were assembled 273[28]
164[12] unequally matched	unable to contend 274[27]
172[11] verse-compositions	versification 288[28]
172[35] exemplified in the practice of men	exemplified in the course of nature 290[1]
173[17] *Additional footnote after:* . . . reform	See Translations of Gaelic Poetry, by James McPherson. 290*n*
177[4] resolute	resolutive 296[26]
178[9] ingenuous	ingenious 298[21]
190[7] unaccountable and obscure	hidden or unobserved 318[11]
190[11] has a great influence	had a great influence 318[17]
190[35] he must form one, in order to be great.	he must lead one, in order to be great 319[19]
194[21] the detail of facts	external effects 326[2]
194[25] proceeding towards	treatment of 326[8]
200[12] in early periods	in an early period 335[18]
205[3] *Addition after:* . . . laws and government;	and men civilized were men practised in the duty of citizens. 342[17]
205[5] *Addition after:* . . . and in commerce,	and men civilized are scholars, men of fashion and traders. 342[21]
206[6] for himself	for a separate fortune 344[17]

1767	1814
page	*page*
206[6] the confidence and the affection he should entertain for his fellow-creatures.	the confidence and the affection with which he should unite with his fellow-creatures, for their joint preservation. 344[17]
208[2] among nations	among many nations 347[21]
215[36] nor curiosity	nor the curiosity of the learned 360[26]
216[2] who are worst furnished with the conveniencies of life	whose manner of life is most simple 360[30]
216[4] the knowing and the polished	those who are best furnished with knowledge and the conveniences of life 361[3]
216[6] in their rude and in their polished condition	in the beginning and in the advanced age of commercial arts 361[6]
216[8] in the advanced ages of society	in the result of commerce 361[10]
218[8] form	mere forms and rules of art 364[17]
218[16] spirit of society itself.	spirit that ought to prevail in the conduct of nations. 364[28]
221[33] secure the person	secure only the person 370[23]
222[3] may now enjoy	may on this supposition enjoy 371[1]
222[10] may find	may in that very struggle have found 371[12]
223[6] the empire of the unknown world	so great an empire 372[25]
224[20] *Addition of footnote after:* . . . or of riches	Adeo in quæ laboramus sola crevimus Divitias luxuriamque. Liv. lib. vii. c. 25 375*n*
225[1] while they study to improve their fortunes	while they are engaged in what is accounted the most selfish of all pursuits, the improvement of fortune 376[1]
225[17] Polished nations	Commercial nations 376[23]

1767	1814
page	*page*
226[7] ordinary occasions	domestic affairs 377[25]
241[34] *Addition of footnote after:*	Sallust. Bell. Catilinarium 404*n*
. . . fettered by laws.	
247[11] change our fashions, without increasing the measures of our vanity or folly.	change our fashions without multiplying coxcombs, or increasing the measures of our vanity and folly. 413[12]
247[20] preferred to friends, to a country or to mankind	preferred to their character, to their country, to mankind 413[25]
264[23] intrusted with any measure of influence	intrusted with power in any degree 442[2]
267[31] will serve, in another, to settle its foundations, and to give it stability	will serve, in another, to remove obstructions, and to smooth its way 447[8]
270[26] fully explained	fully declared 452[2]
279[35] The institutions of men, are, indeed, likely to have their end as well as their beginning; but their duration is not fixed to any limited period; and no nation	The institutions of men, if not calculated for the preservation of virtue, are indeed, likely to have an end as well as a beginning; but so long as they are effectual to this purpose, they have at all times an equal principle of life, which nothing but an external force can suppress; no nation 467[22]

INDEX